TEACHERS,
LEADERS,
AND
SCHOOLS

Teachers, Leaders, and Schools

Essays by John Dewey

Edited by Douglas J. Simpson and
Sam F. Stack Jr.

Southern Illinois University Press
Carbondale and Edwardsville

13 12 11 10   4 3 2 1

Library of Congress Cataloging-in-Publication Data
Teachers, leaders, and schools : essays by John Dewey /
edited by Douglas J. Simpson and Sam F. Stack Jr.
    p. cm.
Includes index.
ISBN-13: 978-0-8093-2999-1 (pbk. : alk. paper)
ISBN-10: 0-8093-2999-9 (pbk. : alk. paper)
ISBN-13: 978-0-8093-8580-5 (ebook)
ISBN-10: 0-8093-8580-5 (ebook)
1. Dewey, John, 1859–1952—Criticism and interpretation.
2. Dewey, John, 1859–1952—Philosophy. 3. Education—
Philosophy. I. Simpson, Douglas J. II. Stack, Sam F., 1954–
LB875.D5T43 2010
370.1—dc22   2010004769

To
   Judy and our daughters, Letitia and Melanie
and
   Linda and our children, Katie, Ashley, and Sam

Contents

Acknowledgments

WE WANT TO EXPRESS OUR appreciation to a variety of people who have worked with us to help bring this collection of Dewey's essays to the public. Among them are two eminent Dewey scholars—A. G. Rud Jr. and Lynda Stone—who spent extensive time analyzing our proposal, reading the proposed essays, making suggestions regarding alternative essays, and contributing general ideas about the book's overall content. Their feedback was invaluable for several reasons, but particularly because one of our most challenging responsibilities as editors was to determine which of the hundreds of relevant essays should be included. In addition, we are grateful that we were able to have two richly experienced and reflective school practitioners—David Snelgrove and Aron Strickland—read the originally proposed essays through their understanding of Dewey, teaching, and leadership in present-day schools. Moreover, we want to extend our thanks to the anonymous reviewers who made recommendations regarding our initial proposal and offered critiques of earlier drafts of the book. Furthermore, our current and former research assistants—Raymond Flores, Heejin Son, William J. Hull Jr., Xiaoming Liu, Jing Wang, and Penny Pollart—who read many of Dewey's essays, analyzed our ideas, and scrutinized drafts, helped us more than we are able to say. Likewise, we are extremely thankful that Michael J. B. Jackson and Joseph DeVitis were able to read portions of our essay introductions and make recommendations for organizational, substantive, and stylistic changes. Finally, we greatly appreciate the suggested editorial changes of Alice Denham, a generous friend and invaluable colleague. For the contributions of each of those noted, we are deeply indebted and appreciative. We have been struck by their willingness to share their knowledge, insights, and critiques. Naturally, the final product is exclusively the responsibility of the editors.

The assistance of several staff members of Southern Illinois University Press has also been immensely helpful in the development of this work. In particular, we need to thank Karl Kageff and Bridget Brown for their initial and ongoing interest in the book. We are also immensely appreciative of the permission of Southern Illinois University Press to reprint the essays used in this work, which are taken from *The Collected Works of John Dewey, 1882–1953: The Electronic Edition*, edited by Larry A. Hickman (Charlottesville, Va.: InteLex Corp., 1996), which is based on the print edition edited by Jo Ann Boydston (Carbondale: Southern Illinois University Press, 1969–91).

Inasmuch as the *Collected Works* were published in three series, titled *The Early Works: 1882–1898*, *The Middle Works: 1899–1924*, and *The Later Works: 1925–1953*, we have used a citation system devised by the Center for Dewey Studies at Southern Illinois University, Carbondale, that identifies the series, volume, and pages for each essay and for other textual references to Dewey's works. Thus, "My Pedagogic Creed" is cited EW5.84–95, or *The Early Works: 1882–1898*, volume 5, pages 84–95. For the convenience of the reader, the source note that follows each essay indicates the original place and date of publication, information that has been culled from the appropriate volume of the *Collected Works*.

Selected Chronological Dates and Events

1859 Born, 20 October, Burlington, Vermont

1879 B.A., University of Vermont

1879–81 Teacher and Assistant Principal, Oil City High School, Pennsylvania

1882 Teacher, Lake View Seminary, Charlotte, Vermont

1884 Ph.D., Johns Hopkins University

1884–88 Professor, University of Michigan

1888–89 Professor, University of Minnesota

1889–94 Professor and Department Chair, University of Michigan

1894–1904 Professor, Department Chair, and Director of the University Elementary School, University of Chicago

Created University Laboratory School, 1896

The School and Society, 1899

The Educational Situation, 1901

Educational Lectures before Brigham Young Academy, 1901–2

The Child and the Curriculum, 1902

1905–30 Professor, Columbia University

Moral Principles in Education, 1909

How We Think, 1910

Interest and Effort in Education, 1913

Schools of To-Morrow, with Evelyn Dewey, 1915

Democracy and Education, 1916

Visited schools in Turkey, 1924

Visited schools in Mexico, 1926

Visited schools in Russia, 1928

The Sources of a Science of Education, 1929

The Quest for Certainty, 1929

1930–52 Professor Emeritus, Columbia University

The Way Out of Educational Confusion, 1931

American Education Past and Future, 1931

Education and the Social Order, 1934

Art as Experience, 1934

Experience and Education, 1938

Human Nature and Conduct, 1944

Problems of Men, 1946

1952 Died, 1 June, New York City

General Introduction: John Dewey and His Educational Writings

WHY, YOU MAY BE THINKING, should I study the ideas of John Dewey? Dewey was probably the most prominent educational thinker in the Western democracies of the twentieth century, and his influence in the twenty-first century continues. The reasons for his being thought-provoking to many teachers, administrators, researchers, curriculum developers, and others are numerous, and at least some of them are related to his ideas and questions about (a) what kinds of teachers should we prepare and employ, (b) which kinds of curricula should students study, (c) which qualities should educational leaders develop and manifest, (d) how do we know when we have a good school, and (e) in what ways are teachers, curricula, leaders, and schools related to a democratic society? Indeed, what is the purpose of education, and what are the means to becoming educated? These questions are posed implicitly and explicitly in the five sections of this book: Part 1, The Classroom Teacher; Part 2, The School Curriculum; Part 3, The Educational Leader; Part 4, The Ideal School; and Part 5, The Democratic Society. In this general introduction, we hope to give readers a better perspective on why Dewey continues to be relevant to those who are interested in education. If you are an aspiring or practicing teacher, we particularly recommend you read "To Those Who Aspire to the Profession of Teaching" (LW13), the second Dewey essay in part 1. Current and future educational leaders are urged to take up "Democracy and Educational Administration" (LW11), the second essay in part 3.

In order to understand the background for Dewey's writings about education, it helps to have an acquaintance both with his historical and intellectual biography and with the ways his educational writings have been interpreted by others. Here, however, we can offer only a short introduction to how Dewey was raised, educated, and thought, noting a few highlights and some of the interpretive challenges facing the reader. The reader is encouraged to access the rich and growing literature on these themes for a fuller appreciation of the context in which Dewey lived and constructed his ideas. The "Reflection and Discussion Questions" that follow the chapter introductions point out some of the ways his and our schools and worlds were both alike and quite different and how these similarities and differences may or ought to influence our thoughts, decisions, and actions as educators.

The Historical Context

Dewey was born on 20 October 1859, to Archibald Sprague Dewey and Lucina Rich Dewey in Burlington, Vermont, and into a country that was on the verge of sweeping intellectual, social, and political changes. That was the year people in the United States and much of the world were challenged in their core beliefs by the publication of Darwin's *Origin of Species* and John Stuart Mill's *On Liberty*. These events would have influenced Dewey's early, informal education through his mother's evangelical (Congregationalist) religious views and values. That same year, the abolitionist John Brown attacked the federal arsenal in Harper's Ferry, Virginia. Five months after the election of Abraham Lincoln as president in 1860, eleven Southern states seceded from the United States, and the American Civil War began with the firing on Fort Sumter in 1861. In part, Dewey grew up in a military family, for his father served as a quartermaster in the Union army. In the later war years, Dewey and his mother traveled south to be with him for a short period in northern Virginia. One can only speculate about what the young Dewey saw and how this experience influenced his thinking.

Dewey understood that one's life and thinking were shaped by early experiences, and he developed a concept of *experience* as an ongoing interaction and transaction in and with the environment that became central to his views of teaching and philosophy. In addition, he claimed that living in Burlington gave him an understanding of both the existing rural/agrarian and emerging industrial worlds. Burlington had a bustling timber industry employing many local and Canadian lumberjacks, and his grandparents' farm introduced him to life in a rural community. In these settings, then, he learned early that education was more than formal schooling, and that the world around him was teeming with educative and miseducative forces. These ideas he later combined in the compact book *Experience and Education* (LW13).

As a child and young man, Dewey was a serious student and an avid reader but not always interested in what his teachers assigned. His love of reading served him well in high school and later in the classical curriculum at the University of Vermont. At the time, he showed less interest in Plato and Herodotus than in Herbert Spencer and August Comte, and in Kant, Hegel, Leibniz, Spinoza, and T. H. Huxley. Upon graduating in 1879 without having made a definite career choice and troubled by emotional, spiritual, and intellectual questions, Dewey took a teaching position in Oil City, Pennsylvania, a boom-town literally fueling the steel industry of Pittsburgh, Pennsylvania. In Oil City, he taught algebra, science, and Latin in addition to serving as assistant principal. Although he found the atmosphere of Oil City stressful, it allowed him to pursue his intellectual and spiritual questions. Ultimately, he resolved to study philosophy and returned to Burlington in the fall 1881 to study with H. A. P. Torrey, his former Vermont professor. During the winter term, he taught at nearby Lake View Seminary in Charlotte, Vermont.

Wanting to continue his formal studies, Dewey decided to attend Johns Hopkins University, a new institution founded on the German research model in 1876. He earned his Ph.D. two years later in 1884. During his graduate study, he was influenced by the idealist philosopher George Morris and the psychologist G. Stanley Hall. He also studied with Charles Sanders Pierce, one of the intellectual founders of American pragmatism. On graduating, Dewey taught at the University of Michigan over the next ten years, with one year spent at the University of Minnesota. He met his first wife, Alice Chipman, at the University of Michigan. Alice had a substantial influence on Dewey's thought, challenging his religious beliefs and stimulating his social-reformist zeal. During these years, he was attracted to the absolute idealism in the works of Kant, Hegel, Leibniz, and Spinoza because it seemed to answer many of his personal and intellectual questions. Yet he was in the process of making a philosophical turn that would eventually lead him to pragmatism. Dewey later chronicled his philosophical and religious journey in "From Absolutism to Experimentalism" (LW5). Early in his career, he began writing about ethics, teaching methods, mathematics, science, psychology, history, and the education of women and of young children.

In 1894 Dewey left Michigan with a colleague, James Tufts, to teach at the University of Chicago. Dewey was attracted to the intellectual atmosphere of Chicago and to an academic department that combined psychology, philosophy, and pedagogy. The department seemed to be an excellent fit for him inasmuch as he rejected traditional academic boundaries and promoted an interdisciplinary approach to curriculum development. One of his early attempts at the integration of these disciplines was his reevaluation of the "reflex arc" in psychology. He criticized Descartes's mind/body dualism and explained the integration of the mind and the body in experience, an understanding that became central in his thinking about how children learn by active experience (EW5.96–109).

During his years in Chicago, Dewey addressed the concern that the problems created during the Industrial Revolution both resulted from and led to the loss of community. He emphasized that one of the primary roles of the school was to help restore community life, a theme often proposed by progressive schools in the early decades of the twentieth century. He was greatly concerned by a growing individualism in society, a lack of understanding that a democratic way of life is social in nature, and an insufficient understanding of democracy as a form of ethical association. He further believed the growing materialism and unrestrained capitalism of the early twentieth century were misguided values that fostered an economic environment inhospitable to democracy and, in fact, inimical to it. He criticized rampant individualism that had no concern for the consequences of action wherever it appeared in society, including schools, in works such as *Schools of To-Morrow* (MW8).

Chicago proved to be influential for Dewey from several other perspectives. For example, Jane Addams and Ellen Starr, cofounders of Hull House, challenged and broadened his intellectual and social horizons. As an early settlement house, Hull House helped meet a broad range of material, physical, cultural, emotional, vocational, and educational needs of thousands of children and adults through its informal educational activities. In this intentionally fashioned community context, Addams and Starr also promoted a feminism and pragmatism that enriched Dewey's views of justice and social action, prompting him to rethink aspects of his evolving philosophy and theory of education. At Hull House, then, Dewey became an eager student of successful efforts to enact a multitude of measures that addressed educational and social justice needs. He also became a more diligent student of feminism, women's rights, and political activism. Clearly, he grew a deeper understanding of important educational forces that existed outside of schools and their planned curricula.

In the realm of formal schooling, Dewey became intrigued by the educational work of Colonel Francis Parker of the Cooke County Normal School in Chicago (an early teacher-preparation institution). Influenced by the educational philosophies of Johann Heinrich Pestalozzi, Johann Friedrich Herbart, and Friedrich Froebel, Parker envisioned the school as an extension of society, a miniature community, and one attentive to the interests and emotions of the child. At the time, Parker was experimenting with new teaching techniques in art, mathematics, and science and the integration of subject matter. Emphasizing the social and psychological growth of children, Dewey, like Parker, came to believe that the school was an "embryonic society" and that true learning came through experience broadly understood and not through books alone. He experimented during these years with connecting subject matter to life, interests, and emotions and grounded this approach in people's work. He developed a view of the child as both an individual and a member of a community and society and realized that the school as an institution could nurture both individuality and social membership, preparing the child for participation in a democratic society. He regarded the student as a member of a social learning group, rejecting an individualistic, child-centered view of education. His educational themes during this time included play, work, imagination, manual training, ethics, interest and effort, how children learn, and the significance of good instruction.

Due to the poor conditions of the Chicago schools and Dewey's interest in Parker's work, he and Alice decided to send their children to Parker's nontraditional school. Dewey began his own school in 1896, referred to as the Dewey laboratory school but officially named the University Elementary School, which was under his supervision and Alice's direction. He used the school as an experimental laboratory to promote the study of teaching, learning, and administration, not as a model for other educators and schools to imitate. Two of his most celebrated books—*The School and Society* (MW1) and *The Child and the Curriculum* (MW2)—were published while he was in Chicago, and he experimented with his ideas in the university school until 1904, when his increasingly contentious disagreements with William Rainey Harper, the president of the University of Chicago, led him to resign. In the winter term of 1894–95, he became a professor at Columbia University in New York City, an association that lasted the rest of his life.

At Columbia, Dewey continued to emphasize the relationship between philosophy, psychology, and pedagogy and published several of his most important books on education, including *How We Think* (LW8) and *Democracy and Education* (LW9). Although he did not oversee a laboratory school, he developed strong associations with influential faculty members at Teachers College, such as William H. Kilpatrick, George Counts, and John Childs. He also immersed himself in the educational and political climate of New York, influencing the work of many, including women educators such as Lucy Sprague Mitchell, Elsie Ripley Clapp, and Caroline Pratt. His writings during this time reaffirmed the fact that he believed not only that education, like society, was constantly changing but also that both needed to be reflectively guided. Moreover, he emphasized that a truly democratic society, including its schools, was alive, organic, and in need of constant renewal through education. His continuing belief in the critical role of education in a democratic society led him to try to better understand not only social, political, and economic forces but also their underlying nature. Education, like life and knowledge, he believed, was not static or fixed, a view that clearly challenged traditional teacher- or text-centered schools. Similarly, he attacked education that was removed from the lived experience of students, that had no connection to their world or their community.

World War I and the Roaring Twenties brought other related concerns to the forefront, such as outspoken attacks on intellectual freedom and freedom of speech, which Dewey thought were essential qualities of a democratic society and school. Never an advocate of violence as an answer to social and political problems because he believed that democratic means and ends were necessary for a genuine democracy, Dewey argued that with pressure from the United States, Europe could be democratically reorganized following World War I. Obviously, his hopes were never fully realized, as he confessed in "America in the World" (MW11.71–73).

During these turbulent times, Dewey asked, what role should the educator play in social and political change? For him, it was creating the proper conditions and environment for nurturing the child in a democratic way of life. The child—being immature and inexperienced—needed guidance and direction. Promoting a democratic way of life includes developing traits of fundamental educational value: reflection, imagination, creativity, inquiry, communication, and judgment. In school, then, the student should experience and practice, not by chance but in an organized way, the freedom, choice, and responsibility of the participating democrat. In the process of being a participating democrat, a citizen as it were, the student should learn how to solve problems by working with others, a lesson that, Dewey saw, was as demanding as it was crucial.

Dewey also emphasized that this created at least two substantial responsibilities for teachers. To be successful, they had to have a depth of understanding in at least one area of inquiry or creativity, to be liberally educated as professionals and persons, and to understand the world around them. Moreover, he stressed that teachers should be politically astute and conscious of the social and economic issues of the day in order to promote political and social freedom and justice. In the academic, political, and social realms, then, Dewey expected the teacher to exemplify intelligence, the ability to solve problems through inquiry, to ask appropriate questions, but also to show students that answers are not always as clear as classroom materials, the media, or people might suggest.

The 1920s and the Depression era reinforced his belief that the public and society were disorganized and in need of a guiding purpose, one that would replace their emphasis on individualism and materialism. That purpose, he believed, could be broadly found in a reflectively oriented democratic set of processes and values. On the other hand, he attacked as morally wrong the growing attraction of fascism in the 1930s and economic policies he deemed not directed at solving the real problems and hardships of the Depression. He also attacked misrepresentations associated with both progressive and traditional education in the late 1930s, believing that neither was being accurately portrayed at times, in *Experience and Education* (LW13), his last major work on education, published in 1938. These critiques on dichotomous thinking seem nearly as relevant today at they did when he wrote them.

In the later years of Dewey's intellectual development, from the Depression to the end of his life, he concentrated more on issues of individualism, freedom, religion, and aesthetics, including aesthetic experiences in schools and other institutions and settings that were not set apart as artistic enclaves. He wrote a string of works on these topics, including *Reconstruction in Philosophy* (MW13), *Human Nature and Conduct* (MW 14), *The Public and Its Problems* (LW2), *Individualism, Old and New* (LW5), *A Common Faith* (LW9), *Art as Experience* (LW10), and *Liberalism and Social Action* (LW11). As well, he continued to refine his influential theories of inquiry in *Logic: The Theory of Inquiry* (LW12) and experience in the aforementioned *Experience and Education* and the roles they play in both life and education, areas that some viewed as separate and distinct but that he attempted to connect and integrate.

After the Depression and World War II ended, Dewey and his educational colleagues found themselves on the defensive in the sociopolitical climate of the Cold War in which the school was often viewed as an essential bulwark of the state rather than an institution to nurture democracy, inquiry, and freedom. Progressive educators, Dewey among them, were blamed for the decline of American education by traditionalist and political conservatives, including the creation of school conditions that were too radical, failed to be sufficiently academic, leaned toward socialism, and glorified the state over the individual. Most of these attacks, he countered in speeches, short essays, and reviews, were based on an ongoing misunderstanding of progressive education or, at least, his version of it. He was particularly on the defense regarding his believed betrayal of democratic ideals when he concurred with the entrance of the United States into World War II.

Up until his death in 1952, Dewey reflected further on the difficulties of a changing world even as the changes themselves often added credibility to his view that children needed to be taught how to think for themselves and about societal problems in all realms of inquiry and creativity, not *what* to think. Consequently, he continued to promote the idea that teachers need to be educated as professionals, capable of judging what is in the best interest of each pupil and a democratic society, rather than conditioned and coerced to respond to the mandates of the state or powerful economic forces. While his ideas became less popular late in his life, interest in them was renewed, especially during the final quarter of the twentieth century. That interest continues in the present.

The Interpretive Challenges

How shall we interpret Dewey's educational writings? Of course, there is no easy and definitive way to interpret him, because questions of hermeneutics are intrinsically debatable. On the other hand, understanding his historical and intellectual biography is unquestionably important in our efforts to interpret him. But it is also valuable to examine how others interpret his writings, especially here his educational works. Dewey has had many interpreters, and he wrote on occasion to explain himself to readers who found his prose cumbersome and difficult to understand as well as to those who yielded to the temptation to misrepresent his views. Since there are many possible ways of misunderstanding Dewey, both his supporters and his critics have attributed to him ideas that he rejected. The fact that his ideas evolved for approximately seventy-five years and through several religious and philosophical paradigms also contributes to the ease with which his ideas can be misunderstood. Since our focus is on his educational views, we concentrate on them and not his religious and philosophical beliefs although, admittedly, they can not be fully separated from his other ideas—as they developed largely during his middle and later years. Dewey's social and educational thought grew out of and influenced his understanding of *pragmatism*, a philosophical attempt to clarify how to think about or inquire into questions regarding knowledge, reality, values, human behavior, and related matters. Pragmatism also devoted attention to understanding action and its consequences, the benefits and disadvantages of action, and the need to seek beneficial consequences for the individual as well as for society. At the core of his pragmatism is the concept of *experience*, noted earlier and vital to understanding Dewey's philosophy and theory of education. Experience for him was a type of connected interaction or transaction, with and within an environment in which we live and learn. We may triumph and grow; or engage in meaningless activities and stagnate; or make mistakes and experience ungrowth. So experience can be educative, noneducative, or even miseducative. An integral part of this conceptualization of experience is that we have the freedom to try out or experiment with ideas. Ideas for the pragmatist, then, are like tools or instruments, serving a constructive function in helping us solve the problems of everyday life. In short, these ideas are tools or means to help us operate effectively, efficiently, and ethically.

Dewey was informed by the work of Charles Sanders Peirce, William James, Oliver Wendell Holmes, Chauncey Wright, and C. S. Schiller, among others, in developing his pragmatism. Unlike some of them, he clearly tied his thinking to the public school. For instance, he believed that the school should serve as a place to integrate theoretical and experiential knowledge through doing, and in so doing, attempt to tear down a dualism or dichotomy between thought and action that too often characterized education. So for Dewey, a teacher- or text-centered classroom or school that separated thinking and knowing from actual human experience was inadequate. To the contrary, he argued that knowledge is not a static instrument but rather a dynamic one with which to learn more and to solve problems. Importantly, he held that part of what a person should learn to do in school is how to be democratic, and the only way to do that is to engage in, experience, or *do* democracy in the school. One of the challenges of evaluating Dewey's thought is to answer the practical question: How do we design and operate schools so that the values of democracy infuse them? Among other works, Dewey's *Democracy and Education* (MW9) stimulates ideas, suggests directions, and provides insights for us.

In order for students to experience democratic learning and living processes and outcomes, Dewey envisioned the school as a miniature community. The school should be designed for students both to engage in deliberative learning and living and to participate as productive citizens and contributors to a democratic society by being imaginative problem solvers. To do this well, open communication should be embedded in the ethos and social fabric of the school. In this way, students would come to understand and construct themselves as individuals in a social setting and the responsibilities they have to the community and others. Education, for Dewey, then, is a reflective process of democratic socialization, and it needs to be flexible, open to change, but also cognizant of the past, preparing in the present for the future.

Because of Dewey's nuanced and complex view of the relationship of the individual to society, he was often misunderstood to be promoting the individual at the expense of the community. This misunderstanding was perpetuated by many associated with what became known as *progressive education*, a loose and diverse group of educators and policymakers. While adherents of progressive education tended to be united in emphasizing the importance of and respect for children, their interests, and their experiences, progressivists often held different perspectives and used assorted practices in operationalizing their views. Dewey was quite critical of those whom he believed had misinterpreted his work, regardless of their specific loyalties. He was equally concerned with those educators who claimed to be child-centered, social reconstructionist, or administrative progressivists who misconstrued his work as he was with traditionalists who attempted to discredit his ideas by associating them with the views of extreme progressivists (LW13).

Even today, many educators see Dewey as primarily child-centered; however, his philosophy of experience precludes any such simplistic notion. He never advocated an educational process predicated on the whims, transient attractions, or mere emotional interests of the individual child. That sort of romantic view of the child fails to notice the crucial role played by the teacher, tends to ignore the learning of content, and refuses to acknowledge the connections between freedom and responsibility. In contrast to such a view is Dewey's strong emphasis in *Experience and Education* (LW13) on the teacher's responsibility to help the student grow from uncultivated impulses, to nurtured desires, to reflective planning and purposing. In a very precise way, however, it would be correct to say—without confusion—that Dewey was focused on the child as *an individual and social being*, as someone with a unique background and valuable talents who could contribute to the well-being of others, and along with the teacher and classmates could become both a colearner and coteacher in a learning community. Hence, Dewey's laboratory school was best understood as community-centered, because education is largely a social process of participation and interaction (LW11.206).

In his view of the child, education, experience, democracy, community, and growth are interwoven. Notably, he defines education as growth, because he views both ideas as the building on and reconstruction of experience. Learning how to become a democratic citizen requires experience but not in a context of absolute freedom. Indeed, there is no such thing in a democratic society. Freedom, for Dewey, demands responsibility and an awareness of the potential consequences of a choice or action. Thus he believed that neither teachers nor administrators should base their pedagogy or administrative style on a belief in absolute freedom for anyone—child, teacher, or administrator (MW9).

Related to the concept of freedom, Dewey was and is often accused of promoting a crude moral relativism or subjectivism that ignores the development of moral inquiry, the identification of relevant data, the search for sound reasoning, and the importance of weighing moral arguments. Much of this mistaken criticism may derive from Dewey's critique of institutionalized religion and the challenge he and other pragmatists made to the notion of absolute truth. However, in reality, morality and ethics are deeply embedded in Dewey's theory of education and are derived in large part from his views of social philosophy as evinced in *Reconstruction in Philosophy* (MW12) and other works. Ethics, in short, involves the careful study of every relevant source of understanding and the act of examining grounds for the conduct of individual and social moral life. His concept of democracy is also rooted in his view of ethics: democracy is a means, an end, and an exercise of ethical association supported by personal dispositions fundamental to public communications, interactions, deliberations, concerns, and interests. This behavior—associated living—relies upon what he described as sympathetic disposition or character. So, in viewing the school as a miniature community, Dewey stressed that democratic values are important as the glue that holds the community together. He included among his list of virtues a reflective manifestation of tolerance, temperance, courage, justice, respect, freedom, wisdom, and conscientiousness. The intellectual abilities underlying these virtues include inquiry, open-mindedness, creativity, analysis, imagination, and judgment. These abilities are life skills, the tools that are needed to think, live, and participate fully in a democratic school and society. The role of the teacher is, in part, to create a set of learning opportunities, fully utilizing subject matter to nurture these abilities and related virtues (EW4.353–62).

Dewey understood that having these abilities meant the potential of contesting the status quo, including professed democratic values, policies, practices, procedures, and products. Challenging democratic claims is critical, he believed, for democracy to remain a dynamic experience, not a stagnant ideology. He challenged those traditions that viewed education as an acquisition of old ideas and information, arguing that it should be seen as a process of inquiry; namely, learning how to solve problems in a changing world and having the freedom to experiment and make mistakes in that process.

Change, however, is not always worthwhile. In particular, Dewey believed the transition from a rural, agrarian society to an industrial one had disrupted community life during his own lifetime. Many people had lost their sense of place and a sense of how they contributed to the greater social whole. He thought that this loss could be partially addressed by reconstructing communities, valuing creative work, and incorporating both community—the human context for democratic, associated living—and work—the fulfillment of creativity, problem solving, and the human need to contribute to society—into school curricula. He experimented with and wrote about the conception of work as aesthetic fulfillment in the laboratory school of the University of Chicago. As he observed in *The School and Society* (MW1), learning about occupations can stimulate the interest of children, aid in the development of their understanding of school subjects, and bring creativity and work together in ways that are usually ignored by both educators and employers.

Unsurprisingly, Dewey's understanding of work was far too often misinterpreted, especially within the field of manual training. Many educators believed they were following Dewey's lead in preparing children for life by training them for a specific job. One of Dewey's objections to such an interpretation was that this kind of preparation too often sorted out working-class children, destining them to manual labor and undermining equality of educational and economic opportunity. Moreover, the approach was narrowly vocational and failed to develop the liberalizing elements of learning and working as well as the capability of reflective thinking that is needed for involvement in broader career and social matters.

This narrow approach to schooling—manual training— was based on a mind-body dualism embedded in much of traditional education philosophy. Dewey wanted to resolve the dualism between intellectual labor and manual labor, not promote it. But the contemporary practice of hands-on activities may also reflect a misinterpretation of Dewey's concept of work. For Dewey, hands-on means more than sensory manipulation and must be connected to the cognitive growth and experience of students with the world around them, helping them to understand their association to the world of work. Ideally students would work together, communicate, and cooperate as they solved problems in the school. But he wanted this same learning to contribute to the development of skills conducive to life in a democratic society. Teachers and students engage in developing and studying appropriate subject matter to work through this process.

As mentioned earlier, Dewey was often misinterpreted during his lifetime, and even today he has more than his share of interpreters, though they may differ in their criticisms or their affinities and whether their focus is on longstanding hermeneutic issues or more recent ones. Currently, interpretive controversies include debates about whether it is best to approach him through a classical or neopragmatic lens, modernist or postmodernist orientation, constructivist or nonconstructivist paradigm, and so forth. Our own inclination is to interpret Dewey through a historical perspective on pragmatism, although our personal philosophical positions are more complex and layered.

Of course, interpreting anyone's philosophy is in part a matter of degree and, at times, intent. Thus, no one consistently reads Dewey as he intended to be understood, if, indeed, he always had one thing in mind for every statement that he made. Equally important, no one is likely to misconstrue his ideas all of the time; neither his overly zealous political, religious, and philosophical proponents nor opponents. Furthermore, he would strenuously object to the idea that we are obligated to remain fixed on the perspective of the 1952 Dewey. All of this means simply that there are no infallible interpreters of Dewey because the process of interpreting his writings is an ongoing public dialogue. Moreover, the reader is encouraged to read carefully the essays we have included while keeping in mind that they were composed in particular historical circumstances and from a specific philosophical background. Dewey wrote for particular audiences entrenched in historical and cultural circumstances that differ in important ways from our own. As a result, while at times it may sound as if he were responding to a present-day situation, the reality is that for us to apply his thinking to our current challenges may require that we understand, reconstruct, and use—as adapted contemporary instruments—his ideas in imaginative ways. Indeed, it is a given from Dewey's perspective that each problem—regardless of the age and context in which it emerges—must be seen as an original or unique challenge that requires drawing from prior learning, engaging in new inquiry, and integrating all that we understand. We think that Dewey can be an invaluable part of our stock of knowledge that is relevant to contemporary educational issues if we remain reflective and open to learning from other sources as well. To state the thought somewhat differently, we think that Dewey's ideas may serve us well as tools by which we can understand, analyze, and reconsider our own theories, assumptions, and practices about school and society, democracy and education, beauty and truth, values and meaning making. Of course, some readers of Dewey may not agree with or care for his ideas. We can only say to such readers that it will reward them to make the extra effort to study and seek to understand Dewey, even if they strongly disagree with him, precisely because he has had such a profound influence on our profession.

At this juncture, it may be helpful to pull together Dewey's philosophy and educational theory and see how they are conjoined with or inclusive of his theories of the teacher, curriculum, educational leader, school, and democratic society. First, Dewey was a pragmatist (instrumentalist or experimentalist) who attempted in his philosophy to offer practical and theoretical insights to societal and educational institutions, including government, businesses, schools, universities, charities, museums, homes, libraries, communities, organizations, media, entertainment venues, political parties, and others in a liberal democracy. Second, he attempted to clarify the interrelatedness of every realm of inquiry and experience and how they interact with, shape, and form one another: so, for example, learning in the corporate office is related to learning on the soccer field and physics laboratory. Third, his educational theory is an inclusive one linking formal, nonformal, and informal education and proposing multiple subtheories regarding teaching, learning, organization, administration, curriculum, and so forth, all of which derives from the previously mentioned realms of inquiry and understanding. The selected readings in this volume spotlight formal schooling (students, teachers, pedagogy, curriculum, educational leaders, and school) and related societal matters (democracy, communities, power, economics, and politics). His writings frequently weave together these themes in ways that make it challenging to place them under one heading or another. They often address multiple strands of thought and flow in a serendipitous rather than systematic fashion. Frequently, they are more conversational than academic. Whatever our view of his style of thinking and writing, they are a part of who he was. Through them, he invites us to engage him in a conversation that reflects his democratic and educative propensities.

This Collection of Essays

A word about the title of this volume and about the selection and arrangement of the essays seems warranted. The title—*Teachers, Leaders, and Schools: Essays by John Dewey*—is meant to suggest that the essays were selected with aspiring and practicing teachers and educational leaders in mind although we hope many other educators and students will find the selections informative and stimulating. The articles were chosen for their user-friendliness, relevancy, scope, and, ideally, because they aim at helping us to understand and reassess something fundamental about ourselves, our schools, and our society. We believe the issues, arguments, and theorizing Dewey undertakes offer the potential for serious reflection and conversation about the nature of education, both its means and ends, in a democratic society. As he often reiterated, democracy is creative and always in process—and this includes education and schooling as well as other dimensions of society.

Our choice of essays, to seriously understate the challenge, was immensely difficult even with and partly because of the excellent feedback we received from others. In the end, we had to rely on our judgment about which of the hundreds of Dewey's essays were more accessible and especially vital for those readers who are, or who aspire to become, educational practitioners and want to begin thinking about educational and societal questions from a Deweyan perspective. We decided to bring together for the first time several of Dewey's educational essays that were previously published in different volumes rather than rely on his educational books, which are less accessible to readers. Our selections, then, are primarily for the new student of Dewey's educational theory interested in his ideas about teaching, learning, and leading in democratically oriented schools and societies. Of course, we strongly encourage readers to explore other educational collections and Dewey's educational books, especially *The School and Society*, *The Child and the Curriculum*, *How We Think*, *Democracy and Education*, and *Experience and Education*.

Our arrangement of Dewey's essays under five headings—The Classroom Teacher, The School Curriculum, The Educational Leader, The Ideal School, and The Democratic Society—was primarily determined by the topics of Dewey's essays and the interests of our intended audience and does not represent an ideological way of looking at his educational theory. For example, Dewey never wrote a book on the roles, responsibilities, qualities, challenges, and ideas of either classroom teachers or educational leaders, but as the essays we have chosen to place under those headings demonstrate, that does not mean that he considered them inconsequential. To the contrary, his educational theory treats them as essential parts of the leadership of classrooms, schools, and school districts, the builders of educative learning environments and policies, and guides of and colearners with one another and students.

A more important matter, however, is whether the essays we have selected represent the heart of Dewey's educational theory and his subtheories about children, teachers, leaders, curriculum, schools, organization, education, experience, pedagogy, inquiry, and so forth. Manifestly, Dewey wrote more on some aspects of his educational theory than he did others, and he frequently commingled his ideas in a single essay, embedding other ideas in addition to those that appear in his title. For example, the first selection in this volume—"My Pedagogic Creed"—outlines his beliefs in such ideas as education, school, curriculum, methodology, and social progress. But while he does not emphasize children, teachers, democracy, experience, inquiry, and other terms, there are many references to children, democracy, and so on. The point is that just as a single title cannot reflect the entire scope of Dewey's educational theory, readers will invariably have to synthesize their own, albeit incomplete interpretation of Dewey's ideas on education. This challenge of developing an educational philosophy should be a lifelong process, and if Dewey's ideas stimulate the thinking of intellectually and professionally growing teachers and leaders, so much the better.

PART ONE. THE CLASSROOM TEACHER

Introduction: The Classroom Teacher

IN WHAT WAY DOES DEWEY'S teaching in public and private schools, serving as an assistant principal, overseeing a university laboratory school, investigating child development, studying schools in several countries, examining the issues of professional educators, and scrutinizing the many needs of society contribute to our understanding of what classroom teachers face today? Or, we might more pointedly inquire, what does Dewey have to say about the importance of the various roles of the classroom teacher as teacher, private person, professional educator, and citizen today? The set of essays in this section were selected to address these and associated questions and to appeal to aspiring and practicing teachers. The articles also offer insights about teachers and schools for educational leaders to consider and evaluate. We believe that if both teachers and educational leaders were to study these essays, Dewey's ideas could make their dialogue with each other even more powerful and thought-provoking.

Although Dewey never wrote a major volume on teachers, he was unwavering in his belief that well-educated, reflective, professional teachers should have a voice in the direction of their own school work and in the preparation of future teachers (MW8, MW15.171–79, LW5.1–40). When teachers have the power to create learning conditions and to select subject matter based on the developing needs and interests of students, it serves the broader purposes of education, which include nurturing students to become reflective thinkers and informed participants in democratic classrooms and societies. Moreover, he argues, teachers also have responsibilities as members of a profession and as citizens in a democratic society. Those are just some of the themes he takes up in the following essays.

In "My Pedagogic Creed" (EW5.84–95), perhaps Dewey's most succinct and clear statement of his educational thought, we find hints of a comprehensive philosophy, or at least a general theory, of education. Utilizing belief statements, and building on the core principle that the process and the goal of education are one and the same—the participation of individuals in the social consciousness of society—the creed asserts the nature of, and relationships among, the multiplicity of elements that go into making education what it is, including school, subject matter, curriculum, methodology, students, teachers, nature, and society. In one sense, it is a concise introduction to this volume that makes explicit or implicit reference to most of the major themes in these essays, with the notable exception of Dewey's view of the educational leader or administrator, a profession that was just emerging at the time. Using religious language that connotes his early interest in the spiritual and perhaps anticipates his later attraction to religious experience, he describes teaching as a *calling* that involves the teacher in the preparation of educational conditions for students that are conducive to their individual and social growth. In view of the nature of the ongoing development of students, he avers that classroom teachers need more than knowledge, pedagogical expertise, psychological insight, and theoretical understanding: they also need to have good character, compassion, and sympathy.

Dewey's implied advice to teachers in his creed becomes explicit in his article "To Those Who Aspire to the Profession of Teaching" (LW13.342–46). From the outset, he asks prospective teachers to reflect on their answers to three questions: What opportunities does teaching offer? How do I measure up to the demands of teaching? What disappointments and challenges will I face as a teacher? As he explores these questions with readers, Dewey identifies a series of indispensable passions that teachers will need throughout their careers and points out that their lives will be characterized by stressful situations, long hours, and limited financial rewards that can challenge these passions. As a result, he reasons, teachers need to be strong, caring, patient, and sympathetic individuals who also know their subjects and model the quest for knowledge. According to Dewey, teaching is not for those who lack personal integrity, respect for students, and passion but for those who are emotionally and intellectually committed to advancing the well-being of individuals and society.

In the "Professional Spirit among Teachers" (MW7.109–12), Dewey argues that a professional spirit is missing from many teachers for several reasons, but especially because they are too infrequently called upon or allowed to be professionals or to use their minds to help improve schools. In the context of this assumption, Dewey makes two normative or value claims, asserting that a professional spirit is present when a teacher is a permanent student of school-related questions and a leader of public opinion about what children need in their communities. As a student, the teacher has only begun learning when she or he completes a teacher-education program. Inquiry—the continuous pursuit of understanding of students, content, pedagogy, and society—is the professional means to becoming and remaining both a reflective teacher and a leader of community thinking about the out-of-school needs of children. Studying individual children, particular classrooms, distinctive schools, unique communities, and academic matters throughout life enables the teacher to be both a teacher and a leader. As a leader or civic servant, in contrast to a civil servant, the teacher has a responsibility to become politically astute and socially engaged. Moreover, Dewey implies that schools and districts and their leaders need to show respect for the ideas and experiences of teachers if schools are to become more than places of mechanical routine. For Dewey, then, the professional spirit extends far beyond simply being a member of a professional organization. But, he believes, the professional spirit of teachers is seriously undermined by the way schools and districts are organized, operated, and controlled by a small group at the top.

Dewey notes two additional matters that need the attention of current and future teachers in "The Educational Balance, Efficiency and Thinking" (LW17.77–82). Here, being both an efficient-effective and reflective-purposive educator is stressed. Dewey asserts that while developing efficiency in teaching skills is necessary, teaching is more than a mechanical act, or routine. While traditional education methods and educators favored acquisition of information, well-ordered classrooms, and students' passivity over their engaging in active and open inquiry, Dewey rejects this scenario, again points out that teachers ought to be artists who have the creative freedom to encourage originality, imagination, inquiry, and problem solving. In effect, Dewey says, the teacher needs to be thoughtfully engaged in getting students "into the attitude of the artist" in order to grapple with the challenges of reality.

Written a decade after he left his high-school teaching position, "Teaching Ethics in High School" (EW4.54–61) may provide insight into both how Dewey theorized about and engaged in the art of teaching. After dissociating himself from certain perceptions and practices of teaching ethics, he delineates his own views and interests, especially his belief that high-school teachers should lead students to understand the importance of ethical relationships and actions in the world, not simply teach ethics per se. He then offers a different—both practical and scientific—ethical theory and pedagogical approach to studying ethics or, stated from his perspective, international ethical relationships. In his classroom, the teacher, at least initially, would try to avoid moral lecturing and discourse and instead ask open-ended questions such as, How do you determine whether "x situation" should be addressed? If you decided to address the situation, how would you go about it? The teacher would encourage students to use their imaginations, relevant data, and reflection to construct their answers, with the immediate goal not to disseminate rules or stimulate explicit ethical theorizing but to promote at least a fourfold classroom orientation: the crucial nature of ethical inquiry, the necessity of understanding the interrelatedness of everyone, the importance of forming imaginative and sympathetic dispositions, and the connection between ethical thinking and action. The essay well illustrates why Dewey's pedagogy is sometimes described as problem solving and why his view of scientific thinking applies to all fields of inquiry, including ethics.

In "Philosophy of Education" (MW7.297–311), Dewey provides a picture of philosophy of education in his day and inklings of his own philosophy. In several ways, he notes the importance of studying philosophy of education, for example, so that an educator can better explain her or his own educational ideals, understand others' educational views, discuss controversial educational issues, recognize the motives for educational philosophy, and clarify the similarities and differences among philosophy of education, science of education, and principles of education. Ultimately, Dewey sees philosophy as a general theory of education that demonstrates the interconnections of all communication and learning, formal and informal, intentional and accidental, educative and miseducative. Given the existing nature of schools and society, he argues, a new philosophy or general theory of education is needed, one that would clarify the issues that both school and society face. Without clarity regarding which goals to pursue, neither school nor society could adequately work toward addressing problems of class, race, culture, equality, so forth. While there are reasons for disagreeing with many of his claims, it may not be easy to argue with his claim that the educator needs to learn to philosophize well in order to attend to numerous controversial assumptions about schooling. Is it embellishing his view to claim that philosophizing educators contribute in important ways to the development of both schools and society? This and other essays constitute, in part, his attempt to help us think clearly about educational issues as we develop a theory of education.

As you read and reflect on the following essays, you may wish to consider the following questions:

REFLECTION AND DISCUSSION QUESTIONS

1. Dewey viewed teaching as an artistic activity. How did he make the connection between teaching and art?
2. Dewey held a very high view of the teacher as a person and professional and also set a high standard for entering and remaining in the field. When schools are staffed by the kind of teachers he envisioned, how might they differ from many contemporary schools?
3. Dewey described philosophy as "the general theory of education." What do you think he meant? What role does a philosophy of education or educational theory play in the act of teaching?
4. For Dewey, teaching was an ethical endeavor. What is the significance of ethics in his philosophy or theory of education?

5. What contradictions, if any, do you see with Dewey's view of the classroom teacher and the role of the teacher today?

6. Beyond clarifying his theory of the teacher and teaching, what other theories do these essays help clarify? Why do you think Dewey discussed these theoretical dimensions in the context of his discussing teachers?

My Pedagogic Creed (1897)

What Education Is

I BELIEVE THAT ALL EDUCATION proceeds by the participation of the individual in the social consciousness of the race. This process begins unconsciously almost at birth, and is continually shaping the individual's powers, saturating his consciousness, forming his habits, training his ideas, and arousing his feelings and emotions. Through this unconscious education the individual gradually comes to share in the intellectual and moral resources which humanity has succeeded in getting together. He becomes an inheritor of the funded capital of civilization. The most formal and technical education in the world cannot safely depart from this general process. It can only organize it; or differentiate it in some particular direction.

I believe that the only true education comes through the stimulation of the child's powers by the demands of the social situations in which he finds himself. Through these demands he is stimulated to act as a member of a unity, to emerge from his original narrowness of action and feeling and to conceive of himself from the standpoint of the welfare of the group to which he belongs. Through the responses which others make to his own activities he comes to know what these mean in social terms. The value which they have is reflected back into them. For instance, through the response which is made to the child's instinctive babblings the child comes to know what those babblings mean; they are transformed into articulate language and thus the child is introduced into the consolidated wealth of ideas and emotions which are now summed up in language.

I believe that this educational process has two sides—one psychological and one sociological; and that neither can be subordinated to the other or neglected

First published in *School Journal* 54 (January 1897): 77–80.

without evil results following. Of these two sides, the psychological is the basis. The child's own instincts and powers furnish the material and give the starting point for all education. Save as the efforts of the educator connect with some activity which the child is carrying on of his own initiative independent of the educator, education becomes reduced to a pressure from without. It may, indeed, give certain external results but cannot truly be called educative. Without insight into the psychological structure and activities of the individual, the educative process will, therefore, be haphazard and arbitrary. If it chances to coincide with the child's activity it will get a leverage; if it does not, it will result in friction, or disintegration, or arrest of the child nature.

I believe that knowledge of social conditions, of the present state of civilization, is necessary in order properly to interpret the child's powers. The child has his own instincts and tendencies, but we do not know what these mean until we can translate them into their social equivalents. We must be able to carry them back into a social past and see them as the inheritance of previous race activities. We must also be able to project them into the future to see what their outcome and end will be. In the illustration just used, it is the ability to see in the child's babblings the promise and potency of a future social intercourse and conversation which enables one to deal in the proper way with that instinct.

I believe that the psychological and social sides are organically related and that education cannot be regarded as a compromise between the two, or a superimposition of one upon the other. We are told that the psychological definition of education is barren and formal—that it gives us only the idea of a development of all the mental powers without giving us any idea of the use to which these powers are put. On the other hand, it is urged that the social definition of education, as getting adjusted to civilization, makes of it forced and external process, and results in subordinating the freedom of the individual to a preconceived social and political status.

I believe each of these objections is true when urged against one side isolated from the other. In order to know what a power really is we must know what its end, use, or function is; and this we cannot know save as we conceive of the individual as active in social relationships. But, on the other hand, the only possible adjustment which we can give to the child under existing conditions, is that which arises through putting him in complete possession of all his powers. With the advent of democracy and modern industrial conditions, it is impossible to foretell definitely just what civilization will be twenty years from now. Hence it is impossible to prepare the child for any precise set of conditions. To prepare him for the future life means to give him command of himself; it means so to train him that he will have the full and ready use of all his capacities; that his eye and ear and hand may be tools ready to command, that his judgment may be capable of grasping the conditions under which it has to work, and the executive forces be trained to act economically and efficiently. It is impossible to reach this sort of adjustment save as constant regard is had to the individual's own powers, tastes, and interests—say, that is, as education is continually converted into psychological terms.

In sum, I believe that the individual who is to be educated is a social individual and that society is an organic union of individuals. If we eliminate the social factor from the child we are left only with an abstraction; if we eliminate the individual factor from society, we are left only with an inert and lifeless mass. Education, therefore, must begin with a psychological insight into the child's capacities, interests, and habits. It must be controlled at every point by reference to these same considerations. These powers, interests, and habits must be continually interpreted—we must know what they mean. They must be translated into terms of their social equivalents—into terms of what they are capable of in the way of social service.

What the School Is

I believe that the school is primarily a social institution. Education being a social process, the school is simply that form of community life in which all those agencies are concentrated that will be most effective in bringing the child to share in the inherited resources of the race, and to use his own powers for social ends.

I believe that education, therefore, is a process of living and not a preparation for future living.

I believe that the school must represent present life—life as real and vital to the child as that which he carries on in the home, in the neighborhood, or on the playground.

I believe that education which does not occur through forms of life, forms that are worth living for their own sake, is always a poor substitute for the genuine reality and tends to cramp and to deaden.

I believe that the school, as an institution, should simplify existing social life; should reduce it, as it were, to an embryonic form. Existing life is so complex that the child cannot be brought into contact with it without either confusion or distraction; he is either overwhelmed by multiplicity of activities which are going on, so that he loses his own power of orderly reaction, or he is so stimulated by these various activities that his powers are prematurely called into play and he becomes either unduly specialized or else disintegrated.

I believe that, as such simplified social life, the school life should grow gradually out of the home life; that it should take up and continue the activities with which the child is already familiar in the home.

I believe that it should exhibit these activities to the child, and reproduce them in such ways that the child will gradually learn the meaning of them, and be capable of playing his own part in relation to them.

I believe that this is a psychological necessity, because it is the only way of securing continuity in the child's growth, the only way of giving a background of past experience to the new ideas given in school.

I believe it is also a social necessity because the home is the form of social life in which the child has been nurtured and in connection with which he has had his moral training. It is the business of the school to deepen and extend his sense of the values bound up in his home life.

I believe that much of present education fails because it neglects this fundamental principle of the school as a form of community life. It conceives the school as a place where certain information is to be given, where certain lessons are to be learned, or where certain habits are to be formed. The value of these is conceived as lying largely in the remote future; the child must do these things for the sake of something else he is to do; they are mere preparation. As a result they do not become a part of the life experience of the child and so are not truly educative.I believe that moral education centres about this conception of the school as a mode of social life, that the best and deepest moral training is precisely that which one gets through having to enter into proper relations with others in a unity of work and thought. The present educational systems, so far as they destroy or neglect this unity, render it difficult or impossible to get any genuine, regular moral training.

I believe that the child should be stimulated and controlled in his work through the life of the community.

I believe that under existing conditions far too much of the stimulus and control proceeds from the teacher, because of neglect of the idea of the school as a form of social life.

I believe that the teacher's place and work in the school is to be interpreted from this same basis. The teacher is not in the school to impose certain ideas or to form certain habits in the child, but is there as a member of the community to select the influences which shall affect the child and to assist him in properly responding to these influences.

I believe that the discipline of the school should proceed from the life of the school as a whole and not directly from the teacher.

I believe that the teacher's business is simply to determine on the basis of larger experience and riper wisdom, how the discipline of life shall come to the child.

I believe that all questions of the grading of the child and his promotion should be determined by reference to the same standard. Examinations are of use only so far as they test the child's fitness for social life and reveal the place in which he can be of the most service and where he can receive the most help.

The Subject-Matter of Education

I believe that the social life of the child is the basis of concentration, or correlation, in all his training or growth. The social life gives the unconscious unity and the background of all his efforts and of all his attainments.

I believe that the subject-matter of the school curriculum should mark a gradual differentiation out of the primitive unconscious unity of social life.

I believe that we violate the child's nature and render difficult the best ethical results, by introducing the child too abruptly to a number of special studies, of reading, writing, geography, etc., out of relation to this social life.

I believe, therefore, that the true centre of correlation of the school subjects is not science, nor literature, nor history, nor geography, but the child's own social activities.

I believe that education cannot be unified in the study of science, or so-called nature study, because apart from human activity, nature itself is not a unity; nature in itself is a number of diverse objects in space and time, and to attempt to make it the centre of work by itself, is to introduce a principle of radiation rather than one of concentration.

I believe that literature is the reflex expression and interpretation of social experience; that hence it must follow upon and not precede such experience. It, therefore, cannot be made the basis, although it may be made the summary of unification.

I believe once more that history is of educative value in so far as it presents phases of social life and growth. It must be controlled by reference to social life. When taken simply as history it is thrown into the distant past and becomes dead and inert. Taken as the record of man's social life and progress it becomes full of meaning. I believe, however, that it cannot be so taken excepting as the child is also introduced directly into social life.

I believe accordingly that the primary basis of education is in the child's powers at work along the same general constructive lines as those which have brought civilization into being.

I believe that the only way to make the child conscious of his social heritage is to enable him to perform those fundamental types of activity which make civilization what it is.

I believe, therefore, in the so-called expressive or constructive activities as the centre of correlation.

I believe that this gives the standard for the place of cooking, sewing, manual training, etc., in the school.

I believe that they are not special studies which are to be introduced over and above a lot of others in the way of relaxation or relief, or as additional accomplishments. I believe rather that they represent, as types, fundamental forms of social activity; and that it is possible and desirable that the child's introduction into the more formal subjects of the curriculum be through the medium of these activities.

I believe that the study of science is educational in so far as it brings out the materials and processes which make social life what it is.

I believe that one of the greatest difficulties in the present teaching of science is that the material is presented in purely objective form, or is treated as a new peculiar kind of experience which the child can add to that which he has already had. In reality, science is of value because it gives the ability to interpret and control the experience already had. It should be introduced, not as so much new subject-matter, but as showing the factors already involved in previous experience and as furnishing tools by which that experience can be more easily and effectively regulated.

I believe that at present we lose much of the value of literature and language studies because of our elimination of the social element. Language is almost always treated in the books of pedagogy simply as the expression of thought. It is true that language is a logical instrument, but it is fundamentally and primarily a social instrument. Language is the device for communication; it is the tool through which one individual comes to share the ideas and feelings of others. When treated simply as a way of getting individual information, or as a means of showing off what one has learned, it loses its social motive and end.

I believe that there is, therefore, no succession of studies in the ideal school curriculum. If education is life, all life has, from the outset, a scientific aspect; an aspect of art and culture and an aspect of communication. It cannot, therefore, be true that the proper studies for one grade are mere reading and writing, and that at a later grade, reading, or literature, or science, may be introduced. The progress is not in the succession of studies but in the development of new attitudes towards, and new interests in, experience.

I believe finally, that education must be conceived as a continuing reconstruction of experience; that the process and the goal of education are one and the same thing.

I believe that to set up any end outside of education, as furnishing its goal and standard, is to deprive the educational process of much of its meaning and tends to make us rely upon false and external stimuli in dealing with the child.

The Nature of Method

I believe that the question of method is ultimately reducible to the question of the order of development of the child's powers and interests. The law for presenting and treating material is the law implicit within the child's own nature. Because this is so I believe the following statements are of supreme importance as determining the spirit in which education is carried on:

1. I believe that the active side precedes the passive in the development of the child nature; that expression comes before conscious impression; that the muscular development precedes the sensory; that movements come before conscious sensations; I believe that consciousness is essentially motor or impulsive; that conscious states tend to project themselves in action.

I believe that the neglect of this principle is the cause of a large part of the waste of time and strength in school work. The child is thrown into a passive, receptive or absorbing attitude. The conditions are such that he is not permitted to follow the law of his nature; the result is friction and waste.

I believe that ideas (intellectual and rational processes) also result from action and devolve for the sake of the better control of action. What we term reason is primarily the law of orderly or effective action. To attempt to develop the reasoning powers, the powers of judgment, without reference to the selection and arrangement of means in action, is the fundamental fallacy in our present methods of dealing with this matter. As a result we present the child with arbitrary symbols. Symbols are a necessity in mental development, but they have their place as tools for economizing effort; presented by themselves they are a mass of meaningless and arbitrary ideas imposed from without.

2. I believe that the image is the great instrument of instruction. What a child gets out of any subject presented to him is simply the images which he himself forms with regard to it.

I believe that if nine-tenths of the energy at present directed towards making the child learn certain things, were spent in seeing to it that the child was forming proper images, the work of instruction would be indefinitely facilitated.

I believe that much of the time and attention now given to the preparation and presentation of lessons might be more wisely and profitably expended in training the child's power of imagery and in seeing to it that he was continually forming definite, vivid, and growing images of the various subjects with which he comes in contact in his experience.

3. I believe that interests are the signs and symptoms of growing power. I believe that they represent dawning capacities. Accordingly the constant and careful observation of interests is of the utmost importance for the educator.

I believe that these interests are to be observed as showing the state of development which the child has reached.

I believe that they prophesy the stage upon which he is about to enter.

I believe that only through the continual and sympathetic observation of childhood's interests can the adult enter into the child's life and see what it is ready for, and upon what material it could work most readily and fruitfully.

I believe that these interests are neither to be humored nor repressed. To repress interest is to substitute the adult for the child, and so to weaken intellectual curiosity and alertness, to suppress initiative, and to deaden interest. To humor the interests is to substitute the transient for the permanent. The interest is always the sign of some power below; the important thing is to discover this power. To humor the interest is to fail to penetrate below the surface and its sure result is to substitute caprice and whim for genuine interest.

4. I believe that the emotions are the reflex of actions.

I believe that to endeavor to stimulate or arouse the emotions apart from their corresponding activities, is to introduce an unhealthy and morbid state of mind.

I believe that if we can only secure right habits of action and thought, with reference to the good, the true, and the beautiful, the emotions will for the most part take care of themselves.

I believe that next to deadness and dullness, formalism and routine, our education is threatened with no greater evil than sentimentalism.

I believe that this sentimentalism is the necessary result of the attempt to divorce feeling from action.

The School and Social Progress

I believe that education is the fundamental method of social progress and reform.

I believe that all reforms which rest simply upon the enactment of law, or the threatening of certain penalties, or upon changes in mechanical or outward arrangements, are transitory and futile.

I believe that education is a regulation of the process of coming to share in the social consciousness; and that the adjustment of individual activity on the basis of this social consciousness is the only sure method of social reconstruction.

I believe that this conception has due regard for both the individualistic and socialistic ideals. It is duly individual because it recognizes the formation of a certain character as the only genuine basis of right living. It is socialistic because it recognizes that this right character is not to be formed by merely individual precept, example, or exhortation, but rather by the influence of a certain form of institutional or community life upon the individual, and that the social organism through the school, as its organ, may determine ethical results.

I believe that in the ideal school we have the reconciliation of the individualistic and the institutional ideals.

I believe that the community's duty to education is, therefore, its paramount moral duty. By law and punishment, by social agitation and discussion, society can regulate and form itself in a more or less haphazard and chance way. But through education society can formulate its own purposes, can organize its own means and resources, and thus shape itself with definiteness and economy in the direction in which it wishes to move.

I believe that when society once recognizes the possibilities in this direction, and the obligations which these possibilities impose, it is impossible to conceive of the resources of time, attention, and money which will be put at the disposal of the educator.

I believe it is the business of every one interested in education to insist upon the school as the primary and most effective instrument of social progress and reform in order that society may be awakened to realize what the school stands for, and aroused to the necessity of endowing the educator with sufficient equipment properly to perform his task.

I believe that education thus conceived marks the most perfect and intimate union of science and art conceivable in human experience.

I believe that the art of thus giving shape to human powers and adapting them to social service, is the supreme art; one calling into its service the best of artists; that no insight, sympathy, tact, executive power is too great for such service.

I believe that with the growth of psychological science, giving added insight into individual structure and laws of growth; and with growth of social science, adding to our knowledge of the right organization of individuals, all scientific resources can be utilized for the purposes of education.

I believe that when science and art thus join hands the most commanding motive for human action will be reached; the most genuine springs of human conduct aroused and the best service that human nature is capable of guaranteed.

I believe, finally, that the teacher is engaged, not simply in the training of individuals, but in the formation of the proper social life.

I believe that every teacher should realize the dignity of his calling; that he is a social servant set apart for the maintenance of proper social order and the securing of the right social growth.

I believe that in this way the teacher always is the prophet of the true God and the usherer in of the true kingdom of God.

To Those Who Aspire to the
Profession of Teaching (1938)

THERE ARE THREE QUESTIONS WHICH I should want answered if I were a young man or woman thinking of choosing an occupation. I should want to know first what opportunities the vocation offers, opportunities for cultural development, intellectual, moral, social, and its material rewards along with its opportunities for usefulness and for personal growth. In the second place I should want to know what special demands it makes so that I could measure my personal qualifications against those which are required for genuine success in that calling. And thirdly, I should want to know something of the discouragements and "outs," the difficulties connected with the vocation I had in mind.

It does not require any long argument to show that teaching is pre-eminent among the callings in its opportunities for moral and spiritual service. It has always ranked with the ministry in that respect. Without drawing any invidious comparisons there are certain traits in the profession of education that are especially appealing at the present time. In the first place, it deals with the young, with those whose minds are plastic and whose characters are forming. Horace Mann said, "Where anything is growing one former is worth a thousand reformers." One who deals with the young does not have the obstacles to overcome that one has to meet who is dealing with adults. Educational work is moreover free from sectarian divisions and other divisions which depend upon dogma. The teacher can meet all pupils on a common ground. This fact adds to the ready approach afforded by the youthful mind. Again all modern psychology increasingly emphasizes the formative character of the earlier years of life. In very many cases, the adjustments which are made then are those which control the activities of adult life, normal adjustments to others being the foundation of

First published in *My Vocation, by Eminent Americans; or, What Eminent Americans Think of Their Callings*, comp. Earl Granger Lockhart (New York: H. W. Wilson Co., 1938), 325–34.

a normal life in the later years, and failures in sane and wise social and personal adaptations being the chief source of later unhappiness and morbid states. The teacher shares with the parent the opportunity to have a direct part in promoting the mental and moral life which is healthy and balanced. The teacher has not only the advantage of dealing with a greater number of children, but also is in a condition to judge more wisely and impartially because of not being involved in emotional ways as the parent is.

The opportunities for intellectual development are so obvious that they hardly need extended exposition. All of the so-called learned professions bring those who pursue them in intimate contact with books, studies, ideas. They stimulate the desire for increased knowledge and wider intellectual contacts. No one can be really successful in performing the duties and meeting these demands who does not retain his intellectual curiosity intact throughout his entire career. It would not, therefore, be just to claim that there is anything unique in the opportunities for intellectual growth furnished by the vocation of teaching. But there are opportunities in it sufficiently great and varied so as to furnish something for every taste. Since literature and science and the arts are taught in the schools, the continued pursuit of learning in some or all of these fields is made desirable. This further study is not a side line but something which fits directly into the demands and opportunities of the vocation.

The social opportunities of teaching, in the narrower sense of the word "social" differ widely in different sections and places, so that no unqualified statement can be made. It is said, and probably with a great deal of truth, that in the large cities teachers are not as much looked up to as they once were; that in some places they are classed almost as household servants. These conditions, however, are exceptional. In general, the profession ranks high in the esteem of the public, and teachers are welcomed because of their calling as well as for their own sake.

The material or pecuniary rewards of the calling are not the chief reason for going into it. There are no financial prizes equalling those to be obtained in business, the law, or even, if we take the exceptional physician as the measure, in medicine. On the other hand, there are not the great disparities and risks which exist in most other callings. The rewards, if not great, are reasonably sure. Until the depression they were, moreover, pretty steadily increasing. If we include vacation periods as part of the material reward of teaching, the profession ranks high. There is no other calling which allows such a prolonged period for travel, for study, and recreation as does the educational. To many temperaments, this phase of teaching counterbalances all the material drawbacks.

The personal qualifications which are needed are indicated in a general way by the opportunities which the vocation presents, since from the standpoint of the individual who is thinking of going into the profession, these are demands made upon him. Good health is, under usual conditions, a prerequisite for success in all callings. One special feature of it may, however, be emphasized in connection with teaching. Those persons who are peculiarly subject to nervous strain and worry should not go into teaching. It is not good for them nor for the pupils who come under their charge. One of the most depressing phases of the vocation is the number of care-worn teachers one sees, with anxiety depicted on the lines of their faces, reflected in their strained high pitched voices and sharp manners. While contact with the young is a privilege for some temperaments, it is a tax on others, and a tax which they do not bear up under very well. And in some schools, there are too many pupils to a teacher, too many subjects to teach, and adjustments to pupils are made in a mechanical rather than a human way. Human nature reacts against such unnatural conditions.

This point of nervous balance and all-round health connects slowly with the next point. Those who go into teaching ought to have a natural love of contact with the young. There are those who are bored by contact with children and even with youth. They can be more useful in other professions. Their contacts soon become perfunctory and mechanical, and children even if they are not able to express the matter in words, are conscious of the lack of spontaneous response, and no amount of learning or even of acquired pedagogical skill makes up for the deficiency. Only those who have it in themselves to stay young indefinitely and to retain a lively sympathy with the spirit of youth should remain long in the teaching profession.

The point which I would emphasize next is a natural love of communicating knowledge along with a love of knowledge itself. There are scholars who have the latter in a marked degree but who lack enthusiasm for imparting it. To the "natural-born" teacher learning is incomplete unless it is shared. He or she is not contented with it in and for its own sake. He or she wants to use it to stir up the minds of others. Nothing is so satisfactory as to see another mind get the spark of an idea and kindle into a glow because of it. One of the finest teachers I have ever known said to me, "I have never known a first-class teacher who did not have something of the preacher about him"—or her. And he went on to explain that what he meant was the love of arousing in others the same intellectual interests and enthusiasms which the teacher himself experienced.

Finally, the teacher should combine an active and keen interest in some one branch of knowledge with interest and skill in following the reactions of the minds of others. I would not say that a teacher ought to strive to be a high-class scholar in all the subjects he or she has to teach. But I would say that a teacher ought to have an unusual love and aptitude in some one subject; history, mathematics, literature, science, a fine art, or whatever. The teacher will then have the feel for genuine information and insight in all subjects; will not sink down to the level of the conventional and perfunctory teacher who merely "hears" recitations, and will communicate by unconscious contagion love of learning to others.

The teacher is distinguished from the scholar, no matter how good the latter, by interest in watching the movements of the minds of others, by being sensitive to all the signs of response they exhibit; their quality of response or lack of it, to subject-matter presented. A personal sympathy is a great thing in a teacher. It does its best work, however, when it is in sympathy with the mental movements of others, is alive to perplexities and problems, discerning of their causes, having the mental tact to put the finger on the cause of failure, quick to see every sign of promise and to nourish it to maturity. I have often been asked how it was that some teachers who have never studied the art of teaching are still extraordinarily good teachers. The explanation is simple. They have a quick, sure and unflagging sympathy with the operations and process of the minds they are in contact with. Their own minds move in harmony with those of others, appreciating their difficulties, entering into their problems, sharing their intellectual victories.

I am not interested in putting any obstacles in the way of those who think of becoming teachers by dwelling on the obstacles it presents. To an active and energetic character, these will prove only stimuli to greater effort. But few things are more disastrous than the round peg in the square hole, than a person in a work to which he or she is not suited. Those who go into the profession of teaching should then realize in advance that for some temperaments it is too safe, too protected, a calling. There is not enough stimulus from competition with their equals to call out their best energies. There are those to whom the young are inferiors; they tend to teach down to them from above, and to acquire a manner which is either tyrannical or patronizing. Such persons should refrain from teaching. There are communities in which political influences operate with great strength. Would-be teachers should ask themselves whether they have the strength of character to sustain their integrity against these influences; whether they can play their part with others without becoming timeservers, chair-warmers, place-holders. The so-called educator who is little more than a cheap politician looking out for his own interests is a sorry spectacle. In fact, every one can call up in his own experience the hard places he is likely to run into and ask whether he has the force to meet and overcome the difficulties which arise.

For those who are fitted for the work, the calling of the teacher combines three rewards, each intense and unique. Love of knowledge; sympathy with growth, intellectual and moral; interest in the improvement of society through improving the individuals who compose it.

Professional Spirit among Teachers (1913)

YOU AND I KNOW, we all know, how much time, effort and energy are spent in attempting to develop a professional spirit among teachers. We all know that it is said over and over, and truly said, that if we could achieve a thoroughly professional spirit, permeating the entire corps of teachers and educators, we should have done more to forward the cause of education than can be achieved in any other way. Now it is not my affair to tell of all the ways by which the formation and development of a professional spirit may be promoted or hindered.

It is not my business to attempt even to define very closely just what a professional spirit among teachers is; but I think we would agree that there would be two marked features characterizing the teachers who have a distinctly professional spirit. One of these traits is manifested in the every-day school work with the children, in the questions of instruction and of discipline arising from the teacher's daily contact with the children. It consists in the teacher being possessed by a recognition of the responsibility for the constant study of school room work, the constant study of children, of methods, of subject matter in its various adaptations to pupils. The professional spirit means that the teachers do not think their work done when they have reasonably prepared a certain amount of subject matter and spent a certain number of hours in the school room attempting in a reasonably intelligent way to convey that material to the children. Teachers of a professional spirit would recognize that they still had a problem to deal with. There would be the continued intellectual growth that comes from diverted intellectual interest in the methods and material of the teachers' occupation, so that we should have not mere artisans but artists.

The other element in a professional spirit consists, I think, of a recognition of the responsibility of teachers to the general public. It is a commonplace that

---

First published in *American Teacher* 2 (1913): 114–16, from an address given to the organization meeting of the Teachers' League of New York, 28 February 1913.

our young are the chief asset of society, and that their proper protection and their proper nurture is the most fundamental care of society. Now a professional spirit would mean not merely that the teachers would be devoted to the continuous study of the questions of teaching within the school room; but that they would also bear a responsibility as leaders, as directors in the formation of public opinion.

Now I am going to say in passing that it is a somewhat striking fact, and, to one who is himself a teacher, perhaps a somewhat humiliating fact, that in the last of these matters, teachers and professional educators have not been especially active. The larger questions about the protection of childhood, the movements for the abolition of child labor, movements for playgrounds, for recreation centres, even for the adequate use of the school plant, these and the thousand and one problems relative to children that have come forward with the great congestion of population in cities in the last generation—the initiative in the agitation of these questions and the formation of public opinion has to a surprisingly small extent proceeded from the teachers. It has come from social settlements, from philanthropists, from charity workers, from people whose interest was not stimulated by education in a professional way.

Now, why is this? As I said, I have no intention of attempting to go into all the causes. But why is it that there has been so comparatively little done in this latter direction? Why is it that it is necessary to harp so continuously upon the formation of a professional spirit among teachers with respect even to the ordinary affairs, the subject matter, the methods and discipline in the classroom? We do not find, I think, for example, in the medical profession that it is necessary constantly to urge the formation of a professional spirit. We hear more or less about professional ethics; but not of professional spirit in the sense of the duty and responsibility of the physician to study his cases, to inform himself of improvements in methods of diagnosis, methods of surgery and therapeutic methods through the country. It is taken for granted that it is for the physician's own interest to be intellectually growing, intellectually alive, and concerned with these things.

Now, if I am asked for a reply as to the chief cause, not the sole cause, but the chief cause, of the relative backwardness of the formation of professional spirit among teachers and the consequent need of urging them, of preaching to them, and of almost driving them to develop this more enlightened interest in the work and recognition of making contributions to its improvement, my answer would be: the lack of adequate impetus.

It is not enough simply to teach people, and preach to people, and to urge them to do certain things. There must be something in the very nature of the work which makes the thing desirable, makes it their own vital concern.

When teachers have as little to do, as they have at present, with intellectual responsibility for the conduct of the schools; when the teachers who are doing most, if not all, of the teaching have nothing whatsoever to say directly about the formation of the courses of study and very little indirectly; when they have nothing save ways of informal discussion and exchange of experience in teachers' meetings, or very little to say about methods of teaching and discipline; when they have no means for making their experience actually count in practice, the chief motive to the development of professional spirit is lacking. There is not a single body of men and women in the world engaged in any occupation whatsoever among whom the development of professional spirit would not be hampered if they realized that no matter how much experience they got, however much wisdom they acquired, whatever experiments they tried, whatever results they obtained, that experience was not to count beyond the limits of their own immediate activity; that they had no authorized way of transmitting or of communicating it, and of seeing it was taken account of by others.

The situation would be ridiculous if it were not serious: that teachers who come in contact with the students should have nothing to do directly, and so little to do indirectly, with the selection, formation and arrangement of subject matter; that they should find that in printed manuals provided by other people, simply with the instruction to purvey so much of that per year, or per month or per week, or, even in some cases, per day.

Now, either teaching is an intellectual enterprise or it is a routine mechanical exercise. And if it is an intellectual exercise, and the professional spirit means intellectual awakening and enlightenment, there is, I repeat, no way better calculated to retard and discourage the professional spirit than methods which so entirely relieve the teachers from intellectual responsibility as do the present methods.

We hear a good deal about the concentration of responsibility. Now, there is one responsibility that can be concentrated only by distributing it. An intellectual responsibility has got to be distributed to every human being who is concerned in carrying out the work in question, and to attempt to concentrate intellectual responsibility for a work that has to be done, with their brains and their hearts, by hundreds or thousands of people in a dozen or so at the top, no matter how wise and skillful they are, is not to concentrate responsibility—it is to diffuse irresponsibility.

And that describes in the rough the system and organization of schools in the democracy under which we are supposed to be living. I read an article in proof a few days ago—I do not know whether it has come out recently—in which the author says that the question at issue regarding the introduction of industrial education in this country was whether the teachers were to control the new industrial schools, as they, the teachers, controlled all the existing schools; or whether the wide-awake and alert business men were to control these schools. And he pointed out that one reason for the business man's control was the fact that the teachers had made such a mess of the schools of which they are already in control.

Now, I bring to you this happy news—that it is you who are and who have been in control of our public schools. But unfortunately it is only when the schools are to be adversely criticised that the power of the mass of the teachers to control their own work is in evidence.

The Educational Balance, Efficiency and Thinking (1916)

THERE ARE TWO TRAITS WHICH have to go together and which have to be balanced with each other in order that we may get an adequate and rounded development of personality, and for that reason there are two factors which have to be constantly borne in mind in all teaching and borne in mind in such a way that we do not first tend to one and develop one, and then, forgetting that, develop the other, but that we keep the two balanced together all the time.

I call those two factors efficiency and thought.

Efficiency, or skill in execution and good, orderly, effective method and technique of doing things which is under control. The other, thinking, or the recognition of the meaning of what we do, having a definite, well-thought-out and comprehensive plan or purpose in our actions.

Now, I do not care whether it is in school or out, in business, in politics, in science, or art, I find everywhere that these two factors are required for real, successful accomplishment. The business man has got to have his orderly habits of work. He has got to have his skill which belongs to his particular business, just as must the physician or the lawyer have a method of skillful operation which enables him to do promptly and without confusion in a regular, consecutive way, without waste, without constant faults and wasted moves, the things which he needs to do. So the scientific man in his laboratory has to have command of the technique of his particular method of inquiry. If he is a chemist, he has got to be able to handle and manipulate his materials and his tools in the way that they call for. If he is a mathematician, he has got another set of tools and apparatus and another mode of skill. But he has to have that same definite control of materials. So with the housewife in the household; so on through all these undertakings. At the same time, just as the artist might have a fine technique

First published in Indiana State Teachers' Association, *Proceedings* (1916), 188–93, from address given on 27 October 1916, at the annual meeting in Indianapolis, 25–28 October 1916.

with the instrument and yet the use of that instrument would not move people, would not affect them on any very deep level, because there was no feeling back of it or because there were no ideas expressed in it, so, of course, a business man might have a certain technique or skill but never rise above the level of a bookkeeper or accountant, never become able or competent really to take hold of the entire business and manage it for himself, because of the lack of ability intellectually to analyze situations, to see what the factors are and to form a broad plan, form a mental synthesis, that would bring these things together. So, I take it, while I have not any particular experience in that line, a housekeeper might know enough to handle a broom and the dishpan and the dishrag and all the other particular things where skill is needed in the household, and yet be a poor housekeeper for lack of ability to control these activities intellectually and make a plan, which would make the different details of the day's work and the day's duties that had to be attended to, fit into each other in some kind of harmonious and effective way.

Now, before we go on I want to generalize, in a way, what I have been saying. What elements of life is it that those two factors correspond to? Why do we need both this regular formed habit of action on the one hand, ability to do a thing with uniformity and promptness twice over, and on the other hand require this capacity to think? It is because there are two factors in every situation that we have to deal with. On the one hand there are certain factors that are stable, that are uniform, that are repeated from place to place, from time to time, from situation to situation. Now, if everything in life were fixed and uniform, habits, skilled habits, would answer every purpose and all that would ever be needed would be for teachers in the schoolroom to train for efficiency. They would drop the element of thought practically out of consideration. What we would get, of course, then, would be efficient machines. A well constructed machine will work as long as its structure remains uniform and constant and the conditions under which it is worked remain constant. If the conditions of life, if the conditions of our natural and social surroundings, were the same from hour to hour and day to day and year to year, all that would be necessary would be for a person to get stocked up with the right set of skilled habits, and having got started they would go on. But it is because beside these stable and constant elements in our lives there are changing elements, unexpectedly varying ones, that we cannot rely simply upon the element of habit to take care of ourselves. We have to have also the training and the variety in thinking to take care of these emergencies that come up because of the unexpected and changing elements in the situation. Wherever the conditions are routine conditions, I repeat, persons do not need to think. A horse in a treadmill would never have any particular occasion for thinking after he got his legs going and the treadmill going around; and persons that are engaged in these routine activities, all they need is a particular skill or habit in doing the particular thing that they have got started on. But when a machine breaks down the habits of the operator running that machine won't help him out. He will be perfectly helpless unless he can call science to his aid, unless he can call thought to his aid, unless he understands the operations of the machine; unless he understands, as we say, the theory of this machine and its workings, he will be helpless and he will have to call in somebody else who has this thought ability, this understanding, in order to help him out. We need these formed habits of skill and execution in so far as there are constant and regular elements in our surroundings and consequently things that can be dealt with two or three times or any number of times the same way, over and over, so when we have got the right habit formed we can dismiss that from further consideration and let that work. But we go through life in a world of variety and change and if we stop to think we know that the average person comes up against complex and varied circumstances in life. A few generations ago there was a time when society was pretty well stratified into classes, when it was known of a child at his birth in a general way what kind of thing he was going to do all his life, that he was going to follow the profession of his father, with the same social status. Under those conditions they could put the emphasis much more on forming the particular habits that would enable him to fit into his particular pre-ordained niche in life. But our life today, and especially our American life, is very mobile and changeable. Things are flexible and fluid and elastic. A person meets one situation today and tomorrow another, and if he is following the same business calling, the changes under which that is done, or he has to drop behind and be abandoned or be able to understand things and think out and make his changes.

A man who employs labor, to whom it is a very important practical matter to be able to pick out people not in the factory but in another type of pursuit, told me that for his own protection he had evolved, as many men have nowadays under the stress of modern business conditions, certain ways of picking out young people particularly who were intellectually promising, that he could trust to take hold of a certain thing and go ahead with it and carry it out in a way that would be advantageous to themselves and to him. He said that one of his devices was to take one of these young men and tell him to go down and look up certain things in the files, look up a certain order and see what the date of the order was and the date upon which it had been filed. When he would come back he would ask him not only that, but ask him more questions about where the order came from and just what it was for, and so on. And he said there was always a certain percentage of people who could answer just the particular question they had been sent to get the information upon. Those were the people that he got rid of and found it profitable to get rid of as soon as possible. He would send him back again to get something else and he would come back again with just that one particular item of information he had been sent after. Then there were the various grades up to those who had sufficient intellectual interest, sufficient curiosity, that when they went down there to find out this one thing, would take in other things, too, or at least after they had been sent back a few times to get these other items of information, made it their business to find out all they could the first time and be ready to answer this variety of scope of questions the next time, and they were the people he found it profitable to take, people who could take intellectual responsibility later on and go ahead for themselves. That is one practical instance of what I mean about the ability to think as a very effective central factor in efficiency in action itself, because, as I said before, if our conditions were perfectly uniform and rigid then we could get efficiency from mere routine, mechanical method, but because we have to change conditions, because we have to readapt our habits that we have formed, we have to have this breadth of intellectual insight and foresight also to control.

The third point that I wish to make in this connection is that when our mere mechanical habits, our forms of skill and our thinking do fall out of balance with each other something happens also on the mental side. We not only become routine, mechanical and slavish in our outward activities, but our mental life becomes very irregular.

You cannot stop people's minds; you cannot stop people's thinking, if you mean by thinking their thoughts, their imaginations, their ideas in their head, not when they are awake. The only way to stop it is to go to sleep and to get into a deep sleep. What we can do, however, is to make a split, make a division, between our outward actions, our forms of skill and power of accomplishment, and our inner life. The extremely absent-minded person is, of course, an example of a person who has had a split between two things, when his actions are going on in one direction and his thoughts and ideas are going in some other direction. So we have a story of a man who pulls out his watch to see if he has time to go back home and get his watch. He performs one action automatically and it has no connection with his thinking.

Now, there is a technique of teaching, a technique of the management of the schoolroom, keeping order, treating children, of asking questions, even of giving out, assigning lessons; assigning the different school work and so forth, is just as much a part of the art of teaching as the particular technique of the artist is a part of the calling of the artist, but over and above that is the need for that sense of the purpose and meaning of it that results in sympathy with a development of the life of the children, what is going on not in their more outward motions, in the things they do, but what is going on in their feelings, their imagination, what effect the schoolroom is having on the permanent disposition, the side of their emotions and imagination, without which the teacher cannot be an artist, no matter how complete and adequate the teacher's command is of the technique of teaching, that is, of the various forms of outward skill which are necessary to make the successful teacher. The teacher as an artist needs to be one who is engaged in getting the pupils as much as possible into the attitude of the artist in their relations in life, that is, to solve what is after all the great problem, the moral, the intellectual problem of everyone, to get habits of efficient action, so that the person won't be a mere day-dreamer or theorist, or a wasteful or incompetent person, but to get that unity with certain affections and desires and sympathies and with power to carry out intellectual plans. That can be got only when we give as much attention to the thinking side of the life of the pupils from the first day as we give to their forming these good outward habits. For this reason it seems to me that so far as the teaching is concerned the great problem of the teacher is the problem of keeping a balance between these two factors of efficiency in action and insight and foresight, ability to have the purpose to perform plans in thought.

Teaching Ethics in the High School (1893)

IT WOULD BE, I AM inclined to believe, comparatively easy to bring arguments in support of the conclusion that there has never been such a widespread interest in teaching ethics in the schools as at present; or of the conclusion that there is a general consensus among experts against teaching it. I am not going to try to draw out this antinomy, but I want to run over two or three of the reasons in favor of the latter conclusion. One is the pretty widespread conviction that conscious moralizing in the schoolroom has had its day—if it ever had any; that the mistake has been made of identifying ethical instruction with the conning over and drumming in of ethical precepts; that the most efficient moral teaching is that afforded by the constant bearing in upon the individual of the life-process of the school; that set moral instruction other than grows directly out of occurrences in the school itself, or other than that which calls to the attention of the pupil the meaning of the life of which he is a part, is pretty sure to be formal and perfunctory, and to result rather in hardening the mind of the child with a lot of half-understood precepts than in helpful development. And if moral instruction is conceived not so much as set instruction in regulations for conduct, as cultivation of the child's own conscience, there is the danger of cultivating in some a morbid conscientiousness always prying and spying into the state of feelings, instead of allowing those feelings to develop in their normal intimate connection with action; and in others there is the danger of creating offensive prigs, possibly hypocrites. With all this I agree; indeed, I do not think that the movement against teaching ethics in the schools has gone as far as it is likely to go, or as it should go—provided, that is, ethics is conceived in this spirit. Some of the books which the last year or two have produced, and which are being gradually urged into the schools on account of the great revival of interest in the moral side of school work, seem to me to be based upon an

---

First published in *Educational Review* 6 (November 1893): 313–21.

utterly wrong idea of ethics—upon the assumption that if you can only teach a child moral rules and distinctions enough, you have somehow furthered his moral being. Against all this, we cannot too often protest. From the side of ethical theory, we must protest that all this is a caricature of the scientific method of ethics and of its scientific aims. From the standpoint of practical morals, we have to protest that the inculcation of moral rules is no more likely to make character than is that of astronomical formulæ.

If this reaction, however, is simply against all instruction in ethical science in the schools; if it does not rather ask how right instruction in morals may be substituted for wrong, I think we shall not get its full benefit. Rightly read, it is a movement against a false view of morals and a false theory of ethics; the danger is that we are likely to interpret it as meaning that the ethical theory in question may be all right in itself, but is out of place in the schools. At all events, I wish to submit a certain conception of ethical theory upon which that theory seems to me thoroughly teachable in the schoolroom; not only teachable, indeed, but necessary to any well-adjusted curriculum. It is generally admitted, for example, that there has been a talking about number in the school instead of intelligent use of it; that there has been altogether too much attention paid to the examination of the logic of quantity, in the abstract, and altogether too little logic in the attitude of the pupil's mind toward quantity. The one who should, on account of this, urge that mathematical relations, in their reality, had no place in the schools, would be quite on a par with the one who draws a similar conclusion in ethics, because of the similar abuse there. The greater the evil resulting from a false conception of the nature of number or of moral action, the greater the demand for introducing instruction based on a right idea.

Ethics, rightly conceived, is the statement of human relationships in action. In any right study of ethics, then, the pupil is not studying hard and fixed rules for conduct; he is studying the ways in which men are bound together in the complex relations of their interactions. He is not studying, in an introspective way, his own sentiments and moral attitudes; he is studying facts as objective as those of hydro-statics or of the action of dynamos. They are subjective, too, but subjective in the sense that since the pupil himself is one who is bound up in the complex of action, the ethical relations have an interest and concern for him which no action of fluid or of dynamo can possibly have. While this subject-matter should be taught from the lowest grade up, I shall choose an illustration of the mode of teaching it better adapted for high schools, or, possibly, the grades just below the high school. In making it, I need hardly say, I suppose, that the method indicated is simply a way; an illustration of the character and spirit of ethical teaching, rather than a method.

Let the teacher, at the outset, ask the pupils how they would decide, if a case of seeming misery were presented to them, whether to relieve it and, if so, how to relieve. This should be done without any preliminary dwelling upon the question as a "moral" one; rather, it should be pointed out that the question is simply a practical one, and that ready-made moral considerations are to be put one side. Above all, however, it should be made clear that the question is not what to do, but how to decide what to do. As this is the rock on which the method is likely to split, let me indicate the force of the distinction. Anyone who is acquainted with the methods in which the well-organized Associated Charities do their work knows that they never discuss giving relief to someone on the basis of abstract principles of charity. They construct, from all available data, an image of the case in question, and decide the particular question upon the basis of the needs and circumstances of that particular case. Now the whole object of the method I am bringing forward is not to get children to arguing about the moral rules which should control the giving of charity—that is a relapse into the method of precepts against which I have protested. The object is to get them into the habit of mentally constructing some actual scene of human interaction, and of consulting that for instruction as to what to do. All the teacher's questions and suggestions, therefore, must be directed toward aiding the pupil in building up in his imagination such a scene. To allow them to discuss what to do, save as relative to the development of some case, is to fall back into the very moral abstractions we are trying to avoid. So when children begin to argue (as they are almost sure to do) about the merits of some proposed plan of action, care must be taken not to let them argue it in general, but to introduce their ideas into the case under consideration so as to add new features and phases. The whole point, in a word, is to keep the mental eye constantly upon some actual situation or interaction; to realize in the imagination this or that particular needy person making his demand upon some other particular person. It follows from this, of course, that the line of illustration chosen, that of charity, has no value in itself; it is taken simply as a basis with reference to which to get the child to fix his mind carefully upon the typical aspects of human interaction. The thought which underlies the method is that if instruction in the theory of morals has any practical value it has such value as it aids in forming, in the mind of the person taught, the habit of realizing for himself and in himself the nature of the practical situations in which he will find himself placed. The end of the method, then, is the formation of a sympathetic imagination for human relations in action; this is the ideal which is substituted for training in moral rules, or for analysis of one's sentiments and attitude in conduct.

I have tried the method with a class of college students, and a rapid summary of questions which one member of the class or another said he would put in order to decide what to do may give an idea of the character of the ethical material thus placed at the disposal of the teacher. Find out whether the want is real or assumed; investigate its character, e.g., whether immediate, as for food, or remote; whether material or spiritual. Inquire into causes of want: lack of energy, incapacity, accident, sickness, vice as intemperance, loss of work. Search out the past record of individual, his station in life; his family, neighbors, cronies; power of work, any special skill. Find out his character and temperament so as to adjust a method to that. Examine into one's own needs and powers, the demands upon one's own time and money, etc., etc. These are selected from the answers given in the first day; of course, further discussion and question would evolve multitudes more.

We now have our teacher with his ideal and his material more or less definitely before him. How shall he deal with it? The answer in the general is plain. Deal with it so that in and through the special situation chosen the pupil shall have gradually brought home to him some of the typical features of every human interaction. These typical features are the content of ethical theory: that is to say, there is no ethical analysis, however advanced and however scientific, which can do more than discover the generic phases of human activity in society. In order to carry out this plan, the teacher should unite, it seems to me, a pretty definite idea of the typical phases which he wishes to bring out, with great freedom in detail. Unless he has the latter, he will fail to take due advantage of the suggestions arising from the pupils' answers; will fail to be alive to their interests and, in general, will be likely to relapse into a formal and rigid mode. But if the freedom is carried so far that the teacher does not have an idea of the goal at which he intends the pupils shall bring up, the work will be so random that its object, the realization by the pupil of human action in its typical features, will be lost.

One of these typical phases is the proper place of the emotions in conduct. In these days; the attacks upon "indiscriminate giving" have permeated a good way, and it is safe to say that some pupil will urge the need of not giving from the mere impulse of the moment. This will open the way for a discussion of the part to be played by sympathy, benevolent impulses, etc. Any teacher who is even moderately acquainted with the literature of charity organizations will have no difficulty in showing the necessity of not giving way to the feelings of the moment. He can show that to do so is not to act for any moral or practical reason, but simply to gratify one's own feelings—and that this is the definition of all selfishness; he can show that, by encouraging idleness and beggary, it does an injustice to society as a whole, while it wrongs the person supposably helped, by robbing him of his independence and freedom. Now all this, I submit, is valuable in itself; treated by a teacher who knows his business (or who is even interested in it, if he does not know it), it can hardly fail to rank in importance with any subject taught in the high school. But it is more than valuable in itself. Any pupil who has worked out these facts day by day for weeks, for a year, who has learned what careful study of conditions and weighing of expedients is necessary to treat many a case of relief, is prepared to understand the true meaning of the term "motive" in ethical discussion better, far better, I submit, than nineteen-twentieths of our college students who have analyzed it at large. The pupil is in position to understand what the relative place and bearing of both impulse and reason in conduct are, and to understand the meaning of those theories which attach such importance to the reasonableness of action.

Another typical phase of all action which the pupil will be in a position to appreciate after carrying on for some weeks a study of this kind, is that of the interrelation of all individuals. When he sees the stress upon the social relations of the person to be helped, upon the dependence of his family upon him, upon the fact that he is out of work, possibly because of a strike, possibly because of speculative movements five hundred miles away, possibly because of some caprice of fashion; when he realizes the pains which must be taken in dealing with him not only not to weaken his own self-respect, but also not to weaken the ties of neighborhood unity—when he sees all this, and a multitude of other details which will develop in the course of the discussion, the interdependence of interests in a single action (though he never hears the phrase) cannot but become a vital fact.

Since, in view of the breakdown of so many of the older motives for morality, the youth of the next generation must more and more draw their inspiration from a realization of the unity of the interest of all in any one and of one in all, there is no need to dwell upon the practical bearing of this.

These two factors of ethical action, namely, the place of impulse and of intelligence, and the multitude of relations to be considered and focused in any human action, may, I think, be taught to all youth as far advanced as the high-school grades. How much further the analysis is carried will have to depend upon the maturity, previous training, and home surroundings of the pupils. In some cases, it might be possible to carry the study of this or some other typical case far enough to indicate the nature of moral law and obligation, and this without detriment to the concreteness of the study. Or, again, it might be possible to introduce a study of the various ideals currently proposed for conduct and test them by application to the problem under consideration. But all this would be a matter of detail. I am concerned only to point out in general in what spirit ethics may and should be taught in the schools, and to suggest an outline of a method for realizing this method in the higher grades. Above and beyond any formal analysis is the result in the way of a new interest in, and a new sense for, human relations in action.

I may be called on to say something of the practicability of introducing this study into the high school; I may be reminded of the already crowded state of the curriculum, and asked to show the interrelations of this study to others. I should only be expressing what I myself feel, if I were to say that if other studies do not correlate well with this one, so much the worse for them—they are the ones to give way, not it. For it is not the study of ethics I am urging; it is the study of ethical relationships, the study, that is, of this complex world of which we are members. Where there is one reason for the ordinary student to become acquainted with the intricacies of geometry, of physics, of Latin, or of Greek, there are twenty for him to become acquainted with the nature of those relations upon which his deepest weal and woe depend, and to become interested in, and habituated to, looking at them with sympathetic imagination. And so far as the fetich of discipline, or the culture-value of studies, or anything of that sort, is concerned, one need have no fear that the world of ethical activities will not afford scope for all the powers of analysis, of interpretation, and of observation, of which any pupil may be possessed. The subject here is so important, the mental power brought into play in dealing with it is of such quality and kept at such pitch, that, ultimately, the subject-matter of ethics must furnish the measure for other studies and not vice versa. But it is not necessary to carry the argument to this extreme. Except through a study of ethical material from the standpoint here outlined, and with the ideal here suggested (though not, of course, necessarily with just the material I have employed), it is impossible for the pupil to get the full meaning either of literature or of history—the two studies of whose future we may be certain, happen what may to the others now entering into our curricula. Such a study of ethics as I am pleading for will play at once into the study and appreciation of both literature and history, while the latter will constantly introduce new material, new problems, new methods for the ethical imagination—the imagination that is occupied with making real for the individual the world of action in which he lives.

No one can be more conscious than I am myself of the apparent gap between the meager outline of the study I have presented and the claims made for it. There is, however, in my own mind no fear that I have exaggerated the importance of a study of ethics conceived in the spirit I have indicated, and I am glad to seem to exaggerate if the seeming will lead any to question for even a moment the highly formal character of high-school instruction as at present administered; and to entertain, if but for a moment, the possibility of a time when the central study shall be human life itself; a time when science shall be less a quantity constant in itself and more a method for approaching and dealing with this human life; a time when language and literature, as well as history, shall be less realms of thought and emotion by themselves and more the record and the instruments of this human life.

Philosophy of Education (1913)

RELATION OF PHILOSOPHY AND EDUCATION.—A clear conception of the nature of the philosophy of education in distinction from the science and principles of education is not possible without some antecedent conception of the nature of philosophy itself and its relation to life. Is philosophy capable of being generated and developed without any reference to education? Then a philosophy of education will be simply the application to educational ideas of an outside ready-made standard of judgment, with all its dangers of forcing the facts of education so that they conform to and support the philosophy already formed. In this case, we shall have as many philosophies of education as are required to illustrate diverging philosophic systems. The case will stand quite otherwise if there is an intimate and vital relation between the need for philosophy and the necessity for education. In this case the philosophy of education will simply make explicit the reference to the guiding of life needs and purposes which is operative in philosophy itself. It will not be an external application of philosophy, but its development to the point of adequate manifestation of its own inner purpose and motive. While different philosophies of education will still exist, they will not be so many corollaries of divergent pure philosophies, but will make explicit the different conceptions of the value and aims of actual life held by different persons. It will be seen that different philosophies exist because men have in mind different ideals of life and different educational methods for making these ideals prevail. The chief point of this article is to develop the conception of the internal and vital relation of education and philosophy.

Every seriously minded person may be said to have a philosophy. For he has some sort of a working theory of life. He possesses, in however half-conscious fashion, a standpoint from which weight and importance are attached to the

First published in *A Cyclopedia of Education*, ed. Paul Monroe (New York: Macmillan, 1913), 4:697–703.

endless flow of detailed happenings and doings. His philosophy is his general scheme and measure of values, his way of estimating the significance that attaches to the various incidents of experience. If pressed to state and justify his working principle, he might reply that while it would not satisfy others, it served its owner and maker. No individual, however, is so eccentric that he invents and builds up his scheme except on the general pattern that is socially transmitted to him. The exigencies and the perplexities of life are recurrent. The same generic problems have faced men over and over; by long-continued cooperative effort men have worked out general ideas regarding the meaning of life, including the connections of men with one another and with the world in which they live. These conceptions are embodied not only in the codes of moral principles which men profess and the religions in which they find support and consolation, but in the basic ideas which have become commonplace through their very generality: such ideas as that things hang together to make a world; that events have causes; that things may be brought into classes; the distinctions of animate and inanimate, personal and physical, and so on throughout the warp and woof of our intellectual fabric. Philosophy aims to set forth a conception of the world, or of reality, and of life which will assign to each of these interests its proper and proportionate place. It aims to set forth the distinctive role of each in a way that will harmonize its demand with that of other ends.

Need of a Philosophy of Education.—Three classes of motives, unconsciously blended with one another, usually operate in making the need for systematic and rational ideas felt, and in deciding the point of view from which the need is dealt with. These motives are the conflict of conservative and progressive tendencies; the conflict of scientific conceptions of the world with beliefs hallowed by tradition and giving sanction to morals and religion; and the conflict of institutional demands with that for a freer and fuller expression of individuality. (1) Some philosophies are marked by a reforming, almost revolutionary, spirit. They criticize the world and life as they exist, and set in opposition to them an ideal world into conformity with which the existent scheme of things ought to be brought. Other philosophies tend rather to justify things as they are, pointing out that if we penetrate to their true nature and essential meaning, each class of things is found to serve a necessary purpose and embody a necessary idea. Plato and Aristotle, Fichte and Hegel, for example, are all of them classified as idealists, but the tendency of Plato and Fichte is to set up an ideal over against the actual; while that of Aristotle and Hegel is to exhibit the rational nature or ideal already embodied in the actual—a difference that clearly corresponds to the ordinary division of men into reformers and conservatives.

(2) Different philosophers interpret their material very differently according to the respective weight they instinctively attribute on the one hand to scientific conceptions of the world, and on the other to ethical tendencies and aspirations.

If one takes his departure from the former, he will explain men's moral and religious beliefs on the basis of the principles furnished by contemporary science, and will deny the validity of all ideas, no matter how influential in life, that do not harmonize with these principles. To others, men's moral aims and efforts are the most significant thing in life and are taken as the key to the nature of reality. The results of science are reinterpreted to bring them into line. During the rapid development of natural science since the seventeenth century, many philosophies have thus made it their chief business to provide a view of reality in which the seemingly divergent claims and standpoints of natural science and morals should be reconciled.

(3) The third moving force concerns the value attached to the principle of free individuality—individuality that confers upon each person a distinctive worth not supplied by any other person and not capable of being summed up or exhausted in any general formula or principle. Some thinkers start by natural preference with the standpoint of law or a general order, or a pervasive and unifying force. Strictly individual traits are then brought into line by reduction (or at least approximation) to the universal. If individuality is not denied as an ultimate reality, it is explained and justified from the standpoint of a comprehensive uniform principle. Such philosophies tend to be deductive in character and to assign greater value to reason, which deals with general conceptions, than to perception, which reveals particulars. Persons with a strong interest in individuality reverse the standard of value and the method of consideration. Specific individuals are taken to be the primary facts; general principles, laws, classes, are derived from comparison of the individuals or are subordinate to them. In method, such philosophies tend to be empirical and inductive, accepting the observations of sense and the particular situations of conduct as the most certain data, and employing rational conceptions only as secondary means of connecting particulars or filling their gaps.

The totality or completeness at which philosophy aims is not quantitative; it is not the greatest possible sum of accurate knowledge. As to this sort of completeness or wholeness, philosophy cannot compete with the special sciences taken in their totality. For all its special facts, philosophy must depend upon these sciences, and so far as organization of the facts into a larger system of knowledge is concerned it must also walk humbly in the path beaten by science. But there is another kind of unity and wholeness with which science is not concerned: unity of attitude and wholeness of outlook. But wholeness means also balance, interaction, and mutual reenforcement of the various values and interests of life: religion, poetry, industry or the business of making a living, politics or the art of living together, morals, science itself. An account of "experience as a whole" is a conception of experience that shows the special contribution which each of these typical interests makes, and the claim for recognition it may legitimately put forth. The only "experience as a whole" that concerns man is an experience whose parts change continuously, but all change into one another as there is occasion, with ease and flexibility, and so as to enrich one another. Its opposite is not our everyday experience with its fluctuations and its endless running out into the new, but one-sided exaggerations of some phase of this everyday experience, or an isolation of its interests so that they restrict one another, and thus impoverish life.

Philosophy of Education, Science of Education, and Principles of Education.—Education is such an important interest of life that in any case we should expect to find a philosophy of education, just as there is a philosophy of art and of religion. We should expect, that is, such a treatment of the subject as would show that the nature of existence renders education an integral and indispensable function of life. We should expect an interpretation and criticism of the materials and methods currently used in education, using this necessary function as the standard of value. Such a treatment is usually presented under the title of "Principles of Education." While no rigid line marks off this discussion from what is termed the "Science of Education," there are differences of aim and spirit that are worth noting, because of the light they shed upon the nature of a philosophy of education. It is possible to start with education as an established fact, with education as it is currently practiced, and to describe and analyze the various factors that enter into it, factors of school organization and administration, of management and discipline, of instruction and the various branches of study. So far as the analysis reveals general principles of individual growth and of social grouping which are operative in the degree that teaching and training are effective, its result rises above the level of recounting and cataloguing relevant phenomena. Hence it deserves the name of a science. This science affords the basis for a critical comparison of the various processes that are currently employed. As teachers are put in intelligent possession of it, their own work becomes less blind and routine; the science, as in other cases, develops a corresponding art which lifts its practitioners from artisans into artists.

Notwithstanding its intellectual and practical value, such an account of education does not cover the whole ground. It works, so to speak, inside of education as a given fact. Another and larger view is possible and desirable, a less professional and a more human view. Education is a concern not merely of school administrators and teachers, of pupils and their parents, but of society. We may have a definite and systematic knowledge of the principles that are at the bottom of the most effective current practice of the day, and may be able to use this knowledge to criticize and correct defective phases of this practice, and yet be thrown back upon mere opinion or mere custom for a judgment as to the value of an educational system as a whole. The general spirit and trend of an established education might be wrong, and yet make possible a scientific account of itself which would be available for rectifying it in details. But the improvement would still be within a scheme which in its main direction and purport was not what it should be.

We have to judge every educational institution and practice from the standpoint of that "whole of experience" which calls it into being and controls its purpose and materials. There exist not merely the principles by which the existing system of education is made effective, but also the principles that animate the entire range of interests of the whole life of the community and that make the existing system what it is. An interpretation and valuation of the educational system in the light of this inclusive social context is the larger and more human view of which we spoke. It utilizes the contributions of science in all its branches to give society an insight into what sort of thing it is undertaking in the training of its members, and it gives society a clearer consciousness of the meaning of the educational office so largely performed by instinct and custom.

Philosophy Is the General Theory of Education.—The connection of education and philosophy is, however, even closer and more vital than this sketch of the principles of education, as distinct from the science of education, would indicate. Philosophy may be defined as the general theory of education; the theory of which education is the corresponding art or practice. Three interlinked considerations support this statement: (i) Men's interests manifest their dispositions; (ii) these dispositions are formed by education; (iii) there must be a general idea of the value and relations of these interests if there is to be any guidance of the process of forming the dispositions that lie back of the realization of the interests. (i) If at any time the various values of experience are out of harmony with one another, the ultimate cause of the difficulty lies in men's habitual attitudes toward life: the habits of judging and of emotional appreciation that are embodied in their habits of action. Interests, attitudes, dispositions, fundamental habits of mind are mutually convertible terms.

(ii) If we but consent to extend the term education beyond its narrow limitation to schooling, we shall find that we cannot stop short in this extension till we have broadened it to cover all the agencies and influences that shape disposition. Not merely books and pictures, but the machinery of publication and communication by which these are made accessible must be included—and this means the use made of railway and telegraph as well as of the printing press, the library, and the picture gallery. Ordinary daily intercourse, the exchange of ideas and experiences in conversation, and the contacts of business competition and cooperation are most influential in deciding the objects upon which attention is fixed and the way in which attention is given to them. Every place in which men habitually meet, shop, club, factory, saloon, church, political caucus, is perforce a schoolhouse, even though not so labelled. This intercourse is in turn dependent upon the political organization of society, the relations of classes to one another, the distribution of wealth, the spirit in which family life is conducted, and so on. Public agitations, discussions, propaganda of public meeting and press, political campaigns, legislative deliberations, are in this regard but so many educational agencies. In brief, every condition, arrangement, and institution that forms the emotional and imaginative bent of mind that gives meaning to overt action is educational in character.

(iii) There are but two alternatives. Either these agencies will perform their educational work as an incidental and unregulated by-product, molding men's minds blindly while conscious attention is given to their other more tangible products; or men will have an idea of the results they wish to have attained, will judge existing agencies according as they achieve or come short of these ends, and will use their idea and their estimate as guides in giving the desired direction to the working of these agencies. This brings us, again, to philosophy, which, as we have seen, is the attempt to develop just such an idea. This is what is meant by saying that philosophy is, in its ultimate extent, a general theory of education; or that it is the idea of which a consciously guided education is the practical counterpart.

It is, of course, possible to exaggerate the importance of philosophy even when it is conceived in this vital and human sense. Reflection is only one of the forces that move our action, and in the thick of events it gives place to necessities of more urgency. But on the other hand, reflection is the only thing that takes us out of the immediate pressure and hurly-burly of overt action. It is a temporary turning aside from the immediate scene of action in order to note the course of events, to forecast probable and possible issues, to take stock of difficulties and resources, to bring to explicit consciousness evils that may be remedied, to plan a future course of action. Philosophy cannot create values by thinking about them, by defining and classifying and arranging them. But by thinking about them, it may promote discrimination as to what is genuinely desirable, and thereby contribute to subsequent conduct a clearer and more deliberately settled method of procedure in attaining what is desired.

There is always danger that the student of philosophy will become simply a student of philosophic traditions, of something that is conventionally called philosophy but from which philosophic life has departed because the genuine problem in life which called out the formulation has departed from consciousness. When philosophic distinctions are approached from the standpoint of their bearing upon life through the medium of the educational process in which they take effect, the perplexity, the predicament, of life which generates the issue can never be far from recognition.

Relation of the History of Philosophy to Education.—The conception of the intimate connection of philosophy with the fundamental theory of education is borne out by reference to the history of philosophic thought. So far as European history is concerned, philosophy originated at Athens from the direct pressure of educational questions. The earlier philosophy, that of the Greek colonies, was really a chapter in the history of science, dealing with the question how things come to be what they are and how they are made. Then the traveling teachers, known as the Sophists, began to apply its results to the conduct of life, and to use the same methods to discuss moral and social matters. Up to their time, men had attained skill and excellence in the various callings of life and in the business of citizenship through apprenticeship in the customs of the community. The Sophist professed to be able to teach "virtue"; that is, ability in the various functions of life. Some limited their claims to ability to teach the arts of poetry and oratory; others gave instruction in the various industrial arts or in military tactics. Others broadened these pretensions, professing ability to convey power in the management of human affairs, private, domestic, and public. It is impossible to exaggerate the historic significance of these claims. They implied that matters which had always been left to practice, and to practice controlled by the habitudes and ideals of the local community, could be set free from their customary provincial setting and be taught on theoretical grounds, on grounds of intellect. Naturally these pretensions evoked violent protests from conservatives, who felt that the life of the community was at stake. This conflict of devotion to social customs with a reliance upon abstract knowledge provoked the first great speculative issues. What is the real basis of social organization and of moral responsibilities? Do these rest upon custom, upon enactment by superiors, or upon universal principles of nature?

At first these questions were discussed, as was natural, in a casual and superficial way. But Socrates, Plato, and others disentangled the basic questions involved. What is the nature of the state and of law? What is the true end of life? How shall man know this end? Can virtue or excellence be taught? Is it a matter of practice and habit, or something intellectual—a kind of knowledge? If so, what kind? What is knowledge? What is its standard? If virtue can be learned, how is learning related to knowledge?

These questions might be multiplied almost indefinitely, but it is more profitable to note that they tended to group themselves into three main problems: (i) What is the relation of knowledge, of reason, to practice, custom, and the opinions that go with custom? (ii) What is the relation of human life, especially of social organization and its virtues and responsibilities, to the nature of the universe, of reality itself? (iii) What is the relation of change, and of the particular things that change, to the universal and permanent? In a generation or two these questions were largely cut loose from their original connection with education. Their discussion developed into distinct disciplines, often isolated from reference to practical or social matters: into logic, as a theory of knowledge; into metaphysics, as a definition of the nature of things; into cosmology, or a general account of the constitution of nature. But the fact that the stream of European philosophic thought arose out of the discussion of educational ends and means, remains an eloquent witness to the ulterior motive and purport of philosophic reflection. If philosophy is to be other than an idle and unverifiable speculation, it must be animated by the conviction that its theory of experience is a hypothesis that is realized only as experience is actually shaped in accord with it. And this realization demands that man's dispositions be made such as to desire and strive for that kind of experience. The philosophy of education is not the external application to educational affairs of a conception of reality ready made independently of education; it is just the philosophic conception of a balanced and articulated experience stated so as to be available for shaping intellectual and emotional disposition, so that the existence it describes may become a living fact, not the dream of a philosopher's brain.

Problems of Philosophy and of Education the Same.—Since upon education falls the burden of securing the practical realizing and balancing of the various interests of life, the educator faces, if only in half-conscious, unsystematic form, precisely the same questions that philosophy discusses in the abstract. In the attitude taken to matters of hygiene, physical training, manual training, corporal punishment, etc., there will be expressed, for example, some idea of the connection, or lack of connection, of mind and body, an idea that, made explicit and fitted in with other beliefs, corresponds to some typical philosophical theory of the relation of bodily and mental action. Some practices imply that man is an external compound of body and soul, in themselves two independent forces. Others proceed on the assumption that the body is a temporary shell in which mind is housed, or that the body is a clog upon the development of spirit. Other projects imply that only through the adequate functioning of the bodily organs can there be realized a symmetrical and sound mental life. The various theories held by philosophers as to the relation of knowledge to practice are paralleled in educational procedure. Some assume that contemplative knowledge is an end in itself; others, that knowledge is a mere external prerequisite for successful action, success being measured on the basis of material possessions and power; others that knowledge is an intrinsic condition of a practice that is free and full of meaning. In educational discussion, one or other of these ideas appears in some disguised form in every dispute about cultural versus professional or vocational education, and shows itself in most debates concerning the relation of the acquisition of knowledge to the formation of character. The old (almost the first) philosophic question as to the relation of the individual to the established objective order appears in instruction as the question of individual initiative and choice over against the accumulated body of organized knowledge which forms the ready-made subject matter of teaching. The philosophical controversy as to the method of knowledge, with its division of camps into sensationalist and rationalist, has a counterpart in the different methods of learning that are encouraged in schools. The philosophic split between mind and physical nature corresponds to the educational antagonism of humanistic and scientific studies, which also has a genuine, even if indirect, bearing upon the philosophic issue of idealism versus realism.

To sum up: Various partial tendencies and interests of life are reflected in native homespun intellectual schemes possessed of strong emotional coloring. These are traditionalized; they float, so to speak, upon the institutions of a society, giving them their sanction and explanation. Philosophies in the formal and technical intellectual sense are generated when these traditional systems are subjected to independent intellectual examination with a view to their rational criticism and supplementation. As the more popular schemes express the standard and the subject matter of the educational procedures of a community, since they naturally aim to shape disposition in the continued acceptance of the customary beliefs and ideals,—so the more conscious philosophies can be tested and objectively embodied only as they are made the working bases of educational processes that develop an experience in harmony with themselves. To convince a small number of the theoretical soundness of the philosophy, while men's lives are still ordered in the mass upon quite another basis, furnishes such a contradiction of the claim of the philosophy to evaluate "experience as a whole" as to place the latter in a ludicrous position.

Character of the New Philosophy of Education.—Every generation and period has its own special problems which decide where the emphasis is thrown. When social conditions and scientific conceptions and methods are both in a state of rapid alteration, the tendency to philosophic reconstruction is especially marked, and the need of working out the newer point of view so that it will throw light upon the spirit and aims of education is especially urgent. The present time is characterized by at least three great movements, of which education must take account in the most radical way if it is to bear any relation to the needs and opportunities of contemporary life—and otherwise intellectual and moral chaos must be the result. These movements are: (i) the rapid growth of democratic ideals and institutions; (ii) the transformation of industrial life—the economic revolution that began in the later eighteenth century with the application of steam to manufacturing and commerce; (iii) the development of experimental science, culminating in the idea of evolution and the thoroughgoing modification of older beliefs about the processes and organs of life.

(i) The democratic movement radically influences education if only because it inevitably produces the demand for universal education. It is impossible that the type of education adapted to the small class in aristocratic and feudal societies, that alone had an opportunity for an intellectual culture, should be adapted to the needs of a democratic society which demands the development of all. By no possibility could the education of a class become the education of all, for a class education is made what it is by the exclusion of most of the people from the opportunities for which it prepares. A democracy, moreover, signifies a social organization which is maintained, upon the whole, by the voluntary wish of the mass of the people, and which is responsive to changes in their purposes. This implies a much greater dependence upon the intelligence and sympathetic good will of all the members of society than is required in communities where authority and precedent are the mainstays of social arrangements. A distinct type of education is demanded to meet the need for individual freedom and initiative combined with respect for others and an instinct for social unity.

(ii) The industrial revolution, with the changes it brought about in modes of association, habits of mind, and increase of commodities, is both cause and effect of the democratic development. From every standpoint it exacts modifications of educational ideas and practices. The importance of labor which it proclaims is a note new in the world's history. The effect of the new inventions in eliminating distance and bringing all mankind within the same circle makes interdependence, which had been preached as an ideal, an operative fact. Since the new industrial régime depends upon the application of science to the control of natural forces, men's best and truest knowledge of nature is put in effective circulation. Men's actions are servile or intelligent according as men do or do not have an appreciation of the ideas which govern their occupations. The extreme specialization and division of labor tend to make men simply small parts of the machines they tend, and only the forethought and oversight of education can avert this menace. The multiplication of material goods makes necessary a higher aesthetic taste to prevent general vulgarization. It also affords new opportunities to the masses which they must be educated to take advantage of. Conversely, the luxury and kind of leisure that had been tolerable or even graceful in past régimes becomes a social menace when the social mechanism makes the responsibilities of production and consumption more and more important.

(iii) Philosophers have debated concerning the nature and method of knowledge. It is hardly cynical to say that positiveness of assertion on those points has been in proportion to the lack of any assured method of knowing in actual operation. The whole idea and scope of knowledge-getting in education has reflected the absence of such a method, so that learning has meant, upon the whole, piling up, worshiping, and holding fast to what is handed down from the past with the title of knowledge. But the actual practice of knowing has finally reached a point where learning means discovery, not memorizing traditions; where knowledge is actively constructed, not passively absorbed; and where men's beliefs must be openly recognized to be experimental in nature, involving hypothesis and testing through being set at work. Upon the side of subject matter, the ideas of energy, process, growth, and evolutionary change have become supreme at the expense of the older notions of permanent substance, rigid fixity, and uniformity. The basic conceptions which form men's standards of interpretation and valuation have thus undergone radical alteration.

Even this bare sketch should suggest the new forces at work in education, and the need of a theory corresponding to the new attitudes and tendencies of our times, if the present situation is to be approached in a spirit of clear intelligence. We need to know the difference that the democratic ideal makes in our moral aims and methods; we need to come to consciousness of the changed conception of the nature of existence that its spread imports. We must reckon intelligently with the new and gigantic industrial forces that have come into being, securing by education a disposition to subordinate them to general welfare and to equality of opportunity so that they may not plunge us into class hatreds, intellectual deadness, and artistic vulgarity. Unless our science is to become as specialized and isolated a thing as was ever any scholastic scheme whose elaborate futility we ridicule, we must make the experimental attitude the pervasive ideal of all our intellectual undertakings, and learn to think habitually in terms of dynamic processes and genetic evolution. Clearness upon the issues, problems, and aims which our own period has brought to the foreground is a necessity for free and deliberate participation in the tasks that present-day education has to perform. Attaining this clearness, with whatever revision of stock notions it may entail, is the peculiar problem of a contemporary philosophy of education.

PART TWO. THE SCHOOL CURRICULUM

Introduction: The School Curriculum

MANY EDUCATORS CONSIDER THE SCHOOL curriculum to be one area that is immediately pertinent to what they do. This perception is easily appreciated, especially when we understand that curriculum is defined in many, diverse, and sometimes overlapping ways. For example, curriculum may be seen as the formal or official subject matter of a class, school, or district; the unofficial lessons that are taught by a school culture; the planned or unplanned activities of a person or agency; a story as approached in a classroom; a set of publications in someone's office; the mainly hidden, structural, organizational, and policy-related characteristics and qualities of a school or district; and the assessment instruments of a school, district, or governmental agency. And there are many other definitions, such as the passions and thinking of the teacher; the life stories that students bring to school; the desirable and undesirable encroaching and interrupting ideas and feelings of students; all of the experiences that students have in a school, planned and otherwise. If we wish to move beyond school definitions of curriculum, some suggest, then the curriculum ought to be seen as including every extraschool lesson conveyed by a dynamic society's sanctioned and unsanctioned influences and entities.

As we might imagine, Dewey's understanding of curriculum was complex, many-sided, and multilayered and included, at least obliquely, most of the meanings if not in the same terms noted above. At a minimum, however, he infused the idea of curriculum with his conceptions of experience and inquiry, experience being that ongoing transaction or interaction that one has with and within any environment, and inquiry being the ability to evaluate those interactions and transactions by employing every available source of knowledge and understanding. Inquiry is also a method of questioning, digging, involving curiosity and reflection and may embody an aesthetic character. Consequently, he believed curriculum included, but went far beyond, the more formal/explicit concepts of textbooks, goals, objectives, and standards and the spheres of inquiry and creativity. While he was attentive to the social, psychological, and cultural development of students and the shaping of their likes and dislikes, or interests, into purposes, he observed in *Experience and Education* (LW13) that students' interests, linked to their experiences and reflective and imaginative realms of inquiry, should be guided by teachers toward warranted assertions, democratic values, meaning construction, and aesthetic satisfaction. Teachers should also guide students from an elementary understanding of their worlds toward adult or mature conceptions, developing minds that are sufficiently informed to learn about and grapple with social, economic, and political questions.

In view of these emphases, it was important to Dewey that the school curriculum be connected to past and current experiences and inquiries of students. This grounding does not ignore but builds on the rudiments of reading, writing, and mathematics. This foundation leads to future attempts to connect content to the world of the students and to their future lives. For Dewey, in one sense, subject matter is accumulated human experience, implying it is tied to both culture and community and cannot be defined simplistically by reference to disciplinary boundaries, such as chemistry, music, English, history, and art. He criticized the traditional curriculum of his time that centered itself in teacher and textbook, which by ignoring the connection between knowing and experience, too often became remote and alienating to the student. He promoted a curriculum that would excite and engage students, that pushed them to imagine, reflect, create, and inquire. Through this engagement, students were to learn more than information and facts, but how to analyze and solve problems in an intelligent fashion and, thereby, form the broader traits of a democratic citizen.

Toward this end (an educated, democratic citizen), he recognized that the teacher and students possess and manifest valuable qualities and in an important sense are also curricula, reflecting to varying degrees the qualities or lessons of thinkers, problem solvers, judges, and democratic citizens (MW1; MW9; MW15). They—and others—contributed to what he labeled the *collateral* curriculum of attitudes, preferences, and ways of thinking (LW13). Beyond the school, he saw other collateral curricula extending even farther into the community and beyond. Probably more than any other educational theorist, Dewey stressed the potential of all types of entities—schools, banks, businesses, homes, industries, government bureaus, private agencies, and religious organizations—to be educative forces in the shaping of a genuinely reflective person and democratic society. For teachers, it is critical to understand and calculate the influence of external curricula in the school and on its curricula.

Among the many questions that arise in the consideration of curriculum that Dewey addressed—or at least alluded to—in these essays are the following: What qualities and dispositions should the teacher as curriculum possess? How should the teacher select, build, deliver, and evaluate the curriculum? What is the role of students in curriculum selection and delivery? In what ways is the pedagogy of a teacher also a part of the (hidden) curriculum? To what degree is school culture both pedagogy and curriculum? How do rigorous inquiry and aesthetic experience complement one another in the school curriculum? Such questions arise in the following essays in the context of discussions of scientific thinking, psychological, logical, and social dimensions of the curriculum; moral education; art and aesthetic experience; and curriculum theory.

In "The Psychological Aspect of the School Curriculum" (EW5.164–76), Dewey underlines the importance of understanding the psychology of students in selecting and making use of subject matter. In doing so, he comments on the importance of having teachers consider the interests and abilities of students in their daily decisions, including the choice to allow students to make choices. He also argues that starting with the logical dimensions of a subject can be counterproductive, if not harmful, for it can impose on the child the findings and conclusions of adults without any consideration given to the joys of inquiry and the maturational levels of individual students. Dewey makes special use of the term *interest* that involves recognizing needs, impulses, experience, motives, social environment, and so on, and their connections to how learners and thinkers grow. In the end, then, curriculum ought to be seen as a personalized inquiry or journey by a student in and with a community of learners, a journey that leads to both immediate and long-term outcomes, such as excitement, fulfillment, understanding, and a more reflective citizenship.

In "The Moral Significance of the Common School Studies" (MW4.205–13), Dewey adds to his psychological perspective a moral one. For him, learning, thinking, and growing are inseparable experiences, part of becoming a more fully formed social being, a moral person. He sees all subject matter that is rightly connected to human experience as filled with moral significance because it is the result of human labor, struggle, and triumph. In describing these connections between the content of knowledge and learning, Dewey dismisses memorization and rote learning as antithetical to his view of an active mind grasping at unfamiliar material and remote ideas that become incorporated into the student's life, interest, and experience. Notably, Dewey alludes to a very important aspect of student experience when he hints at aesthetic experience, a topic that emerges more fully in his later writings. Ideally, art leads to consummatory experiences, including thinking and feeling that involves appreciation, imagination, and wholeness. This process and outcome—called aesthetic experience— he refers to as ethically valuable and the work of art in people and society that results from works or products of art. In other writings such as *Art as Experience* (LW10), he describes in greater detail the notion that all students can move from a rather elementary experience to a well-rounded experience (*an* experience) to an aesthetic experience. Here, however, his thinking is more explicitly related to how art, history, geography, science, and mathematics are or may be connected to moral development. In his conclusion, he takes a somewhat new turn and ends with two paragraphs containing ideas that encapsulate important aspects of his entire curriculum philosophy. He asserts that the school curriculum greatly influences the school's ethos, methodology, and management practices and thereby the student's moral development, community spirit, and ecological appreciations. Hence, curriculum planning, development, delivery, assessment, and evaluation cannot be fertile and inclusive without considering, utilizing, and examining all dimensions of the curriculum.

In "Character Training for Youth" (LW9.186–93), written during the midst of the Depression, Dewey takes up a perennial issue, the theme of moral development. In it, he voices concern about the growing materialism and consumerism in society and the priority placed on competition rather than cooperation. He deems both—materialism and competition—potential threats to a democratic society. That is to say, competition often undercuts the cooperative nature of democracy, and materialism often leads people to neglect the legitimate needs and interests of others (LW5). But, he asks, how responsible is the school when it comes to the moral tenor of society? What is its role and degree of influence in the realm of moral education? While skeptical of many aspects of direct moral instruction, he maintains that formal education plays a prominent but not determinative role in character development. So, character can be partially formed in cooperative, communicative, and democratic environments, including the school. An important trait of character that needs to be developed by schools is a respect for people and their differences. In context, he accentuates the responsibility to respect those who have often been excluded from positions of influence and prestige, such as workers, women, immigrants, and the racially different.

Although the place of art, artistic endeavors, and aesthetic experience became more dominant themes later in his life, "Art in Education" (MW6.375–79), along with other writings, illustrates that these realms of understanding were not foreign to Dewey's early and middle works. In this essay, we find five conclusions he reached about the historical rise of the arts and their influence on individuals, schools, and societies: Art has a powerful influence on the development of individuals and society; artistic expression precedes aesthetic appreciation; joint experiences stimulate both artistic expression and aesthetic enjoyment; arts brings together the communally valuable and the psychologically attractive; and literature is the most widely used of the arts in schools. These conclusions, however, might seem sterile if Dewey's elaborations were ignored. For example, he argues that literature ought not to be used to explicitly teach grammar or moral lessons. Instead, foreshadowing his later emphasis on the value of students' aesthetic experiences, he points to literature's capacity for pulling together valued aspects of earlier experiences, extending, enriching, and consummating them.

In "Science as Subject-Matter and as Method" (MW6.69–79), Dewey reveals his broad and, at least for some, rather peculiar notion of science. Science as subject matter, he believed, is more than the natural sciences or other disciplines and certain collections of facts, as the teaching of science in schools sometimes presents it. Instead, he deems science as primarily a method of inquiry and saw the scientifically disposed person as one who has particular intellectual habits, attitudes, inclinations, understandings, and skills. And in this view, science as method constitutes a form of inquiry that can be applied to any domain that requires a systematically rigorous examination of information, facts, and theories. All forms of scientific investigation or thinking are means of constructing secure knowledge that moves us away from unsubstantiated and counterproductive beliefs, speculations, and myths. As a consequence, while Dewey often used scientific metaphors in his writing, his real interest was in the nature of inquiry and how people discover facts, collect data, and construct knowledge and meaning. Inquiry, reflective thinking, and problem solving are important in any course of study, and it is vital that the teacher create conditions within the classroom for thoughtful investigation and not approach subject matter as ready-made. Life—and school—are learning laboratories, and students need to know how to experiment, to ask questions, and to seek understanding if not resolution.

The last essay, "Theory of Course of Study" (MW6. 395–403), indicates the way Dewey thought about curriculum after approximately fifteen years at Columbia University. He looks briefly at what may be termed a practical approach to curriculum before examining philosophical concerns. We are introduced to three major topics and a host of other issues: the importance of curriculum, the relationship of curriculum to a student's experience, and the possibility of classifying curriculum content. Among the motifs he discusses are the historical evolution of the curriculum, the taxing problem of selecting content, the personal-impersonal gap between student- and adult-oriented curricula, the socially impregnated nature of all curricula, and the psychological and logical dimensions of the curriculum. He concludes with a note on art in its aesthetic sense and claims that all educational accomplishments ought to tend to enhance, consummate, and perfect experience.

As implied earlier, the school curriculum is more than the formal studies that are examined in a conscious way. The lessons of school are also taught through the way the schools are organized, managed, and led and are personified in the attitudes, traits, habits, and reflections of school and district administrators, not to mention teachers and other staff members. The weight of this element of the curriculum—the anthropological or human dimension—often proves more powerful than other elements.

As you read the following essays, here are some questions that you may wish to consider:

REFLECTION AND DISCUSSION QUESTIONS

1. Dewey was greatly concerned that traditional education fostered the use of subject matter as acquisition over inquiry. How can subject matter be fully utilized to stimulate inquiry?

2. From what you understand of Dewey's philosophy at this point, what do you think he would say to a group of elementary school teachers who asked him, "How can we act on the theory of curriculum that you suggest and still prepare our students to do well on annual standardized examinations?"

3. What role, if any, should the stakeholders, such as parents, teachers, students, and others, have in the selection of subject matter to be taught in school if Dewey's ideas are acted on?

4. What are some of the differences between the traditional view and Dewey's view of the relationship between knowledge and the curriculum?

5. Beyond clarifying his theory of the school curriculum, what other theories do these essays help clarify? Why do you think Dewey discussed these theoretical dimensions in the context of his discussing the curriculum?

The Psychological Aspect of the School Curriculum (1897)

THERE IS A ROUGH AND ready way, in current pedagogical writing, of discriminating between the consideration of the curriculum or subject-matter of instruction and the method. The former is taken to be objective in character, determined by social and logical considerations without any particular reference to the nature of the individual. It is supposed that we can discuss and define geography, mathematics, language, etc., as studies of the school course, without having recourse to principles which flow from the psychology of the individual. The standpoint of method is taken when we have to reckon with the adaptation of this objective given material to the processes, interests, and powers of the individual. The study is there ready-made; method inquires how the facts and truths supplied may be most easily and fruitfully assimilated by the pupil.

Taken as a convenient working distinction, no great harm is likely to arise from this parceling out of the two phases of instruction. When pressed, however, into a rigid principle, and made the basis for further inferences, or when regarded as a criterion by reference to which other educational questions may be decided, the view is open to grave objections.

On the philosophic side it sets up a dualism which, to my own mind, is indefensible; and which, from any point of view, is questionable. Moreover, many of the writers who hold this distinction on the practical or pedagogical side would certainly be the last to admit it if it were presented to them as a philosophic matter. This dualism is one between mental operation on one side, and intellectual content on the other—between mind and the material with which it operates; or, more technically, between subject and object in experience. The philosophic presupposition is that there is somehow a gap or chasm between

First published in *Educational Review* 13 (April 1897): 356–69.

the workings of the mind and the subject-matter upon which it works. In taking it for granted that the subject-matter may be selected, defined, and arranged without any reference to psychological consideration (that is, apart from the nature and mode of action of the individual), it is assumed that the facts and principles exist in an independent and external way, without organic relation to the methods and functions of mind. I do not see how those who refuse to accept this doctrine as good philosophy can possibly be content with the same doctrine when it presents itself in an educational garb.

This dualism reduces the psychological factor in education to an empty gymnastic. It makes it a mere formal training of certain distinct powers called perception, memory, judgment, which are assumed to exist and operate by themselves, without organic reference to the subject-matter. I do not know that it has been pointed out that the view taken by Dr. Harris in the Report of the Committee of Fifteen regarding the comparative worthlessness of the psychological basis in fixing educational values is a necessary consequence of the dualism under discussion. If the subject-matter exists by itself on one side, then the mental processes have a like isolation on the other. The only way successfully to question this condemnation of the psychological standpoint is to deny that there is, as a matter of fact, any such separation between the subject-matter of experience and the mental operations involved in dealing with it.

The doctrine, if logically carried out in practice, is even less attractive than upon the strictly theoretical side. The material, the stuff to be learned, is, from this point of view, inevitably something external, and therefore indifferent. There can be no native and intrinsic tendency of the mind toward it, nor can it have any essential quality which stimulates and calls out the mental powers. No wonder the upholders of this distinction are inclined to question the value of interest in instruction, and to throw all the emphasis upon the dead lift of effort. The externality of the material makes it more or less repulsive to the mind. The pupil, if left to himself, would, upon this assumption, necessarily engage himself upon something else. It requires a sheer effort of will power to carry the mind over from its own intrinsic workings and interests to this outside stuff.On the other side, the mental operation being assumed to go on without any intrinsic connection with the material, the question of method is degraded to a very low plane. Of necessity it is concerned simply with the various devices which have been found empirically useful, or which the ingenuity of the individual teacher may invent. There is nothing fundamental or philosophical which may be used as a standard in deciding points in method. It is simply a question of discovering the temporary expedients and tricks which will reduce the natural friction between the mind and the external material. No wonder, once more, that those who hold even unconsciously to this dualism (when they do not find the theory of effort to work practically) seek an ally in the doctrine of interest interpreted to mean the amusing, and hold that the actual work of instruction is how to make studies which have no intrinsic interest interesting—how, that is, to clothe them with factitious attraction, so that the mind may swallow the repulsive dose unaware.

The fact that this dualistic assumption gives material on one hand such an external and indifferent character, while on the other it makes method trivial and arbitrary, is certainly a reason for questioning it. I propose, accordingly, in the following pages, to examine this presupposition, with a view to showing that, as a matter of fact, psychological considerations (those which have to deal with the structures and powers of the individual) enter not only into the discussion of method, but also into that of subject-matter.

The general tone of Dr. Harris's criticism of my monograph on Interest as Related to Will is so friendly and appreciative that it would be hypercritical and controversial for me to carry on the discussion longer without raising some deeper problem. I am convinced that much of the existing difference of opinion as regards not only the place of interest in education, but the meaning and worth of correlation, is due to failure to raise the more fundamental question which I have just proposed; and that the thing needed in the present state of discussion is, as it were, to flank these two questions by making articulate the silent presupposition which has been so largely taken for granted.

What, then, do we mean by a study in the curriculum? What does it stand for? What fixes the place which it occupies in the school work? What furnishes it its end? What gives it its limitations? By what standard do we measure its value? The ordinary school-teacher is not, of course, called upon to raise such questions. He has certain subjects given to him. The curriculum is, as we say, laid out, and the individual teacher has to do the best he can with the studies as he finds them. But those who are concerned theoretically with the nature of education, or those who have to do practically with the organization of the course of study—those who "lay out" the course—cannot afford to ignore these questions.

On the whole, the most philosophic answer which has as yet been given to these questions in America is that worked out by Dr. Harris in his deservedly famous St. Louis reports, and more recently formulated by him in the Report of the Committee of Fifteen, as well as in the articles which he has written opposing the Herbartian conception of correlation. In substance, we are told that a study is the gathering up and arranging of the facts and principles relating to some typical aspect of social life, or which afford a fundamental tool in maintaining that social life; that the standard for selecting and placing a study is the worth which it has in adapting the pupil to the needs of the civilization into which he is born.

I do not question this statement, so far as it goes, on the positive side. The objectionable point is the negative inference that this social determination is exclusive of the psychological one. The social definition is necessary, but is the psychological one less pressing? Supposing we ask, for example, how a given study plays the part assigned to it in social life? What is it that gives it its function? How does the study operate in performing this function? Suppose we say not simply that geography does, as a matter of fact, occupy a certain important position in interpreting to the child the structure and processes of the civilization into which he is born; suppose that, in addition, we want to know how geography performs this task. What it is that intrinsically adapts it to this and gives it a claim to do something which no other study or group of studies can well perform? Can we answer this question without entering into the psychological domain? Are we not inquiring, in effect, what geography is on the psychological side—what it is, that is to say, as a mode or form of experience?

Moreover, we must ask how the given study manages to do the work given it before we can get any basis upon which to select the material of instruction in general; and much more before we can select the material for pupils of a certain age or of a certain social environment. We must take into account the distinction between a study as a logical whole and the same study considered as a psychological whole. From the logical standpoint, the study is the body or system of facts which are regarded as valid, and which are held together by certain internal principles of relation and explanation. The logical standpoint assumes the facts to be already discovered, already sorted out, classified, and systematized. It deals with the subject-matter upon the objective standpoint. Its only concern is whether the facts are really facts, and whether the theories of explanation and interpretation used will hold water. From the psychological standpoint, we are concerned with the study as a mode or form of living individual experience. Geography is not only a set of facts and principles, which may be classified and discussed by themselves; it is also a way in which some actual individual feels and thinks the world. It must be the latter before it can be the former. It becomes the former only as the culmination or completed outgrowth of the latter. Only when the individual has passed through a certain amount of experience, which he vitally realizes on his own account, is he prepared to take the objective and logical point of view, capable of standing off and analyzing the facts and principles involved.

Now, the primary point of concern in education is beyond question with the subject as a special mode of personal experience, rather than with the subject as a body of wrought-out facts and scientifically tested principles. To the child, simply because he is a child, geography is not, and cannot be, what it is to the one who writes the scientific treatise on geography. The latter has had exactly the experience which it is the problem of instruction to induce on the part of the former. To identify geography as it is to the pupil of seven or fifteen with geography as it is to Humboldt or Ritter is a flagrant case of putting the cart before the horse. With the child, instruction must take the standpoint not of the accomplished results, but of the crude beginnings. We must discover what there is lying within the child's present sphere of experience (or within the scope of experiences which he can easily get) which deserves to be called geographical. It is not the question of how to teach the child geography, but first of all the question what geography is for the child.

There is no fixed body of facts which, in itself, is eternally set off and labeled geography, natural history, or physics. Exactly the same objective reality will be one or other, or none of these three, according to the interest and intellectual attitude from which it is surveyed. Take a square mile of territory, for example; if we view it from one interest, we may have trigonometry; from another stand-point we should label the facts regarding it botany; from still another, geology; from another, mineralogy; from another, geography; from still another stand-point it would become historical material. There is absolutely nothing in the fact, as an objective fact, which places it under any one head. Only as we ask what kind of an experience is going on, what attitude some individual is actually assuming, what purpose or end some individual has in view, do we find a basis for selecting and arranging the facts under the label of any particular study.

Even in the most logical and objective consideration, we do not, therefore, really escape from the psychological point of view. We do not get away from all reference to the person having an experience, and from the point of how and why he has it. We are simply taking the psychology of the adult (that is to say, of the one who has already gone through a certain series of experiences), of one who has, therefore, a certain background and course of growth, and substituting the mature and developed interest of such a person for the crude and more or less blind tendency which the child has. If we act upon this distinction in our educational work, it means that we substitute the adult's consciousness for the child's consciousness.

I repeat, therefore, that the first question regarding any subject of study is the psychological one, What is that study, considered as a form of living, im-mediate, personal experience? What is the interest in that experience? What is the motive or stimulus to it? How does it act and react with reference to other forms of experience? How does it gradually differentiate itself from others? And how does it function so as to give them additional definiteness and richness of meaning? We must ask these questions not only with reference to the child in general, but with reference to the specific child—the child of a certain age, of a certain degree of attainment, and of specific home and neighborhood contacts.

Until we ask such questions the consideration of the school curriculum is arbitrary and partial, because we have not the ultimate criterion for decision before us. The problem is not simply what facts a child is capable of grasping or what facts can be made interesting to him, but what experience does he himself have in a given direction. The subject must be differentiated out of that experience in accordance with its own laws. Unless we know what these laws are, what are the intrinsic stimuli, modes of operation and functions of a certain form of experience, we are practically helpless in dealing with it. We may follow routine, or we may follow abstract logical consideration, but we have no decisive educational criterion. It is the problem of psychology to answer these questions; and when we get them answered, we shall know how to clarify, build up, and put in order the content of experience, so that in time it will grow to include the systematic body of facts which the adult's consciousness already possesses.

This is a distinctly practical question—a question which concerns the actual work of the schoolroom and not simply the professorial chair. Upon the whole, I believe that the crying evil in instruction today is that the subject-matter of the curriculum, both as a whole and in its various stages, is selected and determined on the objective or logical basis instead of upon the psychological. The humble pedagogue stands with his mouth and his hands wide open, waiting to receive from the abstract scientific writers the complete system which the latter, after centuries of experience and toilsome reflection, have elaborated. Receiving in this trustful way the ready-made "subject," he proceeds to hand it over in an equally ready-made way to the pupil. The intervening medium of communication is simply certain external attachments in the way of devices and tricks called "method," and certain sugar-coatings in the way of extrinsic inducements termed "arousing of interest."

All this procedure overlooks the point that the first pedagogical question is, How, out of the crude native experience which the child already has, the complete and systematic knowledge of the adult consciousness is gradually and systematically worked out. The first question is, How experience grows; not, What experience the adult has succeeded in getting together during his development from childhood to maturity. The scientific writer, having a background of original experience, and having passed through the whole period of growth, may safely assume them and not get lost; the subject-matter standing to him in its proper perspective and relation. But when this adult material is handed over ready-made to the child, the perspective is ignored, the subject is forced into false and arbitrary relations, the intrinsic interest is not appealed to, and the experience which the child already has, which might be made a vital instrument of learning, is left unutilized and to degenerate.

The genuine course of procedure may be stated as follows:

We have first to fix attention upon the child to find out what kind of experience is appropriate to him at the particular period selected; to discover, if possible, what it is that constitutes the special feature of the child's experience at this time; and why it is that his experience takes this form rather than another. This means that we observe in detail what experiences have most meaning and value to him, and what attitude he assumes toward them. We search for the point, or focus, of interest in these experiences. We ask where they get their hold upon him and how they make their appeal to him. We endeavor by observation and reflection to see what tastes and powers of the child are active in securing these experiences. We ask what habits are being formed; what ends and aims are being proposed. We inquire what the stimuli are and what responses the child is making. We ask what impulses are struggling for expression; in what characteristic ways they find an outlet; and what results inure to the child through their manifestation.

All this is a psychological inquiry. It may be summed up, if I am permitted to use the word, under the head of "interest." Our study is to find out what the actual interests of the child are; or, stated on the objective side, what it is in the world of objects and persons that attracts and holds the child's attention, and that constitutes for him the significance and worth of his life. This does not mean that these interests, when discovered, give the ultimate standard for school work, or that they have any final regulative value. It means that the final standard cannot be discovered or used until this preliminary inquiry is gone through with. Only by asking and answering such questions do we find out where the child really is; what he is capable of doing; what he can do to the greatest advantage and with the least waste of time and strength, mental and physical. We find here our indicators or pointers as to the range of facts and ideas legitimate to the child. While we do not get the absolute rule for the selection of subject-matter, we do most positively get the key to such selection. More than this, we here have revealed to us the resources and allies upon which the teacher may count in the work of instruction. These native existing interests, impulses, and experiences are all the leverage that the teacher has to work with. He must connect with them or fail utterly. Indeed, the very words leverage and connection suggest a more external relation than actually exists. The new material cannot be attached to these experiences or hung upon them from without, but must be differentiated from them internally. The child will never realize a fact or possess an idea which does not grow out of this equipment of experiences and interests which he already has. The problem of instruction, therefore, is how to induce this growth.

The phenomena of interest, then, are to be studied as symptoms. Only through what the child does can we know what he is. That which enables us to translate the outward doing over into its inner meaning is the ability to read it in terms of interest. If we know the interest the child has, we know not simply what he externally does, but why he does it; where its connection with his own being can be found. Wherever we have interest we have signs of dawning power. Wherever we have phenomena of a lack of interest, wherever we have repulsion, we have sure tokens that the child is not able to function freely, is not able to control and direct his own experience as he would; or, if I may use what Dr. Harris calls a "glib and technical term," does not "express himself" easily and freely. Once more, these phenomena of interest are not final. They do not say to the teacher: We are your final end, and all your energies are to be devoted to cultivating us just as we are. None the less, they are indices and instruments; they are the only clues which the instructor can possibly have to what experiences are such really, and not simply in name. They reveal the general standpoint from which any subject must be presented in order to lay hold on the child. The problem of the teacher is to read the superficial manifestations over into their underlying sources. Even "bad" interests, like that of destruction, are the signs of some inner power which must be discovered and utilized.

In the second place, in saying that these psychical phenomena afford opportunities, give clues, and furnish leverages, we are virtually saying that they set problems. They need to be interpreted. They have the value of signs, and, like all signs, must be interpreted into the realities for which they stand. Now it is the province of the subject-matter on its logical and objective side to help us in this work of translation. We see the meaning of the beginning through reading it in terms of its outcome; of the crude in terms of the mature. We see, for example, what the first babbling instincts and impulses mean by contemplating the articulate structure of language as an instrument of social communication, of logical thought, and of artistic expression. We see what the interest of the child in counting and measuring represents, by viewing the developed system of arithmetic and geometry. The original phenomena are prophecy. To realize the full scope of the prophecy, its promise and potency, we must look at it not in its isolation, but in its fulfillment.

This doctrine is misconceived when taken to mean that these accomplished results of the adult experience may be made a substitute for the child's experience, or may be directly inserted into his consciousness through the medium of instruction, or, by any external device whatsoever, grafted upon him. Their value is not that of furnishing the immediate material or subject-matter of instruction, any more than the phenomena of interest furnish the final standards and goals of instruction. The function of this ordered and arranged experience is strictly interpretative or mediatory. We must bear it in mind in order to appreciate, to place, the value of the child's interests as he manifests them.

Thus we come, in the third place, to the selection and determination of the material of instruction, and to its adaptation to the process of learning. This involves the interaction of two points of view just considered. It is working back and forth from one to the other. The transitory and more or less superficial phenomena of child life must be viewed through their full fruitage. The objective attainments of the adult consciousness must be taken out of their abstract and logical quality and appreciated as living experiences of the concrete individual.

Then we may see what both subject-matter and method of instruction stand for. The subject-matter is the present experience of the child, taken in the light of what it may lead to. The method is the subject-matter rendered into the actual life experience of some individual. The final problem of instruction is thus the reconstruction of the individual's experience, through the medium of what is seen to be involved in that experience as its matured outgrowth.

We have two counterpart errors: one is the appeal to the child's momentary and more or less transitory interest, as if it were final and complete, instead of a sign of nascent power; as if it were an end instead of an instrument; as if it furnished an ideal instead of setting a problem. The other is taking the studies from the scientific standpoint, and regarding them as affording the subject-matter of the curriculum. As the phenomena of interest need to be controlled by reference to their fullest possibility, so the scientific content of the studies needs to be made over by being "psychologized," seen as what some concrete individual may experience in virtue of his own impulses, interests, and powers. It is the element of control which takes us out of the region of arbitrary tricks and devices into the domain of orderly method. It is the making over and psychological translation of the studies which renders them a genuine part of the Lehrstoff [practical activities] of the pupil. It is because of the necessity of this operation, the transfiguring of the dead objective facts by seeing them as thoughts and feelings and acts of some individual, that we are justified in saying that there is a psychological aspect to the curriculum.

In applying this to the actual studies which make up the present curriculum, no one would deny, I suppose, that language, literature, history, and art, being manifestations of human nature, cannot be understood in their entirety, nor yet fully utilized in the work of instruction, until they are regarded as such manifestation. But we must go a point further, and recognize that in education we are not concerned with the language that has been spoken, the literature that has been created, the history that has been lived, but with them only as they become a part of what an individual reports, expresses, and lives. Even in the sciences, where we appear to be dealing with matters that are more remote from the individual, we need to remember that educationally our business is not with science as a body of fixed facts and truths, but with it as a method and attitude of experience. Science in the sense in which we can find it stated in books, or set forth in lectures, is not the subject-matter of instruction. Anything that can be found in these forms is simply an index and instrument. It sets before us our goal—the attitude of mind and kind of experience which we wish to induce; when it is read over, into psychological terms, it helps us reach our goal; but without the psychological rendering, it is inert, mechanical, and deadening.

Because the actual, as distinct from the abstract or possible, subject is a mode of personal experience, not simply an ordered collection of facts and principles, the curriculum as a whole, and every study in detail, has a psychological side whose neglect and denial lead to confusion in pedagogic theory; and in educational practice to the dead following of historic precedent and routine, or else to the substitution of the abstract and the formal for the vital and personal.

The Moral Significance of the Common School Studies (1909)

IT MAY ASSIST COMPREHENSION OF the more specific portions of this paper if we begin with stating the standpoint from which the paper is conceived. Why should we expect the subject-matter of school studies to have any moral value? How can bodies of knowledge, of information, get transmuted into character? Have we any right to suppose that the miracle of changing facts, ideas, artistic products into the fibre of personal endeavor can be wrought? Unless we bear two principles in mind—bear them in mind by engraving them in practice—the expectation is unreasonable.

The two principles are that the subject-matter of the studies represents the results of past human social struggles and achievements, and that mind—the capacities of knowing by which the subject-matter is laid hold of and digested—is a manifestation of primary impulses in their efforts to master the environments. Because art, natural science, and mathematics have been evolved in the doings and sufferings of man, they are something more than merely intellectual; they are the outcome of human desire, passion, endeavor, success and failure. They have not been produced by some mind in the abstract, interested only in knowing, but have been worked out in the long-continued, arduous struggle of man to come into sound and effective connection with nature and with fellowman. Because of this fact they are full of moral meaning.

In like fashion, the powers with which children assimilate subject-matter are outgrowths of native instincts and reactions, tendencies much more akin to hunger, thirst, reaching, handling, moving about than to separate independent faculties of theoretical knowing.

First published in Northern Illinois Teachers' Association, *Topics for General Sessions: Moral and Religious Training in Public Schools*, 5–6 November 1909, 21–27.

These general statements indicate the source both of failure and of success in using subject-matter as a means of moral nurture. When studies are treated as just so many studies to be learned by pure intellectual faculties of memory, thought, etc., the moral outcome is insecure and accidental. When they are treated as human achievements, appealing to tendencies in childhood which are aiming however unconsciously and partially at similar achievements, the moral connection is positive and direct.

Art, of which literature is only one branch, though the one most readily available for school uses, is perhaps the most unmixed and the simplest record of the consummation of human endeavor. For this reason, it has been overworked in the schools as a moral force compared with other subjects. Children are easily stimulated,—their emotions are stirred,—and teachers are apt to assume that a somewhat momentary reaction of the feelings is a distinct ethical gain. In the early years, serious limitations attend the use of reading matter. The child's capacity to take in ideas through eye-symbols is so slight that "literature" is apt to be puerile intellectually, and the best of intentions to point a moral do not make up for triviality and paucity of ideas. For this reason, the ear is the natural channel, but there is danger that even oral stories and poems be made up on the basis of success in catching momentary attention and arousing signs of excitement. It is not a matter of accident that classic stories, as nearly as possible in their classic form, are more valuable than stories or poems composed for children. They are classics because they have passed through the medium of successive generations and have been proved true to the essentials of human experience. Their endurance is the stamp of their sterling, their genuine nature, while things written for children are mostly only paper money, even if not counterfeit. The chief protection lies in remembering that literature is a branch of art, so that if the literary material, whether prose or poetry, oral or printed, does not show the marks of highly selected, purified and refined experience, its effect upon children, even when striking, is likely to be sensational rather than morally educative. Physical reactions and the emotional thrills that accompany them closely simulate moral responses, and the parent or teacher who judges the worth of story and poems on the basis of the immediate excitement aroused instead of judging the latter on the basis of the intrinsic significance of the experiences condensed in the work of art is turning the scale of values upside down.

Given genuine art, genuine crystallization of what is important in life, in literature and the chief condition of its moral influence is that it be unconsciously absorbed, not consciously driven in, raked over and pulled up. Nothing is more absurd in theory or harmful in practice than first insisting upon the intrinsic ethical value of literature, and then impressing by suggestion, question, and discourse, the moral point or lesson to be derived from the piece of literature.

What this really means is that the teacher has no faith in the moral force of the scene and ideas presented, but has great faith in his own conversation and personal influence. Consequently, while he talks about the moral import of a poem or story, in fact he only uses it as an occasion for his own moralizings. The result is the destruction of the piece in question as a work of art; and whatever accidental moral influence accrues being due to the teacher's personality and method, it could have been got as well from the multiplication table by the exercise of a little ingenuity.

One can hardly remind himself too often that works of art are appreciated, not consciously dissected. To say that they are appreciated means that the organ for taking them in is a sympathetic imagination. They are apprehended in terms of the analogous instincts and experience which they arouse in the spectator or auditor. The appeal is direct and hence unconscious. Somehow, nobody can tell just how, the person responds; he puts himself in tune with the theme and its mode of treatment, he takes on the color of the scene presented. The process is one of silent adjustment, of absorption, of assimilation, involving a gradual making over of personal fibre. Conscious effort to secure the desired moral result may arrest the process of assimilation; it cannot hasten it. Intellectual digestion and reconstruction are slow and organic processes. Conscious and short cuts to the end only leave superficial, perverted, and conventional results behind.

Appreciation of literature is moreover a personal, a highly individual matter. The teacher, like any skilled critic, may heighten another's appreciation of a work of art by indicating how he himself is affected, what memories and expectations are aroused in himself. But when he decides in advance that the moral truth of a given poem or literary transcript is just thus and so, and then enforces this upon a class as a whole, a class composed of individuals of different temperaments, experiences, and preferences, he tends to fix in the pupils' minds a conventional, superficial interpretation, and thus arbitrarily prevent the work of art accomplishing its own and perfect work. There is a certain impertinence in any case in forestalling the deeper and organic responses of other persons, whether children or adults; a certain presumptuous lack of sympathy in insisting upon one's own reaction as typical and essential. And the worst of it is when the teacher undertakes to make a piece of literary art an excuse for tagging on "morals," he rarely gets the benefit even of his own genuine response, but falls back upon nondescript stereotyped generalities.

In short, since art represents the purified consummation, the selected consummation of human experience, its ethical value, at its best, is indeed supreme. But because its work is so vital, its mode of operation is most delicate, is most easily disturbed and disarranged. "Literature" has no magical automatic efficacy simply because it is called literature. Its importance measures also the dangers of its use, and hence while it cannot be said that current pedagogical traditions exaggerate the moral value of literature, it is nevertheless true that they are highly misleading so far as they create the belief that literature is the chief conscious moral resource of the teacher with respect to the various branches of subject-matter.

History, rather than literature, represents doubtless the most effective conscious tool (I am not speaking of the various active occupations and exercises of the pupil, but of the stock studies of the curriculum). Here conscious analysis, the study of motives and results, comes into play. Even here it must be remembered, however, that conscious attention should be directed not to what the teacher regards as the peculiar moral truth embodied in the portion of history under consideration, but to the subject-matter itself, to clear up its obscurities, to render it more vivid and vital, to build up, in short, a complete scene to which pupils may respond as a whole. That the "kingdom of God cometh not with observation" may be taken to mean, among other things, that the reactions which induce moral growth are too total and too personal to be laid out in advance by even the most competent teacher. His work, in the case of history as well as of literature, is to so see that full justice is done in the presentation of the objective subject-matter that the moral response must come in the pupil's assimilative reactions.

This being premised, we naturally ask what it is in the historical subject-matter that specially lends itself to a growth of desirable personal attitudes. Putting the matter first in a somewhat technical way, we may say that as literature affords the occasion for realizing the select consummation, the achieved ideals and standards of human experience, so history affords the materials for apprehending its typical problems, the chief obstructions to development, the chief methods of progress. It gives processes rather than results—and for this reason lends itself so rapidly to analytic discussion.

It is commonly stated that history must be studied from the standpoint of cause and effect. The truth of this statement depends upon its interpretation. Social life is so complex and the various parts of it are so organically related to one another and to the natural environment, that it is impossible to say that this or that thing is the cause of some other particular thing. But the study of history can reveal the main instruments in the discoveries, inventions, new modes of life, etc., which have initiated the great epochs of social advance; and it can present to the child types of the main lines of social progress, and can set before him what have been the chief difficulties and obstructions in the way of progress. This can be done so far as it is recognized that social forces in themselves are always the same,—that the same kind of influences were at work one hundred and one thousand years ago that are now working,—and that particular historical epochs afford illustration of the way in which the fundamental forces work.

Everything depends, then, upon history being treated from a social standpoint; as manifesting the agencies which have influenced social development, and as presenting the typical institutions in which human experience naturally assumes form. The culture-epoch theory, while working in the right direction, has failed to recognize the importance of treating past periods with relation to the present,—as affording insight into the representative factors of its structure; it has treated these periods too much as if they had some meaning or value in themselves. The biographical method is often treated in such a way as to exclude from the child's consciousness (or at least not sufficiently to emphasize) the social values involved, which give the biographies their moral significance. Isolated stories about heroes, about George Washington and Abraham Lincoln, belong to literature rather than to history, and, except when told by a master, to second-rate literature. Of course, it is individuals who are important, not abstract forces and causes; but there is a fundamental difference between methods which dole out isolated anecdotes however thrilling or however calculated to impress a moral, and methods in which the leader is seen as one individual among many, summing up, by guidance, their powers and meeting needs which help in the peculiar social environment in which he lives and works. The individual disconnected from his social situation is ethically unreal, and no devices for instilling, through stories about him, lessons of truth-telling, patriotism, industry, etc., succeed in really concealing the moral unreality of the case.

In short, the ethical value of history teaching is measured by the extent to which past events are made the means of understanding the present,—affording insight into what makes up the structure and working of society today. Existing social structure is exceedingly complex. It is practically impossible for the child to attack it en masse and get any definite mental image of it. But type phases of historical development may be selected which will exhibit, as through a telescope, the essential constituents of the existing order.

The separation of geography from history on one side, and from "nature study" on the other, is quite artificial. History does not go on "in the air," and even if it did, the air would still be intimately one with the earth. Human action takes place under natural conditions; it is modified by geographical conditions, and in turn it transforms them. History would be meaningless if it were writ in water; if it did not leave behind itself permanent changes in nature which make it possible for later generations to take up their work on a higher plane of activity. Reverence for the natural, the physical, conditions of human well-being is perhaps the chief moral accomplishment of the study of science.

Hence, the beginning must be social geography, the frank recognition of the earth as the home of men acting in relations to one another. The essence of any geographical fact is the consciousness of two persons, or two groups of persons, who are at once separated and connected by their physical environment, and that the interest is in seeing how these people are at once kept apart and brought together in their actions by the instrumentality of the physical environment. The ultimate significance of lake, river, mountain, and plain is not physical but social,—the part played in modifying and directing human relationships. This evidently involves an extension of commercial geography, which has to do not simply with business in the narrow sense, but with whatever relates to human intercourse and intercommunication as affected by natural forms. Political geography represents the same social interaction in a static, instead of in a dynamic way; that is, as temporarily crystallized in certain forms.

If it be asked what this has to do with the moral bearing of geography, the answer is not far to seek. The development of character is not exhausted in learning the nature of the various virtues and in having their importance emotionally impressed. Effective character—and this is increasingly true under modern conditions of life—requires intelligence regarding the natural resources and conditions of action. Morality severed from an understanding of the conditions in which action takes effect is sentimental or else routine.

In its broad sense, the study of the earth as genuinely the home of man, geography includes nature study. Plants and animals live on the earth; knowledge of them disconnected from the total scene of which they are a part, results in mere scrappy information, futile intellectually and hence morally. Electricity, heat, light, gravity, etc., may be studied by specialists as separate themes; but in general education they owe their significance to the fact that they too belong to the earth as the home of man, while their laws express the ways in which natural resources have been adapted to human ends.

A word in conclusion about mathematics. What the study of number suffers from in elementary education is lack of motivation. Back of this and that and the other particular bad method is the radical mistake of treating number as if it were an end in itself, instead of the means of accomplishing some end. Let the child get a consciousness of what is the use of number, of what it really is for, and half the battle is won. Now this consciousness of the use or reason implies some end which is implicitly social.

One of the absurd things in the more advanced study of arithmetic is the extent to which the child is introduced to numerical operations which have no distinctive mathematical principles characterizing them, but which represent certain general principles found in business relationships. To train the child in these operations, while paying no attention to the business realities in which they are of use, or to the conditions of social life which make these business activities necessary, is neither arithmetic nor common sense. The child is called upon to do examples in interest, partnership, banking, brokerage, and so on through a long string, and no pains are taken to see that, in connection with the arithmetic, he has any sense of the social realities involved. This part of arithmetic is essentially sociological in its nature. It ought either to be omitted entirely, or else be taught in connection with a study of the relevant social realities.

The training in exactness, neatness, and thoroughness which it is customary to associate with mathematics is real enough, but after all it extends beyond its own particular sphere only when mathematical relations are seen in their connection with the realities, where strictness, definiteness, accuracy and leaving nothing out of account are recognized as important.

In conclusion, we may say that in many respects, the subject-matter used in school life decides both the general atmosphere of the school and the methods of instruction and discipline which rule. A barren "course of study," that is to say, a meagre and narrow field of school activities cannot possibly lend itself to the development of a vital social spirit or to methods that appeal to sympathy and cooperation instead of to absorption, exclusiveness, and competition.

"Studies" are of moral value in the degree in which they enable the pupil sympathetically and imaginatively to appreciate the social scene in which he is a partaker; to realize his own indebtedness to the great stream of human activities which flow through and about him; the community of purpose with the large world of nature and society and his consequent obligation to be loyal to his inheritance and sincere in his devotion to the interests which have made him what he is and given him the opportunities he possesses. If such moral training seems slow and roundabout, we may yet encourage ourselves with the reflection that virtue is not a miracle but a conquest, and character not an accident but the efficacious growth of organic powers.

Character Training for Youth (1934)

THERE IS A GOOD DEAL of alarm just now at what seems to be a deterioration of character among the young. There is a growing increase of juvenile criminality. Revelations of breach of trust and shady practices among men the community had looked up to as leaders have led to questioning of the value of the education they received when they were young. The prevalence of racketeering has added to the force of the question. In consequence, many persons are blaming the school for inattention to the importance of moral education. There are many who demand that systematic moral and religious instruction be introduced into the schools.

How far are the charges against the schools justified?

What is the place of the schools in the moral education of the young?

Anyone interested in these questions should be clear about at least two things. In the first place, the roots of character go deep and its branches extend far. Character means all the desires, purposes, and habits that influence conduct. The mind of an individual, his ideas and beliefs, are a part of character, for thought enters into the formation of desires and aims. Mind includes imagination, for there is nothing more important than the nature of the situations that fill imagination when a person is idle or at work. If we could look into a person's mind and see which mental pictures are habitually entertained we should have an unsurpassed key to his character. Habits are the fibre of character, but there are habits of desire and imagination as well as of outer action.

The second point follows from the first. Just because character is such an inclusive thing, the influences that shape it are equally extensive. If we bear this fact in mind when we ask what the schools are doing and can do in forming character, we shall not expect too much from them. We shall realize that

First published in *Rotarian* 45 (September 1934): 6–8, 58–59.

at best the schools can be but one agency among the very many that are active in forming character. Compared with other influences that shape desire and purpose, the influence of the school is neither constant nor intense. Moral education of our children is in fact going on all the time, every waking hour of the day and three hundred and sixty-five days a year. Every influence that modifies the disposition and habits, the desires and thoughts of a child is a part of the development of his character.

In contrast with their power, the school has the children under its influence five hours a day, for not more than two hundred days a year (on the average much less), and its main business is teaching subject-matter and promoting the acquisition of certain skills, reading, writing, figuring, that from the children's standpoint have little to do with their main interests. The information given is largely from books, is remote from daily life, and is mainly committed to memory for reproduction in recitations rather than for direct manifestation in action outside the school. Industry, promptness, and neatness are indeed insisted upon, but even the good habits formed in these matters are so special-ized that their transfer over into out-of-school matters is largely a matter of accident. Because the material is remote, the effect on character is also remote.

In short, formation of character is going on all the time; it cannot be confined to special occasions. Every experience a child has, especially if his emotions are enlisted, leaves an impress upon character. The friends and associates of the growing boy and girl, what goes on upon the playground and in the street, the newspapers, magazines, and books they read, the parties and movies they attend, the presence or absence of regular responsibilities in the home, the at-titude of parents to each other, the general atmosphere of the household—all of these things are operating pretty constantly. And their effect is all the greater because they work unconsciously when the young are not thinking of morals at all. Even the best conscious instruction is effective in the degree in which it harmonizes with the cumulative result of all these unconscious forces.

Character, in short, is something that is *formed* rather than something that can be taught as geography and arithmetic are taught. Special things about character can be taught, and such teaching is important. It is usually given, both at home and in school, when something is done that is irregular and is disapproved. The child is disobedient, quarrelsome, has shirked doing some assigned task, has told a lie, etc. Then his attention is called to some specific moral matter. Even so, a great deal depends upon the way this moral instruction is managed. Reproof may be given in such a way that dislike of all authority is inculcated. Or a child develops skill in evasion and in covering up things that he knows are disapproved of.

Negativism, fear, undue self-consciousness often result. Consequently the net effect of even direct moral instruction cannot be foretold, and its efficacy depends upon its fitting into the mass of conditions which play unconsciously upon the young.

A few of the indirect forces may be noted by way of illustration. Recent investigations, conducted with scientific care, have shown that many boys and girls have been stimulated in unwholesome ways by the movies. Parents in good homes are likely to underestimate the influences of the movies upon children coming from other kinds of homes. The influence of movies upon children is fixed by the general tone and level of the child's surroundings.

A boy or girl from a cramped environment that provides few outlets reacts very differently from one in which the movie is not the main vent for romance, and for acquaintance with conditions very different from those that habitually surround him. The luxury of scenes depicted on the screen, the display of adventure and easy sex relations, inoculate a boy or girl living in narrow surroundings with all sorts of new ideas and desires. Their ambitions are directed into channels that contrast vividly with actual conditions of life. The things that a boy or girl from a well-to-do and cultivated home would discount or take simply as part of a show are for other children ideals to be realized—and without especial regard for the means of their attainment. The little moral at the close has no power compared with the force of desires that are excited.

A child who is one of a family of from four to six or seven children living in two rooms in a congested tenement district lives also on a congested street. The father is away most of the day and comes home tired from monotonous work. The mother, needless to say, has no servant. The children are under foot save when at school. They are "naughty" and scolded in the degree in which they get in her way or make added work. The street is their natural outlet and the mother gets relief in the degree they are out of the two rooms of the home. The effect of such conditions in creating a type of life in which the discipline and example of the gang count much more than that of family instruction cannot be exaggerated.

The homes of many of the well-to-do suffer from opposite conditions. There is excess of luxury and deficit of responsibility, since the routine of the household is cared for by servants.

To "pass the buck" and to find "alibis" is natural to all of us. When the public is faced by the sum total of the bad results of the conditions—of which only one or two have been selected as illustrations—a cry goes up that the schools are not doing their duty. I am not trying to set forth an alibi in turn for the schools, and I do not mean to assert that they have done and are doing all that can be done in shaping character. But take a look in imagination at the schoolroom. There are forty children there, perhaps fifty since the depression. The children are there five or five and a half hours a day. The teacher takes care of the "order" of the room, hears lessons in six or seven subjects, corrects papers, and has more or less semi-janitorial work to do. In the average schoolroom even today most of the time of the children is spent, when not reciting, in conning their textbooks, doing "sums" and other written work. They are active beings and yet have little outlet for their active impulses. How many parents would undertake to do much training of character, save of a negative and repressive sort, under such conditions?

The answer that is often given is to add one more study. Give direct instruction in morals, or in religion combined with morals. Now I cannot go into the merits and demerits of direct instruction of this sort. But it is a matter of common experience in other subjects that formal instruction often leaves no great impress. It is one thing to learn words and sentences by heart and another thing to take them to heart so that they influence action. At the best, this method has no great force in comparison with the indirect effect of conditions that are operating all the time in school and out. It is an old and true saying that example is more powerful than precept, and example is but one of the forces that act constantly on the young.

Those who are inclined to think that more of direct moral instruction would be almost a panacea for present evils usually look back to earlier times when such instruction was customary in home and school. They forget that it was effective because it was part of the general conditions and atmosphere. It was reinforced by many other things that are now lacking. It is a fallacy to suppose that the social trend and context can be radically changed and special methods be as effective as they were under other conditions.

It would be absurd to omit the effect upon the plastic and forming character of the young of the economic conditions that prevailed about them. Till recently, youth has grown up in a social atmosphere in which emphasis upon material success was enormous, both consciously and unconsciously. The fact that multitudes of persons were engaged in steady and honest industry was not sensational. Save where the young were faced with that fact in their own home and neighborhood, it did not have the effect that conspicuous cases of great financial careers exerted. And many children were faced by the fact that in their own homes, industry and honesty brought no great material reward. They came to feel that possession of money was the key to the things they most desired.

There is no great amount of tangible evidence that can be cited on this point. But the very fact that so many persons have come to think that the great thing is to "get by," and that if a person attains material success no great attention will be paid by society to the means by which he "got away" with it, should be evidence enough. If material success is glorified by current public opinion, the effect of that glorification upon the young cannot be offset by occasional moralizing from pulpit, press, teacher and parent.

In pointing out that the concrete state of social relations and activities is the most powerful factor in shaping character, I do not wish it inferred that

I think schools have no responsibility and no opportunity. The conclusion to be drawn is that the schools are only one among many factors, and that their shaping influence will be most helpful when it falls in line with social forces operating outside the schools.

I think the depression has had one healthy effect. It has led to a more general questioning of the primacy of material values. Events have disclosed the demoralizing effect of making success in business the chief aim of life. But I think that still greater economic reconstruction must take place before material attainment and the acquisitive motive will be reduced to their place. It is difficult to produce a cooperative type of character in an economic system that lays chief stress upon competition, and wherein the most successful competitor is the one who is the most richly rewarded and who becomes almost the social hero and model. So I should put general economic change as the first and most important factor in producing a better kind of education for formation of character.

As long as society does not guarantee security of useful work, security for old age, and security of a decent home and of opportunity for education of all children by other means than acquisition of money, that long the very affection of parents for their children, their desire that children may have a better opportunity than their parents had, will compel parents to put great emphasis upon getting ahead in material ways, and their example will be a dominant factor in educating children.

As I have already intimated, better education of parents would be a large element in bringing about better moral education of children and youth. Psychology is still in its infancy. But the increase of knowledge of human nature, and of how it develops and is modified, has grown enormously in the last generation. It has grown especially with respect to how relations between persons—between parents with respect to each other and with respect to their offspring—affect character. The important movement for parental education has developed out of this increase of knowledge. But there are still multitudes of parents who have not had the most rudimentary contact with the new knowledge and who are totally unaware of the influences that are most powerfully affecting the moral fibre of their children.

I would put parental education second among the factors demanded in the improvement of character education.

In recent years there has been great advance in provision of recreation for the young, and yet hardly more than a beginning in comparison with what remains to be done. There are regions in New York City where "cellar clubs" flourish and are attended by school boys and girls. There are large regions in which, in spite of the efforts of social settlements, public playgrounds, and school fields, the great mass of growing youth resort to the streets for an outlet in the day time, and to dance halls, movies, and the like, in the evening.

The two dominant impulses of youth are toward activity and toward some kind of collective association. Our failure to provide for these two impulses, under the changed conditions of rural as well as city life, is at least a partial measure of why we are getting unsatisfactory results in character development.

If I put the school fourth and last it is not because I regard it as the least important of factors in moral training but because its success is so much bound up with the operation of the three others. I shall mention only two changes that would help. Few schools are organized on a social basis. Moral instruction through conference and discussion would be much more effective if it grew out of concrete situations present in the experience of the young instead of centering about general discussions of virtues and vices in the abstract. The more the school is organized as a community in which pupils share, the more opportunity there is for this kind of discussion and the more surely it will lead to the problems of larger social groupings outside the school. Moreover, such organization would give practice in the give and take of social life, practice in methods of cooperation, and would require assumption of definite responsibilities on the part of the young people—adapted of course to their age and maturity.

The other change is provision of greater opportunity for positive action, with corresponding reduction of the amount of passivity and mere absorption that are still current. The latter style of school organization and instruction involves a degree of suppression that stimulates unguided and unruly activity as compensation beyond the school walls. It does not arouse tastes and desires that would be followed up in constructive ways outside the school. It leaves boys and girls, especially those more active by nature, an easy prey to mere excitement.

In short, as far as schools are concerned, the present interest in more effective character education may have two different results. If it is satisfied by merely adding on a special course for direct instruction in good behavior, I do not think it can accomplish much. If it leads public attention to the changes that are needed in the schools in order that they may do more to develop intelligent and sturdy character in the young, it may well be the beginning of a most important movement.

It seems to me especially important that organizations of business and professional men should exercise an influence along the lines mentioned. They have already done a great deal in promoting the growth of the playground movement. They can determine to a great extent the treatment of delinquents, with respect to both prevention and cure. They are in a better position than any other one class to realize what slums and bad housing do to foster juvenile criminality. They can exercise a powerful influence upon the kind of movies that are shown in the community. Instead of throwing their powerful influence for so-called economy measures that eliminate provision for activity in lines of useful work in the schools, retaining only the driest and most formal subjects, they can effectively cooperate with school authorities to promote school subjects that give a healthy outlet to those impulses for activity that are so strong in the young. Through active parent associations they can bring more of the outside world into the school, breaking down that isolation of the school room from social life which is one of the chief reasons why schools do not do more effective work in the formation of character.

Art in Education (1911)

A STUDY OF EDUCATION IN its earlier forms, not only in savage communities, but in a civilization as advanced as the Athenian, reveals the great role played by the arts. Anthropological investigations have confirmed the obvious educational influence by showing the great part played by the arts in the life of the community and in determining progress. Psychology adds to these convictions the fact of the fundamental character of the impulsive tendencies which are the physiological origin of the activities that lead to the arts. All of these facts are opposed to the common assumption that the arts represent a kind of educational luxury and superfluity.

Various classifications have been made of the arts,—they have been subdivided into the spatial and the temporal, arts of rest and motion, of the eye and the ear, etc. However correct for their own purposes, these divisions are educationally defective in that they start from art products rather than from the psycho-physical acts from which these products originate. More significant from the educational point of view is the classification of Santayana according to which arts are distinguished into those that spring from automatisms, i.e. organic or "spontaneous" movements which, when rhythmically ordered and accompanied by intensified emotion, themselves constitute acts, and those in which the movements, even if similarly induced originally, terminate in effective enduring modifications in natural objects. The dance, pantomime, song, music, etc., belong in the first class; the second class Santayana terms "plastic," including in it architecture, sculpture, painting, and design.

Anthropological and historical inquiry have fairly established the following principles: first, that art is born of primary impulses of human nature when the activity, whether automatic or plastic, has social value; second, that this

---

First published in *A Cyclopedia of Education*, ed. Paul Monroe (New York: Macmillan, 1911), 1:223–25.

social value is conferred by the tendency of the activity or its product to spread an emotional mood favorable to joint or concerted action. Otherwise put, the arts, in their origin, tended to contagion or communication of an emotion, that produced unity of attitude and of outlook and imagination. From this point of view, no sharp line divided the fine and useful arts from each other. Any useful object—a piece of pottery, of weaving, an implement of hunting—that provokes social reminiscences and anticipations attaches contagious emotions to itself, and acquires aesthetic quality. The marked distinction between useful and fine arts is chiefly a product of slave labor or of commercial production, making things for a market, under circumstances where the factor of shared emotional life is eliminated.

Another significant trait of the arts in their simple and more natural form is the prominence of the festal element. Tribal dances are the background, out of which music, poetry, and the drama all gradually differentiated. These pantomime dances were either occasional or ceremonial, i.e. they were either community celebrations of more or less choice episodes happening to attract general attention, or else were stated and recurrent celebrations of important tribal traditions and customs, attaching to changes in the season, return of food animals, gathering crops, war expeditions, etc.

Some of the educational bearings of these considerations, psychological and ethnological, come out conspicuously in the older Athenian education. Music (in the Greek sense) and gymnastic were, in general, and in many of the details of their educational use, very direct outgrowths of the role of the dramatic and communal arts of more primitive societies. It is not difficult to detect in Plato's treatment of gymnastics in the Republic and the Laws the fact that dances, etc., originally associated with industrial and military crises in the life of a people, had become so saturated with elements of rhythm, measure, and order, and with social memories and hopes, as to present great value in the training of the young; while music was frankly a vehicle for carrying what was of typical or idealized value in the traditions of the Greek people, by enhancing their emotional value so that they would deeply, though unconsciously, modify the character of children's tastes and likes and dislikes in the direction that reason would later consciously approve.

If we attempt to summarize the meaning of the facts mentioned in this brief summary for present educational practice, the following points stand out clearly:—

1. There has been great loss in relegating the arts to the relatively trivial role which they finally assumed in schooling, and there is corresponding promise of gain in the efforts making in the last generation to restore these to a more important position. Viewed both psychologically and socially, the arts represent not luxuries and superfluities, but fundamental forces of development.

2. Instead of aesthetic appreciation, the sense of beauty, etc., coming first and leading to artistic expression in order to satisfy itself, the order is the reverse. Man instinctively attempts to enhance and perpetuate his images that are charged with emotional value by some kind of objectification through action. The outcome inevitably is marked by certain factors of balance, rhythm, and constructive order, and by the function of representation, i.e. of recording in some adequate way the values to which emotions cling. The sense of beauty, or aesthetic appreciation, is a reflex product of this attempt at production. A product, which is objectively crude, but which represents a genuine attempt at embodiment of an experienced value of unusual emotional quality, is more likely to be an effective means of cultivating taste and aesthetic sensitiveness than the presentation for passive appreciation of much more perfect works produced by others. The latter are indispensable, but their function is to serve as models which will stimulate to appreciation of crudities and imperfections that may be refined away, and to enlarge the emotional images out of which personal expression springs. In the end, the great majority of pupils are of course to become appreciators of art rather than its producers in any technical sense. But only by taking some part in creative production (and that not for the sake consciously of producing beauty but simply of embodying vital and significant feelings) can a wholesome and natural attitude of appreciation finally be secured.

3. The social, or communicable, character of the emotions from which aesthetic expression naturally springs, emphasizes the values of joint experiences and actions of a more or less domestic nature. Group activity of a joyous character celebrating some event or fact of common value is the natural soil of artistic creation in the school as well as out.

4. Expressive activity is also especially adapted for educational use in that the separation, so usual with adults, between the utilitarian and the artistic does not naturally exist for them. In the absence of economic pressure, the measure of use is simply value contributed to the enhancement of individual and group life. Cooking, even such seemingly utilitarian things as setting a table and serving a meal, easily take on for children an artistic value so far as they represent a consciousness and commemoration of things to which children attach a vague social significance, all the more potent because in its vagueness it represents the mysterious and attractive world of adult life. The separation of the externally and technically useful from emotional and imaginative enrichment is unnatural psychological divorce, and one of the chief functions of the arts in education is to maintain the natural union of the socially important with that which makes strong emotional appeal.

5. Literature is probably the art most generally available for school purposes. In order that it may be a genuine art it is necessary that it be presented as a consummation and perfecting of factors which the child already appreciates

as having value. This means that it is not so much a point of departure for instruction as it is a focus in which other factors gather together in a vivid and ordered way. Literature is not to be used as a means for any other end than this gathering together, in a vital and readily appreciated way, of scattered and inchoate elements of experience. It is not, for example, to be made a means of moral instruction or consciously impressing a specific moral lesson. It is ethically important simply because it presents in a form easily grasped and likely to be enduring values which are themselves felt to be intrinsically important. Any attempt at definite formulation and impressing of these values and the kind of conduct they require is certainly detrimental to the literature as art, and is very likely to be harmful to the moral influence which the values might exercise, if left undisturbed in their proper medium of feeling and imagination. The same principle holds, of course, of methods that utilize literature simply as a means of teaching grammar, information about the history of literary men, antiquities, or any of the diverse topics which have been hung upon literature as upon a peg.

Science as Subject-Matter and as Method (1910)

ONE WHO, LIKE MYSELF, CLAIMS no expertness in any branch of natural science can undertake to discuss the teaching of science only at some risk of presumption. At present, however, the gap between those who are scientific specialists and those who are interested in science on account of its significance in life, that is to say, on account of its educational significance, is very great. Therefore I see no other way of promoting that mutual understanding so requisite for educational progress than for all of us frankly to state our own convictions, even if thereby we betray our limitations and trespass where we have no rights save by courtesy.

I suppose that I may assume that all who are much interested in securing for the sciences the place that belongs to them in education feel a certain amount of disappointment at the results hitherto attained. The glowing predictions made respecting them have been somewhat chilled by the event. Of course, this relative shortcoming is due in part to the unwillingness of the custodians of educational traditions and ideals to give scientific studies a fair show. Yet in view of the relatively equal opportunity accorded to science to-day compared with its status two generations ago, this cause alone does not explain the unsatisfactory outcome. Considering the opportunities, students have not flocked to the study of science in the numbers predicted, nor has science modified the spirit and purport of all education in a degree commensurate with the claims made for it. The causes for this result are many and complex. I make no pretense of doing more than singling out what seems to me one influential cause, the remedy for which most lies with scientific men themselves. I mean that science has been taught too much as an accumulation of ready-made material with which students are

First published in *Science*, n.s. 31 (1910): 121–27, from an address of the vice-president and chairman of Section L, Education, American Association for the Advancement of Science annual meeting, Boston, 29 December 1909.

to be made familiar, not enough as a method of thinking, an attitude of mind, after the pattern of which mental habits are to be transformed.

Among the adherents of a literary education who have contended against the claims of science, Matthew Arnold has, I think, been most discreetly reasonable. He freely admitted the need of men knowing something, knowing a good deal, about the natural conditions of their own lives. Since, so to say, men have to breathe air, it is advisable that they should know something of the constitution of air and of the mechanism of the lungs. Moreover, since the sciences have been developed by human beings, an important part of humanistic culture, of knowing the best that men have said and thought, consists in becoming acquainted with the contributions of the great historic leaders of science.

These concessions made, Matthew Arnold insisted that the important thing, the indispensable thing in education, is to become acquainted with human life itself, its art, its literature, its politics, the fluctuations of its career. Such knowledge, he contended, touches more closely our offices and responsibilities as human beings, since these, after all, are to human beings and not to physical things. Such knowledge, moreover, lays hold of the emotions and the imagination and modifies character, while knowledge about things remains an inert possession of speculative intelligence.

Those who believe, nevertheless, that the sciences have a part to play in education equal—at the least—to that of literature and language, have perhaps something to learn from this contention. If we regard science and literary culture as just so much subject-matter, is not Mr. Arnold's contention essentially just? Conceived from this standpoint, knowledge of human affairs couched in personal terms seems more important and more intimately appealing than knowledge of physical things conveyed in impersonal terms. One might well object to Arnold that he ignored the place of natural forces and conditions in human life and thereby created an impossible dualism. But it would not be easy to deny that knowledge of Thermopylae knits itself more readily into the body of emotional images that stir men to action than does the formula for the acceleration of a flying arrow; or that Burns's poem on the daisy enters more urgently and compellingly into the moving vision of life than does information regarding the morphology of the daisy.

The infinitely extensive character of natural facts and the universal character of the laws formulated about them is sometimes claimed to give science an advantage over literature. But viewed from the standpoint of education, this presumed superiority turns out a defect; that is to say, so long as we confine ourselves to the point of view of subject-matter. Just because the facts of nature are multitudinous, inexhaustible, they begin nowhere and end nowhere in particular, and hence are not, just as facts, the best material for the education of those whose lives are centered in quite local situations and whose careers are irretrievably partial and specific. If we turn from multiplicity of detail to general laws, we find indeed that the laws of science are universal, but we also find that for educational purposes their universality means abstractness and remoteness. The conditions, the interests, the ends of conduct are irredeemably concrete and specific. We do not live in a medium of universal principles, but by means of adaptations, through concessions and compromises, struggling as best we may to enlarge the range of a concrete here and now. So far as acquaintance is concerned, it is the individualized and the humanly limited that helps, not the bare universal and the inexhaustibly multifarious.

These considerations are highly theoretical. But they have very practical counterparts in school procedure. One of the most serious difficulties that confronts the educator who wants in good faith to do something worth while with the sciences is their number, and the indefinite bulk of the material in each. At times, it seems as if the educational availability of science were breaking down because of its own sheer mass. There is at once so much of science and so many sciences that educators oscillate, helpless, between arbitrary selection and teaching a little of everything. If anyone questions this statement, let him consider in elementary education the fortunes of nature study for the last two decades.

Is there anything on earth, or in the waters under the earth or in the heavens above, that distracted teachers have not resorted to? Visit schools where they have taken nature study conscientiously. This school moves with zealous bustle from leaves to flowers, from flowers to minerals, from minerals to stars, from stars to the raw materials of industry, thence back to leaves and stones. At another school you find children energetically striving to keep up with what is happily termed the "rolling year." They chart the records of barometer and thermometer; they plot changes and velocities of the winds; they exhaust the possibilities of colored crayons to denote the ratio of sunshine and cloud in successive days and weeks; they keep records of the changing heights of the sun's shadows; they do sums in amounts of rainfalls and atmospheric humidities—and at the end, the rolling year, like the rolling stone, gathers little moss.

Is it any wonder that after a while teachers yearn for the limitations of the good old-fashioned studies—for English grammar, where the parts of speech may sink as low as seven but never rise above nine; for text-book geography, with its strictly inexpansive number of continents; even for the war campaigns and the lists of rulers in history since they can not be stretched beyond a certain point, and for "memory gems" in literature, since a single book will contain the "Poems Every Child Should Know."

There are many who do not believe it amounts to much one way or the other what children do in science in the elementary school. I do not agree, for upon the whole I believe the attitude toward the study of science is, and should be, fixed during the earlier years of life. But in any case, how far does the situation in the secondary schools differ from that just described? Anyone who has followed the discussions of college faculties for the last twenty-five years concerning entrance requirements in science will be able to testify that the situation has been one of highly unstable equilibrium between the claims of a little of a great many sciences, a good deal (comparatively) of one, a combination of one biological and one exact science, and the arbitrary option of the pupil of one, two or three out of a list of six or seven specified sciences. The only safe generalization possible is that whatever course a given institution pursues, it changes that course at least as often as the human organism proverbially renews its tissues. The movement has probably tended in the direction of reduction, but everyone who has followed the history of pedagogical discussion will admit that every alteration of opinion as to what subjects should be taught has been paralleled by a modification of opinion as to the portions of any subject to be selected and emphasized.

All this change is to some extent a symptom of healthy activity, change being especially needed in any group of studies so new that they have to blaze their own trail, since they have no body of traditions upon which to fall back as is the case with study of language and literature. But this principle hardly covers the whole field of change. A considerable part of it has been due not to intelligent experimentation and exploration, but to blind action and reaction, or to the urgency of some strenuous soul who has propagated some emphatic doctrine.

Imagine a history of the teaching of the languages which should read like this: "The later seventies and early eighties of the nineteenth century witnessed a remarkable growth in the attention given in high schools to the languages. Hundreds of schools adopted an extensive and elaborate scheme by means of which almost the entire linguistic ground was covered. Each of the three terms of the year was devoted to a language. In the first year, Latin and Greek and Sanskrit were covered; in the next, French, German and Italian; while the last year was given to review and to Hebrew and Spanish as optional studies."

This piece of historic parallelism raises the question as to the real source of the educational value of, say, Latin. How much is due to its being a "humanity," its giving insight into the best the world has thought and said, and how much to its being pursued continuously for at least four years? How much to the graded and orderly arrangement that this long period both permitted and compelled? How much to the cumulative effort of constant recourse to what had earlier been learned, not by way of mere monotonous repetition, but as a necessary instrument of later achievement? Are we not entitled to conclude that the method demanded by the study is the source of its efficacy rather than anything inhering in its content?

Thus we come around again to the primary contention of the paper: that science teaching has suffered because science has been so frequently presented just as so much ready-made knowledge, so much subject-matter of fact and law, rather than as the effective method of inquiry into any subject-matter.

Science might well take a leaf from the book of the actual, as distinct from the supposititious, pursuit of the classics in the schools. The claim for their worth has professedly rested upon their cultural value; but imaginative insight into human affairs has perhaps been the last thing, save per accidens, that the average student has got from his pursuit of the classics. His time has gone of necessity to the mastering of a language, not to appreciation of humanity. To some extent just because of this enforced simplification (not to say meagreness) the student acquires, if he acquires anything, a certain habitual method. Confused, however, by the tradition that the subject-matter is the efficacious factor, the defender of the sciences has thought that he could make good his case only on analogous grounds, and hence has been misled into resting his claim upon the superior significance of his special subject-matter; even into efforts to increase still further the scope of scientific subject-matter in education. The procedure of Spencer is typical. To urge the prerogative of science, he raised the question what knowledge, what facts, are of most utility for life, and, answering the question by this criterion of the value of subject-matter, decided in favor of the sciences. Having thus identified education with the amassing of information, it is not a matter of surprise that for the rest of his life he taught that comparatively little is to be expected from education in the way of moral training and social reform, since the motives of conduct lie in the affections and the aversions, not in the bare recognition of matters of fact.

Surely if there is any knowledge which is of most worth it is knowledge of the ways by which anything is entitled to be called knowledge instead of being mere opinion or guess-work or dogma.

Such knowledge never can be learned by itself; it is not information, but a mode of intelligent practice, an habitual disposition of mind. Only by taking a hand in the making of knowledge, by transferring guess and opinion into belief authorized by inquiry, does one ever get a knowledge of the method of knowing. Because participation in the making of knowledge has been scant, because reliance on the efficacy of acquaintance with certain kinds of facts has been current, science has not accomplished in education what was predicted for it.

We define science as systematized knowledge, but the definition is wholly ambiguous. Does it mean the body of facts, the subject-matter? Or does it mean the processes by which something fit to be called knowledge is brought into existence, and order introduced into the flux of experience? That science means both of these things will doubtless be the reply, and rightly. But in the order both of time and of importance, science as method precedes science as subject-matter. Systematized knowledge is science only because of the care and thoroughness with which it has been sought for, selected and arranged. Only by pressing the courtesy of language beyond what is decent can we term such information as is acquired ready-made, without active experimenting and testing, science.

The force of this assertion is not quite identical with the commonplace of scientific instruction that text-book and lecture are not enough; that the student must have laboratory exercises. A student may acquire laboratory methods as so much isolated and final stuff, just as he may so acquire material from a text-book. One's mental attitude is not necessarily changed just because he engages in certain physical manipulations and handles certain tools and materials. Many a student has acquired dexterity and skill in laboratory methods without its ever occurring to him that they have anything to do with constructing beliefs that are alone worthy of the title of knowledge. To do certain things, to learn certain modes of procedure, are to him just a part of the subject-matter to be acquired; they belong, say, to chemistry, just as do the symbols H_2So_4, or the atomic theory. They are part of the arcana in process of revelation to him. In order to proceed in the mystery one has, of course, to master its ritual. And how easily the laboratory becomes liturgical! In short, it is a problem and a difficult problem to conduct matters so that the technical methods employed in a subject shall become conscious instrumentalities of realizing the meaning of knowledge—what is required in the way of thinking and of search for evidence before anything passes from the realm of opinion, guess-work and dogma into that of knowledge. Yet unless this perception accrues, we can hardly claim that an individual has been instructed in science. This problem of turning laboratory technique to intellectual account is even more pressing than that of utilization of information derived from books. Almost every teacher has had drummed into him the inadequacy of mere book instruction, but the conscience of most is quite at peace if only pupils are put through some laboratory exercises. Is not this the path of experiment and induction by which science develops?

I hope it will not be supposed that, in dwelling upon the relative defect and backwardness of science teaching, I deny its absolute achievements and improvements, if I go on to point out to what a comparatively slight extent the teaching of science has succeeded in protecting the so-called educated public against recrudescences of all sorts of corporate superstitions and silliness. Nay, one can go even farther and say that science teaching not only has not protected men and women who have been to school from the revival of all kinds of occultism, but to some extent has paved the way for this revival. Has not science revealed many wonders? If radio-activity is a proved fact, why is not telepathy highly probable? Shall we, as a literary idealist recently pathetically inquired, admit that mere brute matter has such capacities and deny them to mind? When all allowance is made for the unscrupulous willingness of newspapers and magazines to publish any marvel of so-called scientific discovery that may give a momentary thrill of sensation to any jaded reader, there is still, I think, a large residuum of published matter to be accounted for only on the ground of densely honest ignorance. So many things have been vouched for by science; so many things that one would have thought absurd have been substantiated, why not one more, and why not this one more? Communication of science as subject-matter has so far outrun in education the construction of a scientific habit of mind that to some extent the natural common sense of mankind has been interfered with to its detriment.

Something of the current flippancy of belief and quasi-scepticism must also be charged to the state of science teaching. The man of even ordinary culture is aware of the rapid changes of subject-matter, and taught so that he believes subject-matter, not method, constitutes science, he remarks to himself that if this is science, then science is in constant change, and there is no certainty anywhere. If the emphasis had been put upon method of attack and mastery, from this change he would have learned the lesson of curiosity, flexibility and patient search; as it is, the result too often is a blasé satiety.

I do not mean that our schools should be expected to send forth their students equipped as judges of truth and falsity in specialized scientific matters. But that the great majority of those who leave school should have some idea of the kind of evidence required to substantiate given types of belief does not seem unreasonable. Nor is it absurd to expect that they should go forth with a lively interest in the ways in which knowledge is improved and a marked distaste for all conclusions reached in disharmony with the methods of scientific inquiry. It would be absurd, for example, to expect any large number to master the technical methods of determining distance, direction and position in the arctic regions; it would perhaps be possible to develop a state of mind with American people in general in which the supposedly keen American sense of humor would react when it is proposed to settle the question of reaching the pole by aldermanic resolutions and straw votes in railway trains or even newspaper editorials.

If in the foregoing remarks I have touched superficially upon some aspects of science teaching rather than sounded its depths, I can not plead as my excuse failure to realize the importance of the topic. One of the only two articles that remain in my creed of life is that the future of our civilization depends upon the widening spread and deepening hold of the scientific habit of mind; and that the problem of problems in our education is therefore to discover how to mature and make effective this scientific habit. Mankind so far has been ruled by things and by words, not by thought, for till the last few moments of history, humanity has not been in possession of the conditions of secure and effective thinking. Without ignoring in the least the consolation that has come to men from their literary education, I would even go so far as to say that only the gradual replacing of a literary by a scientific education can assure to man the progressive amelioration of his lot. Unless we master things, we shall continue to be mastered by them; the magic that words cast upon things may indeed disguise our subjection or render us less dissatisfied with it, but after all science, not words, casts the only compelling spell upon things.

Scientific method is not just a method which it has been found profitable to pursue in this or that abstruse subject for purely technical reasons. It represents the only method of thinking that has proved fruitful in any subject—that is what we mean when we call it scientific. It is not a peculiar development of thinking for highly specialized ends; it is thinking so far as thought has become conscious of its proper ends and of the equipment indispensable for success in their pursuit.

The modern warship seems symbolic of the present position of science in life and education. The warship could not exist were it not for science: mathematics, mechanics, chemistry, electricity supply the technique of its construction and management. But the aims, the ideals in whose service this marvelous technique is displayed are survivals of a pre-scientific age, that is, of barbarism. Science has as yet had next to nothing to do with forming the social and moral ideals for the sake of which she is used. Even where science has received its most attentive recognition, it has remained a servant of ends imposed from alien traditions. If ever we are to be governed by intelligence, not by things and by words, science must have something to say about what we do, and not merely about how we may do it most easily and economically. And if this consummation is achieved, the transformation must occur through education, by bringing home to men's habitual inclination and attitude the significance of genuine knowledge and the full import of the conditions requisite for its attainment. Actively to participate in the making of knowledge is the highest prerogative of man and the only warrant of his freedom. When our schools truly become laboratories of knowledge-making, not mills fitted out with information-hoppers, there will no longer be need to discuss the place of science in education.

Theory of Course of Study (1911)

THE COURSE OF STUDY MAY be considered from two quite distinct points of view. On the one hand, we may accept the curriculum as it obtains at a given time, and consider how each constituent study may be treated so as to make it most effective; what materials are available and what methods of presentation and enforcement are most successful. Arithmetic, geography, history, reading, spelling, and all the studies may be thus treated. The results constitute a very important part of pedagogy or educational doctrine. Treatment from this practical point of view may also be extended to take into account the arrangement of these studies from the standpoint of the working school program, their proper grouping simultaneous and successive, the allotment of time to each study, the alternation of study and recitation periods appropriate to each subject, etc.

On the other hand, there is the philosophical theory of the Course of Study. From this standpoint, the problem does not grow out of accepting the currently established curriculum and asking how it may be perfected in efficiency, but centres about the ground and justification of any body of subject-matter, and the reason for being of each constituent ingredient as a special means, or division of labor, for fulfilling the function of subject-matter as a whole. However, it is neither necessary nor advisable to draw a sharp line between the more concrete or practical point of view and the more theoretical problem. In a transitional time like the present there is no absolutely fixed and established body of subject-matter. From the practical standpoint certain subjects are relatively retiring from the field; new subjects are being introduced or are clamoring for recognition. A generalized conception of the function to be served by the subject-matter of education, of the various phases and factors of this function, and of the relation of various types of study to these different factors, can

---

First published in *A Cyclopedia of Education*, ed. Paul Monroe (New York: Macmillan, 1911), 2:218–22.

hardly fail to throw some light on the problems of the conflict and respective claims of various studies. Questions of the practical adjustment and sequence of studies and topics also run into problems of *correlation, concentration,* and *isolation,* which have some philosophic basis and bearing. In this article, the philosophic aspect of the course of study is considered, and with reference to the following problems: (1) the significance of subject-matter in general; (2) its relation to experience; (3) its classification.

1. Viewed externally, the various studies present many independent collections of facts and general principles, each of these collections having its own distinctive logical basis and organization. Some of the studies represent forms of skill or of special ability to be acquired,—reading, writing, drawing, etc. Regarded in this external way, there is a great gap between the experience of the pupil and the subject-matter which he studies. Three points of contrast may be noted. The child's experience is intensely social and personal. Every parent and every teacher knows that children naturally respond with a personal association to any incident or fact; what cannot be translated into terms of something which they themselves have done, or something that is connected with the activities of their friends, is not comprehended, or leaves them cold and indifferent. Experience centres about persons; things that are noted and recalled are things that play some part in the lives of persons. The material of studies, on the other hand, is impersonal and objective. It extends beyond the little world of persons with which the child is acquainted; it ignores all that is peculiar and precious to each individual. Over against the limited but social field of familiar friends, studies introduce the external world, infinite in space and time. In the second place, there is a striking contrast between the fluid continuity of children's experience and the hard-and-fast subjects of the curriculum. The child passes quickly and readily from one incident, one place, one idea, to another and each blends insensibly into the other. He is absorbed in the present, and the present melts vaguely in indefinite vistas. His world is too fluid to permit of sharp separations or isolations. There is not even a dividing line between man and nature, to say nothing of between various phases of man's activities and various aspects of nature. The specific studies that form the curriculum represent this dissolving unity precipitated into detached and rigid subjects. Its world of experience is partitioned off into independent compartments. The unity of life appears simply as an aggregate of separate parts, such as arithmetic, geography, astronomy, physics, etc. Finally, the connecting links of direct experience and of a study are of radically different sorts. Affections, sympathies, inclinations, interests are the axes which hold together the diversity of fact and episode of ordinary experience. In a subject of study, facts are torn away from this primitive matrix, and are classed in a new way on the basis of a principle which is abstract and intellectual. The meaning of facts consists no longer in what they

are worth to a person, but in the capacity of one fact to stand, impartially and objectively, for another. The classes, the genera, of natural experience are things that feel alike or that have the same value; studies present groups of facts that may be logically derived from a common principle.

These three contrasts, the personal and narrow world of the child and the impersonal and indefinitely extended world of the studies, the fluid continuity of experience and the specialized divisions of the curriculum, the practical and emotional ties of life and the logical basis and system of subject-matter, define the problem of the significance of subject-matter. The studies represent selections and formulations of what is regarded as most important in the experience of the race, and hence most necessary to transmit for the sake of the future of society. Subject-matter is to be regarded from a social point of view. Every human group, at every stage of development, from the tribes of savages, to the national states of the present day, has certain customs and manners of living, with which are associated certain forms of skill, trained ability, accumulated knowledge, and practical and moral aims. To habituate the young to these customs, to discipline them in the acquired modes of skill, to inform with the knowledge possessed, and, above all, to permeate them with the current ideals, is necessary to the conservation of the type of social life in question. When community life is simple, the function of transmission is performed by personal contact and intercourse and by the sharing of the young and old in common activities. But as associated life becomes more complex, it becomes more and more impossible to secure the requisite continuity of institutions by such informal means. As the tribal traditions become richer and fuller, and the technique of the arts, industrial, military and magical, more elaborated, division of labor occurs, and certain persons are set aside, as it were, to attend particularly to these things and to their perpetuation. These persons become the instructors of the community, and through them certain bodies of knowledge and belief and certain modes of skill are more or less differentiated and isolated. Instead of existing in solution, as it were, in the ordinary experience of the members of the community, they are precipitated. The need of special instruction going along with specialized legends and activities is probably the chief motive force in compelling self-conscious reflection upon naïve and customary experience. Instead of the development of sciences leading to instruction, the demand for instruction led to the selection and formulation into definite bodies of subject-matter of achievements and traditions that had previously been carried by the main stream of direct social intercourse.

It is not intended to trace the historic process by which out of these early crude condensations of various forms of tribal custom, belief, and skill, our present curriculum has been built up. Reference to the simple and more primitive types of education is here made because of the light thrown upon our problem of the significance of subject-matter in general. This reference enables us to see that, fundamentally, geography, history, arithmetic, grammar, physics, etc., do not exist as studies simply for the sake of affording material of discipline or of intellectual improvement or general culture to pupils, nor because knowledge is inherently desirable in the abstract, but because there are certain values, activities, purposes, and beliefs currently existing in social life which absolutely must be transmitted to the succeeding and immature generation if social life itself is not to relapse into barbarism and then into savagery. On its face, geography is so much systematized knowledge about the earth. Fundamentally, however, it does not enter into the course of study just because of the objective facts themselves, but because of the role these facts play in the social organization and intercourse of a people. The same holds true, in its own way, of each factor of the course of study. Summing up, we may say that the significance of the subject-matter that forms the material of the course of study is to present phases and results of community life having such typical value that it is necessary to insure their continuous transmission.

2. What is the relation of this subject-matter to the ordinary, immediate experience of pupils? It is to be noted that when we consider the course of study from the social point of view, we gain a notion of this relationship, which is very different from that entertained when, as is too common, we regard it from a purely intellectual, or logical, point of view. If the course of study is regarded simply as a body of material which has its significance in itself (whether as pure objective information or as a collection of modes of technical skill), the three antitheses already mentioned are much accentuated. It is difficult to discover points of natural community and transition between the everyday experience of children, their activities, purposes, and methods of cognition out of school, and the elaborate intellectual subdivisions and systems of abstract bodies of knowledge regarded as ends in themselves. But if we treat the organized subject-matter of textbooks and formulated curricula as indications of socially important results to be employed not as self-sufficient ends of learning, but as stimuli to the progressive induction of pupils into a richer and fuller life, the situation is quite different.

The experience of pupils is already more or less socialized. It has been built up through suggestions and interpretations derived from the social groups of which the child is already a member. It is already saturated with social values that are akin to those presented in the studies of the curriculum. When taken statically and in cross-section, these studies are ready-made; they are hard-and-fast classifications. But if we take them historically, we find that they are gradual growths and precipitates of the experience of the race. The race also began with a crude immature experience, and out of this condition has gradually evolved the richer and more exact experience represented in the course of study.

Since, therefore, these studies are social products of the same sort of powers and conditions that are now found in child experience, there must be many points of kinship and contact between them and the present embryonic experience of the child. The primary business of education is to discover these points of likeness, and to make them the starting points of a guided development. The child's present experience and the subject-matter of instruction, instead of existing in two separate worlds, one wholly psychological, the other wholly logical, represent two changing or dynamic limits of one continuous social process.

Looking at the problem from the side of the child, we find that his experience is not a static or finished thing needing to be stimulated to grow from without. It is transitive, full of motives and outreaching forces that compel its own modification and reconstruction. It is self-transforming, so that the problem of education is not to engraft foreign and remote material upon an indifferent, passive person, but to supply an environment which will direct the changes that are bound to occur anyway toward the desired social result.

3. Classification of Studies.—What has been said indicates a convenient and fruitful principle for classifying the subject-matter of instruction. First come those studies which, looked at from the standpoint of the child, are not studies but modes of social activity and experience, and which, looked at from the standpoint of the educator, are typical embodiments of social values that represent important ends to be attained in instruction. Elementary education has already included within itself (for a variety of reasons) such activities as gardening, cooking, sewing and weaving, constructive work in paper, leather, wood, metal, care of animals, excursions, singing, story telling, dramatizations, drawing, painting, designing, sand molding, clay modeling, plays and games, etc. These modes of activity are not psychological merely; they do not simply appeal to and express the more native and spontaneous impulses of children; they also present important social processes; they typify occupations that are indispensable to the continued existence of community life. Moreover, as processes they condition intelligent study of social products.

Probably the main motives for introducing these activities into the primary curriculum have been psychological and utilitarian, rather than any conscious perception of their value as social types. That is to say, they have made their way because children were found to be interested in them, because they furnished devices for teaching the three R's more easily, because they afforded relief and recreation from more severe intellectual studies, and because they seemed to prepare children for the later business of making a living. For this reason, they have been inserted into the curriculum, or superimposed upon other studies, without any particular transformation of other studies, or any organic connection with them. They have been for the most part simply additional school studies. It remains to utilize them systematically as foundation stones for the other studies by teaching them as representatives of these social activities which are funda-mental to the knowledge and modes of skill embodied in these other studies.

History and geography (including, for convenience, nature study under the latter term) are the members of our second group. They are to be considered as the background of the direct social processes exhibited in the group just considered. History sets forth the temporal background, the evolution of the gradual control of the activities by which mankind has enriched and perfected its experience. From the pupil's standpoint, the direct activities in which he engages lead constantly out into this historic field. Children must begin naturally with simple operations, whether in cooking, weaving, woodwork, or whatever. These simple operations agree of necessity in their main features of crude material and simple tools and technique with the operations of men in the less developed, the earlier, periods of social life. In their contrast with the elaborate complicated products and machinery of contemporary occupations, they present the problem of the historic step by which the gap has been bridged. They introduce questions regarding the social effects of the industrial activities they typify, and the nature of the inventions by which the progress of society has been effectively secured. They lead, in other words, not only to the economic history of mankind, but to the political and scientific history associated with man's economic development.

On another side, these activities necessitate consideration of the natural background, a study of the globe from which materials are drawn, of the various plants, animals, minerals, etc., that supply the raw material, and the various conditions, climatic, physiographic, etc., under which these materials originate; they also require study of those physical and chemical energies that are involved in the tools and operations employed. In the history of the race, the sciences have been slowly developed out of practical necessities—anatomy and physiology out of sickness, accidents, and the need for keeping well; botany out of agriculture and the search for medicinal remedies; physics out of mechanical devices for getting results more economically and on a large scale; chemistry out of dyeing, metal working, the refining of crude natural products; geometry out of measuring land, erecting buildings, etc. The natural differentiation of studies with pupils follows the same general sequence of evolution.

There are also found in the curriculum various studies and aspects of studies that represent technical skill and intellectual or logical methods in the abstract, i.e. on purely intellectual grounds. From the standpoint of our fundamental criterion, the social, these abstract and technical methods signify the instru-mentalities by which complex and progressive communities are maintained in being. From one standpoint, mathematics is a pure science, organized on logical grounds for the sole sake of the perfecting of knowledge. From another point of view, mathematics represents an absolutely indispensable organ, or method, of any social life that rises above barbarism. In like fashion, written and printed language, while, on its face, a purely symbolic device for the recording and communicating of thought and objective information, is, in its concrete setting and function, a device of social life. Oral language is transitory; it leaves behind itself no permanent deposit. Where it alone has been achieved, social development is restricted to what can be carried by personal memory and communication. When written and printed symbols came into use, the net results of the past could be economically conserved, their transmission was facilitated, and they themselves were emancipated, by their symbolic or abstract representations, from all sorts of local and irrelevant associations. Generalization and organization of future activities were rendered possible. Now it follows, it goes without saying, that the educational significance and motivation of the studies that have to do with the mastery and use of symbols should be based, not upon their purely theoretical values, but upon their value as social methods and instrumentalities. This mode of approach is secured in the degree in which this class of studies is organically connected with the two classes previously described. While the reaction in the elementary curriculum against the domination of the "three R's" has proceeded practically and unconsciously in response to specific exigencies, its philosophical justification lies in the fact that it recognizes that studies dealing with formal or symbolic materials have to be motivated and led up to through educational content of a more direct and social character.

The scheme of classification indicated makes no provision for literature and the fine arts. Art—in the aesthetic as distinct from the technical and industrial sense—is to be regarded as a perfected expression of any crude or primitive mode of activity which has gained a recognized social value. It is essentially a consummation, a refinement and idealization of what is originally done and acquired from more direct and practical motives. It represents the end to which all other educational achievement should tend—its perfected goal.

PART THREE. THE EDUCATIONAL LEADER

Introduction: The Educational Leader

IN EARLIER READINGS, WE GAINED insight into Dewey's views of the teacher, the curriculum, and, at least indirectly, the school, but so far we have seen little of what he has to say about the educational leader or administrator of a school or school district. For instance, he describes the school as a social institution that ideally is designed to promote students' growth and to engage them in a community's activities, preparing them for participation in a democratic society. And schools should be designed to help students develop reflective minds that are prepared to keep learning and wrestling with social, economic, and political questions. In addition, Dewey argues that the best schools are rooted in the experiences of their students and the realities of their society, not artificial enclaves of abstract or alien studies. Moreover, the school should be a community of social groups (i.e., more than a collection of isolated classes) that participate in the construction of an environment that nurtures students' attitudes, learning, thinking, and behavior.

A school, of course, is much more, including being an organization composed of individuals with delegated responsibilities and imaginative opportunities, whether administrators, teachers, support staff, or volunteers. But a school may also be viewed as embodying a culture, a physical plant, and a mission, accompanied by goals, objectives, and related curriculum. Substantial research confirms the importance of a school's having a clear mission or purpose and strong, ethical educational leadership. Other research indicates that a successful school is also characterized by academic focus, parental and community involvement, and shared responsibility for learning and its assessment. These kinds of schools, so we are told, need leaders who have a comprehensive understanding of individual schools and districts as a whole. But these ideas had not been well researched in Dewey's day. Not surprisingly, the roles and responsibilities of supervisors, principals, and superintendents grew more important during his lifetime. Although their contributions to the educational system were initially looked on by many as peripheral or even detrimental, professional educational leaders gradually became major influences in schools and districts. Likewise, the role of informal leaders gradually became better understood. Today, the field of educational leadership represents a major field of inquiry.

Dewey wrote about many of the tensions that hampered relations between teachers and administrators and how the two groups could overcome their differences and collaborate in providing school leadership. Just as he was unquestionably supportive of the artistic teacher personalizing students' educative experiences, his interest in school administration was far-reaching and aimed at encouraging teachers and administrators to contribute to the well-being of students and society. In fact, it is important to note that Dewey's laboratory school was designed to experiment with—not model—a theory of collaborative leadership involving both teachers and administrators. His administrative and organizational theories were shaped and guided by his ideas about curriculum and pedagogy, child development, and interpersonal communication, the ultimate aim of which was to facilitate educative interactions between students, teachers, and administrators (LW11.182–91).

Dewey advises administrators to protect staff and students from a mass of "dogma called pedagogy and a mass of ritualistic exercises called school administration" (MW13.321–22). He argues that leaders should not be dominated by tradition (LW3.260), autocratic inclinations (LW3.279), indolent schoolteachers (MW11.56), or powerful socioeconomic groups (LW7.365). He also urges administrators to guard educational goals, staff, and students from those who would emphasize standardization over imagination (MW8.131), competition over community (MW6.223), and quantitative results over qualitative outcomes (LW3.261).

In a chapter in *John Dewey on Education: Selected Writings*, edited by Richard Archambault (Chicago: University of Chicago Press, 1964) titled "What Psychology Can Do for the Teacher," Dewey provides a framework for many of his administrative, managerial, and organizational concerns by discussing them in the context of two inseparable "functions" of education, namely (a) seeing the school as "an organic whole" and (b) understanding the necessity of adapting "school structure to the individual pupil." These two ideas and a plethora of others, as a result, need sustained attention by leaders to ensure that all children are properly, flexibly, and socially guided in their learning by well-educated, responsible, and creative teachers. Seeing the school as a whole while taking seriously the needs of the individual student, then, become both the perspective on and the grounds for changing schools so that students are better served.

Dewey recognized, then, that part of seeing the school as a whole is to recognize the interaction, commingling, and suffusing of content, methodology, and administration, or the "trinity of school topics" (MW9.171). Correspondingly, he recognizes that a triad of administrators, teachers, and students needs to work together to construct and adapt conditions and environments that will develop the "kind of individuality which is intelligently alive to the common life and sensitively loyal to its common maintenance" (MW11.57). Dewey thought that educational leaders—teachers, principals, superintendents, and so on— should facilitate and manage the resources, energy, focus, and engagement of the school organization toward the freeing of intelligence for the well-being of students to promote their becoming individuals who live democratically with one another (MW3.237–38).

Of course, Dewey was interested in other educational issues as well. For example, personal relationships, coherent districts, genuine communication, educational supervision, administrative practice, and professional development are some of the ideas that he addresses in the essays of this section.

In "Democracy and Educational Administration" (LW11.217–25), Dewey contends that democratic leadership in schools and districts is essential in and for a democratic society. Sensitive to the growing power and influence of fascism in Europe as he wrote, he advises administrators to listen to and learn from the voices of the stakeholders in developing educational methods, goals, and curriculum. As an educational leader for a host of school- and community-related matters, he views the role of the school administrator as more than a bookkeeper or manager, but a person who has the power and responsibility to nurture a cooperative and engaging learning environment. Aware that school administrators face numerous difficult situations, particularly in times of tight budget cuts, as many experienced during the Great Depression, he nevertheless challenges them to lead in ways that will achieve the primary goals of the schools. He frames his argument around two basic questions, What is democracy? and, What does it have to do with school and district administration? Not altogether obliquely, he asks, What are the consequences of nondemocratically organized and operated schools and districts?

His essay "Toward Administrative Statesmanship" (LW11.345–47) moves from the challenges of being a democratic leader to the problems of leaders managing their own lives in professionally fruitful ways. He identifies three problems facing school administrators or educational leaders: the intellectual-professional challenge, the personal-relationships challenge, and the detail-routine challenge. Speaking as an experienced educational leader, he observes that school administrators far too often get bogged down in, if not overwhelmed by, the detail problem. Because of the nearly overpowering demands of the job, the administrator has less time to focus on working with teachers, guiding student growth, analyzing curricular issues, interacting with parents, and developing the necessary personal relationships that, Dewey believed, help to build the school community and make educational efforts more likely to succeed. He shows both compassion and understanding of the plight and privilege of school administrators. In the process, he also issues advice to educational leaders to pay attention to these three problems, thoughtfully integrating the roles they must play and keeping them in balance. To assist in this exercise, he enjoins them to visit and revisit three queries: What is the social function of the school? What type of community should the school be? and, How will the school and district educate the public? Dewey implies that thinking through these questions should facilitate the development of not just an education leader but an educational statesperson.

Dewey's focus in "General Principles of Educational Articulation" (LW5.299–310) is on how to eliminate the waste of time, energy, and resources in schools by working toward an articulation—we would probably say, a better understanding and integration—of school structures, student development, curriculum experiences, and school-home-neighbor interests. Speaking to a group of public school administrators, Dewey shares his concern regarding the integration of theory and practice, especially as it relates to a district's schools, their organization, and their influence on the continuity of services to students, given their developmental, experiential, and curricular needs. Staff, too, must be considered in order to reduce educational waste caused by ineffective utilization of teacher knowledge. School administrators may need to examine challenges from both administrative and psychological angles, understand the latest research, avoid the temptation of being guided by ideology instead of inquiry, and consider the experience of teachers and other administrators. Unsurprisingly, the educational leader should not blindly rely on administrative or pedagogical tradition, convenience, or habit. Instead, they need to be lifelong students of neighborhoods and communities and to learn from new theories and research. He urges that we never forget that education is organic, affecting the structure of living organisms, dynamic schools, and vibrant societies. Thus, educational leaders need to see students as developing persons throughout their school years, schools and universities as dynamic and interrelated institutions, and schools as interactive parts of a broader society.

In "Democracy in Education" (MW3.229–39), a fairly early essay, Dewey summarizes one of the strongest threads of his entire work on education: the need for more democratic practices in all facets of education. Democratically operating schools, he asserts, help to create and maintain democratically functioning societies. Translating that from theory to practice in the classroom means, in part, allowing teachers a greater share of responsibility in the selection and presentation of curriculum, which both empowers them and gives them respect as professionals. It also means freeing children to explore and discover, as opposed to following formulaic teaching units; in a word, to experience learning *first-hand.* Consequently, Dewey argues for an academic environment that welcomes experimentation, free and open interaction, and a stimulating intellectual climate. He concludes that the practice of democratic values in schools would lead to thinking scientifically about the world, constructive work, experimental projects, hands-on experiences, and artistic studies in schools. Dewey prods the reader to reflect on such questions as, What are the most powerful human motives? What do these motives have to do with education and democracy? How are the answers to these questions connected to guiding students toward reflective thinking and ethical actions?

Obviously, the last essay in this section, "The Classroom Teacher" (MW15.180–89) could be placed in Part 1: The Classroom Teacher. We placed it here because it demonstrates Dewey's objections to a mechanical system of schooling that dominates teachers and students and because it illustrates his call for intervention in such schools by educational administrators. He points out that though teachers are often treated as clerks or cooks, who fill educational orders with prepackaged lessons or fixed recipes, in fact much more is required of them as intelligent professionals—or to continue his latter metaphor—chefs, who improvise and invent to make their teaching appeal to students. The essay delineates a list of problems of management, standardization, examination, classification, and assessment that need to be addressed by educators. He urges that teachers be allowed to do their work imaginatively and not be constrained by unnecessary administrative rules and regulations.

Dewey's reflections on school and district administration and leadership, of course, do not end with these essays. Indeed, his essays about the ideal school (Part 4) are overflowing with ideas that are designed to challenge an entire set of assumptions about how schools should be conceived, designed, operated, staffed, evaluated, and reconstructed.

As you read the essays that follow, you may wish to reflect on the questions below:

REFLECTION AND DISCUSSION QUESTIONS

1. Dewey believed that educational leaders are key figures in establishing the most appropriate climate for learning. What do you think are some of the most important characteristics of this learning climate?

2. Dewey saw the learning climate or environment too often stifled by fixed subordination, autocracy, rigid assessment, and what he terms "the problem of detail." How might educational leaders help overcome these obstacles and create a better learning climate?

3. How did Dewey characterize the relationship of teachers and administrators? In what ways can administrators and teachers be both leaders and colleagues in the development of schools?

4. What in Dewey's view are educational leadership's most notable shortcomings? What are the strengths?

5. Dewey believed successful learning must link the school and the community. Why did he think this link so important? How might educational leaders nurture the relationship between the school and the community?

6. Beyond clarifying his theory of educational leadership, what other theories do these essays help clarify? Why do you think Dewey discussed these theoretical dimensions in the context of discussing his theory of leadership?

Democracy and Educational Administration (1937)

MY EXPERIENCE IN EDUCATIONAL ADMINISTRATION is limited. I should not venture to address a body of those widely experienced and continuously engaged in school administration about the details of the management of schools. But the topic suggested to me has to do with the relation of school administration to democratic ideals and methods and to the general subject of the relation of education and democracy, to which I have given considerable thought over many years. The topic suggested concerns a special phase of this general subject. I shall begin, then, with some remarks on the broad theme of democratic aims and methods. Much of what I shall say on this subject is necessarily old and familiar. But it seems necessary to rehearse some old ideas in order to have a criterion for dealing with the special subject.

In the first place, democracy is much broader than a special political form, a method of conducting government, of making laws and carrying on governmental administration by means of popular suffrage and elected officers. It is that of course. But it is something broader and deeper than that.

The political and governmental phase of democracy is a means, the best means so far found, for realizing ends that lie in the wide domain of human relationships and the development of human personality. It is, as we often say, though perhaps without appreciating all that is involved in the saying, a way of life, social and individual. The key-note of democracy as a way of life may be expressed, it seems to me, as the necessity for the participation of every mature human being in formation of the values that regulate the living of men

First published in Department of Superintendence of the National Education Association, *Official Report* (Washington, D.C.: American Association of School Administrators, 1937), 48–55, from an address given on 22 February 1937, read at the general session of the annual meeting of the Department of Superintendence, National Education Association, New Orleans, February 1937.

together:—which is necessary from the standpoint of both the general social welfare and the full development of human beings as individuals.

Universal suffrage, recurring elections, responsibility of those who are in political power to the voters, and the other factors of democratic government are means that have been found expedient for realizing democracy as the truly human way of living. They are not a final end and a final value. They are to be judged on the basis of their contribution to end. It is a form of idolatry to erect means into the end which they serve. Democratic political forms are simply the best means that human wit has devised up to a special time in history. But they rest back upon the idea that no man or limited set of men is wise enough or good enough to rule others without their consent; the positive meaning of this statement is that all those who are affected by social institutions must have a share in producing and managing them. The two facts that each one is influenced in what he does and enjoys and in what he becomes by the institutions under which he lives, and that therefore he shall have, in a democracy, a voice in shaping them, are the passive and active sides of the same fact.

The development of political democracy came about through substitution of the method of mutual consultation and voluntary agreement for the method of subordination of the many to the few enforced from above. Social arrangements which involve fixed subordination are maintained by coercion. The coercion need not be physical. There have existed, for short periods, benevolent despotisms. But coercion of some sort there has been; perhaps economic, certainly psychological and moral. The very fact of exclusion from participation is a subtle form of suppression. It gives individuals no opportunity to reflect and decide upon what is good for them. Others who are supposed to be wiser and who in any case have more power decide the question for them and also decide the methods and means by which subjects may arrive at the enjoyment of what is good for them. This form of coercion and suppression is more subtle and more effective than is overt intimidation and restraint. When it is habitual and embodied in social institutions, it seems the normal and natural state of affairs. The mass usually become unaware that they have a claim to a development of their own powers. Their experience is so restricted that they are not conscious of restriction. It is part of the democratic conception that they as individuals are not the only sufferers, but that the whole social body is deprived of the potential resources that should be at its service. The individuals of the submerged mass may not be very wise. But there is one thing they are wiser about than anybody else can be, and that is where the shoe pinches, the troubles they suffer from.

The foundation of democracy is faith in the capacities of human nature; faith in human intelligence, and in the power of pooled and cooperative experience. It is not belief that these things are complete but that if given a show they will grow and be able to generate progressively the knowledge and wisdom needed to guide collective action. Every autocratic and authoritarian scheme of social action rests on a belief that the needed intelligence is confined to a superior few who because of inherent natural gifts are endowed with the ability and the right to control the conduct of others; laying down principles and rules and directing the ways in which they are carried out. It would be foolish to deny that much can be said for this point of view. It is that which controlled human relations in social groups for much the greater part of human history. The democratic faith has emerged very, very recently in the history of mankind. Even where democracies now exist, men's minds and feelings are still permeated with ideas about leadership imposed from above, ideas that developed in the long early history of mankind. After democratic political institutions were nominally established, beliefs and ways of looking at life and of acting that originated when men and women were externally controlled and subjected to arbitrary power, persisted in the family, the church, business and the school, and experience shows that as long as they persist there, political democracy is not secure. Belief in equality is an element of the democratic credo. It is not, however, belief in equality of natural endowments. Those who proclaimed the idea of equality did not suppose they were enunciating a psychological doctrine, but a legal and political one. All individuals are entitled to equality of treatment by law and in its administration. Each one is affected equally in quality if not in quantity by the institutions under which he lives and has an equal right to express his judgment, although the weight of his judgment may not be equal in amount when it enters into the pooled result to that of others. In short, each one is equally an individual and entitled to equal opportunity of development of his own capacities, be they large or small in range. Moreover, each has needs of his own, as significant to him as those of others are to them. The very fact of natural and psychological inequality is all the more reason for establishment by law of equality of opportunity, since otherwise the former becomes a means of oppression of the less gifted.

While what we call intelligence be distributed in unequal amounts, it is the democratic faith that it is sufficiently general so that each individual has something to contribute whose value can be assessed only as it enters into the final pooled intelligence constituted by the contributions of all. Every authoritarian scheme, on the contrary assumes that its value may be assessed by some prior principle, if not of family and birth or race and color or possession of material wealth, then by the position and rank a person occupies in the existing social scheme. The democratic faith in equality is the faith that each individual shall have the chance and opportunity to contribute whatever he is capable of contributing, and that the value of his contribution be decided by its place and function in the organized total of similar contributions:—not on the basis of prior status of any kind whatever.

I have emphasized in what precedes the importance of the effective release of intelligence in connection with personal experience in the democratic way of living. I have done so purposely because democracy is so often and so naturally associated in our minds with freedom of action, forgetting the importance of freed intelligence which is necessary to direct and to warrant freedom of action. Unless freedom of individual action has intelligence and informed conviction back of it, its manifestation is almost sure to result in confusion and disorder. The democratic idea of freedom is not the right of each individual to do as he pleases, even if it be qualified by adding "provided he does not interfere with the same freedom on the part of others." While the idea is not always, not often enough, expressed in words, the basic freedom is that of freedom of mind and of whatever degree of freedom of action and experience is necessary to produce freedom of intelligence. The modes of freedom guaranteed in the Bill of Rights are all of this nature: Freedom of belief and conscience, of expression of opinion, of assembly for discussion and conference, of the press as an organ of communication. They are guaranteed because without them individuals are not free to develop and society is deprived of what they might contribute.

What, it may be asked, have these things to do with school administration? There is some kind of government, of control, wherever affairs that concern a number of persons who act together are engaged in. It is a superficial view that holds government is located in Washington and Albany. There is government in the family, in business, in the church, in every social group. There are regulations, due to custom if not to enactment, that settle how individuals in a group act in connection with one another.

It is a disputed question of theory and practice just how far a democratic political government should go in control of the conditions of action within special groups. At the present time, for example, there are those who think the federal and state governments leave too much freedom of independent action to industrial and financial groups and there are others who think the Government is going altogether too far at the present time. I do not need to discuss this phase of the problem much less to try to settle it. But it must be pointed out that if the methods of regulation and administration in vogue in the conduct of secondary social groups are non-democratic, whether directly or indirectly or both, there is bound to be an unfavorable reaction back into the habits of feeling, thought and action of citizenship in the broadest sense of that word. The way in which any organized social interest is controlled necessarily plays an important part in forming the dispositions and tastes, the attitudes, interests, purposes and desires, of those engaged in carrying on the activities of the group. For illustration, I do not need to do more than point to the moral, emotional and intellectual effect upon both employers and laborers of the existing industrial system. Just what the effects specifically are is a matter about which we know very little. But I suppose that every one who reflects upon the subject admits that it is impossible that the ways in which activities are carried on for the greater part of the waking hours of the day; and the way in which the shares of individuals are involved in the management of affairs in such a matter as gaining a livelihood and attaining material and social security, can only be a highly important factor in shaping personal dispositions; in short, forming character and intelligence.

In the broad and final sense all institutions are educational in the sense that they operate to form the attitudes, dispositions, abilities and disabilities that constitute a concrete personality. The principle applies with special force to the school. For it is the main business of the family and the school to influence directly the formation and growth of attitudes and dispositions, emotional, intellectual and moral. Whether this educative process is carried on in a pre-dominantly democratic or non-democratic way becomes therefore a question of transcendent importance not only for education itself but for its final effect upon all the interests and activities of a society that is committed to the democratic way of life. Hence, if the general tenor of what I have said about the democratic ideal and method is anywhere near the truth, it must be said that the democratic principle requires that every teacher should have some regular and organic way in which he can, directly or through representatives democratically chosen, participate in the formation of the controlling aims, methods and materials of the school of which he is a part. Something over thirty years ago I wrote: "If there is a single public-school system in the United States where there is offi-cial and constitutional provision made for submitting questions of methods of discipline and teaching, and the questions of the curriculum, text-books, etc., to the discussion and decision of those actually engaged in the work of teach-ing, that fact has escaped my notice." I could not make that statement today. There has been in some places a great advance in the democratic direction. As I noted in my earlier article there were always in actual fact school systems where the practice was much better than the theory of external control from above: for even if there were no authorized regular way in which the intelligence and experience of the teaching corps was consulted and utilized, administrative officers accomplished that end in informal ways. We may hope this extension of democratic methods has not only endured but has expanded. Nevertheless, the issue of authoritarian versus democratic methods in administration remains with us and demands serious recognition.

It is my impression that even up to the present democratic methods of dealing with pupils have made more progress than have similar methods of dealing with members of the teaching staff of the classroom. At all events, there has been an organized and vital movement in the first matter while that in the second is still in its early stage. All schools that pride themselves upon being up-to-date utilize methods of instruction that draw upon and utilize the life-experience of students and strive to individualize treatment of pupils. Whatever reasons hold for adopting this course with respect to the young certainly more strongly hold for teachers, since the latter are more mature and have more experience. Hence the question is in place: What are the ways by which can be secured more organic participation of teachers in the formation of the educational policies of the school?

Since, as I have already said, it is the problem I wish to present, rather than to lay down the express ways in which it is to be solved, I might stop at this point. But there are certain corollaries which clarify the meaning of the issue. Absence of participation tends to produce lack of interest and concern on the part of those shut out. The result is a corresponding lack of effective responsibility. Automatically and unconsciously, if not consciously, the feeling develops, "this is none of our affair; it is the business of those at the top; let that particular set of Georges do what needs to be done." The countries in which autocratic government prevails are just those in which there is least public spirit and the greatest indifference to matters of general as distinct from personal concern. Can we expect a different kind of psychology to actuate teachers? Where there is little power, there is correspondingly little sense of positive responsibility:—It is enough to do what one is told to do sufficiently well to escape flagrant unfavorable notice. About larger matters a spirit of passivity is engendered. In some cases, indifference passes into evasion of duties when not directly under the eye of a supervisor; in other cases, a carping, rebellious spirit is engendered. A sort of game is instituted between teacher and supervisor like that which went on in the old-fashioned schools between teacher and pupil. Other teachers pass on, perhaps unconsciously, what they feel to be arbitrary treatment received by them to their pupils.

The argument that teachers are not prepared to assume the responsibility of participation deserves attention, with its accompanying belief that natural selection has operated to put those best prepared to carry the load in the positions of authority. Whatever the truth in this contention, it still is also true that incapacity to assume the responsibilities involved in having a voice in shaping policies is bred and increased by conditions in which that responsibility is denied. I suppose there has never been an autocrat, big or little, who did not justify his conduct on the ground of the unfitness of his subjects to take part in government. I would not compare administrators to political autocrats. On the whole, what exists in the schools is more a matter of habit and custom than it is of any deliberate autocracy. But, as was said earlier, habitual exclusion has the effect of reducing a sense of responsibility for what is done and its consequences. What the argument for democracy implies is that the best way to produce initiative and constructive power is to exercise it. Power, as well as interest, comes by use and practice. Moreover, the argument from incapacity proves too much. If it is so great as to be a permanent bar, then teachers can not be expected to have the intelligence and skill that are necessary to execute the directions given them. The delicate and difficult task of developing character and good judgment in the young needs every stimulus and inspiration possible. It is impossible that the work should not be better done when teachers have that understanding of what they are doing that comes from having shared in forming its guiding ideas.

Classroom teachers are those who are in continuous direct contact with those taught. The position of administrators is at best indirect by comparison. If there is any work in the world that requires the conservation of what is good in experience so that it may become an integral part of further experience, it is that of teaching. I often wonder how much waste there is in the traditional system. There is some loss even at the best of the potential capital acquired by successful teachers. It does not get freely transmitted to other teachers who might profit by it. Is not the waste very considerably increased when teachers are not called upon to communicate their successful methods and results in a form in which it could have organic effect upon general school policies? Add to this waste that results when teachers are called upon to give effect in the classroom to courses of study they do not understand the reasons for, and the total loss mounts up so that it is a fair estimate that the absence of democratic methods is the greatest single cause of educational waste.

The present subject is one of peculiar importance at the present time. The fundamental beliefs and practices of democracy are now challenged as they never have been before. In some nations they are more than challenged. They are ruthlessly and systematically destroyed. Everywhere there are waves of criticism and doubt as to whether democracy can meet pressing problems of order and security. The causes for the destruction of political democracy in countries where it was nominally established are complex. But of one thing I think we may be sure. Wherever it has fallen it was too exclusively political in nature. It had not become part of the bone and blood of the people in daily conduct of its life. Democratic forms were limited to Parliament, elections and combats between parties. What is happening proves conclusively, I think, that unless democratic habits of thought and action are part of the fiber of a people, political democracy is insecure. It can not stand in isolation. It must be buttressed by the presence of democratic methods in all social relationships. The relations that exist in educational institutions are second only in importance in this respect to those which exist in industry and business, perhaps not even to them.

I recur then to the idea that the particular question discussed is one phase of a wide and deep problem. I can think of nothing so important in this country at present as a rethinking of the whole problem of democracy and its implications.

Neither the rethinking nor the action it should produce can be brought into being in a day or year. The democratic idea itself demands that the thinking and activity proceed cooperatively. My utmost hope will be fulfilled if anything I have said plays any part, however small, in promoting cooperative inquiry and experimentation in this field of democratic administration of our schools.

Toward Administrative Statesmanship (1935)

THE CURRENT MEETING OF THE Department of Superintendence of the N.E.A. makes appropriate a consideration of the problems of public school administration in this country and of the ways of meeting them. It is not necessary to insist upon the fact that the problems are complex and difficult. They present at least three phases, each of which in turn is composed of obscure and conflicting factors.

There is, first, what may be called the intellectual-professional problem. Superintendents, principals, supervisors, etc., are engaged in the direction of an *educational* enterprise. It may seem superfluous to italicize the word "educational." But I do so in order to suggest what is meant by the intellectual phase of the responsibility and function of the administrator. He—or she—not only participates in the development of minds and character, but participates in a way that imposes special intellectual responsibilities. Indeed, the sense of responsibility for distinctively intellectual leadership may take a form that defeats its own purpose. It may take the form of laying out, in a good deal of detail, the whole scheme of the curriculum and promulgating methods to be followed. Even when the idea is not carried to this extent, there are too few cases in which the teaching corps takes an active and cooperative share in developing the plan of education.

In the second place, administrators are particularly charged with problems arising from personal relations. Any one who has faced the task of helping to maintain harmonious and effective personal relations in family life, can imagine the difficulties that emerge in connection with a large teaching staff made up of persons of different temperaments, who have had different training, and are possessed of different outlooks on life. But the problems that arise in connection

First published as "John Dewey's Page," *Social Frontier* 1 (March 1935): 9–10.

with these personal relationships are only a part of those which an administrator has to face. He has to maintain cooperative relations with members of a school board; to deal with taxpayers and politicians; to meet parents of varied views and ideals. Moreover, the problems of personal adjustment that offer themselves are often conflicting, because of the opposed demands of different groups. A superintendent is an intermediary between the teaching staff and the members of the public. He is compelled to face two ways, and is fortunate if he can escape the tendency towards a divided personality. At least, there are some administrators who are "diplomatic" and even subservient in one relation and arbitrary and authoritative in the other.

In the third place, the administrator by the nature of his calling has a large amount of detail and routine to which he must attend. There is always the danger that he will become so immersed in this phase of his work, that the other two phases of his activity are submerged. Especially in large systems is the danger acute. Large systems work almost automatically toward isolation of the administrator. Business and other details are so pressing that connection with the intellectual and moral problems of education is had only at arms' length. Impersonal matters take the place of personal relations, and are always mechanical. The tendency in this direction is increased because the powerful influence of business standards and methods in the community affects the members of an educational system, and then teachers are regarded after the model of employees in a factory.

The reason I have mentioned these rather obvious things is because they indicate, to my mind, that an administrator can deal effectively with these various problems only as he is able to unify them all in some comprehensive idea and plan. If he parcels them out and tries to deal with them separately he is lost. Especially is it important that his conception of the directly educational phase of his work be unified with his conception of the social relations of administration, both inside and outside the school. The different aspects of the administrator's work tend in fact to cut across each other in such ways as to nullify their proper effect. The only way for the administrator to avoid this dispersion is to have a definite idea of the place and function of the school in the ongoing processes of society, local and national. Only from a definite point of view, firmly and courageously adhered to in practice, can the needed integration be attained.

The first step in this integration is a clear and intelligent decision upon a basic issue. Is it the social function of the school to perpetuate existing conditions or to take part in their transformation? One decision will make the administrator a time server. He will make it his business to conform to the pressures exercised by school boards, by politicians allied with heavy taxpayers, and by parents. If he decides for the other alternative, many of his tasks will be harder, but in that way alone can he serve the cause of education. For this cause is one of development, focussing indeed in the growth of students, but to be conceived even in this connection as a part of the larger development of society.

In the second place, in the degree to which the administrator achieves the integration of the educational phase of his work with the human and social relations into which he necessarily enters, he will treat the school itself as a cooperative community. His leadership will be that of intellectual stimulation and direction, through give-and-take with others, not that of an aloof official imposing, authoritatively, educational ends and methods. He will be on the lookout for ways to give others intellectual and moral responsibilities, not just for ways of setting their tasks for them.

In the third place, the administrator will conceive adult education to be a necessary part of his job, not in the sense of providing adult classes and lectures—helpful as these may be—but in the sense that only as the public is brought to understand the needs and possibilities of the creative education of the young, can such education be vitally effective. He will realize that public education is essentially education of the public: directly, through teachers and students in the school; indirectly, through communicating to others his own ideals and standards, inspiring others with the enthusiasm of himself and his staff for the function of intelligence and character in the transformation of society.

General Principles of Educational Articulation (1929)

THERE ARE TWO WAYS OF approaching the problem of elimination of waste in the educative processes of the schools. One is the administrative. This takes the existing system as a going concern, and inquires into the breaks and overlappings that make for maladjustment and inefficient expenditure of time and energy on the part of both pupil and teacher—useless and therefore harmful mental motions, harmful and not merely useless because they set up bad habits. The other may be called personal, psychological or moral. By these adjectives is meant that the method starts from the side of personal growth of individual needs and capacities, and asks what school organization is best calculated to secure continuity and efficiency of development. It sets out from the side of pupils and asks how the successive stages of the school system should be arranged so that there shall be a minimum of blocks, arrests, sudden switches and gaps, futile repetitions and duplications, as the children and youth pass from one stage to another, from kindergarten to elementary, from this to high school, and from the latter to college.

This statement of two modes of approach does not imply that there is a necessary opposition between the two. They should be complementary. What is common to both is that each looks at the educational system as a whole and views each part with respect to what it does in making education really a whole, and not merely a juxtaposition of mechanically separated parts. Each avenue of approach is equally concerned to eliminate isolations and render the function of each part effective with respect to the others. There is no more necessary opposition between the two than there is when engineers in tunneling a mountain

First published in *School and Society* 29 (30 March 1929): 399–406, and in Department of Superintendence of the National Education Association, *Official Report* (Washington, D.C.: Department of Superintendence, 1929), 51–60, from an address given on 26 February 1929, at the annual meeting of the Department of Superintendence, National Education Association, Cleveland, Ohio, 24–28 February 1929.

bore from opposite ends. Before they start work, the tunnel must be considered as a single thing and the work done from either end must be thought out and undertaken with reference to examination of the entire project. But a preliminary intellectual survey of the whole is necessary to make the two modes of approach meet at a centre.

When the consideration of the problem is undertaken from either side without regard to the considerations which necessarily exist at the other side, there are dangers and evils that can not be avoided. Thus an approach from the exclusively personal side will overlook certain administrative necessities that seem to be inherent in the situation. An important consideration here is pointed out in the general introductory report of the commission. The area of the region drawn upon and the different numbers of children and youth who go to school in the elementary and higher grades must be considered. Younger children as a rule must be in buildings nearer their own homes, and because of their greater number there must be a certain amount of physical segregation from older pupils. Moreover, for the older pupils there must be a greater variety of courses, differentiation of teachers and amount of equipment. These facts demand a large number of pupils in the high school and this in turn demands that they be drawn from a wide area. Hence consideration from the personal development side must take into account administrative necessities.

Consideration of the latter must, however, be checked at every point by taking into account the conditions that make for effective mental and moral growth of individuals as individuals. Undue attention to the administrative side tends toward "rationalization" of the divisions that happen at a given time to be institutionalized. Reasons are found which justify their continued existence as more or less independent units. Then the problem of articulation becomes an external one, that of smoothing transitions from one to another and getting rid of the more obvious sources of friction. This is a gain as far as it goes, but it does not go far enough to touch the basic matter of securing adequate and complete personal growth. In consequence of this external approach, there will be a tendency to assume that mental and moral growth is marked by "epochs" which correspond, at least roughly, to the isolated units of the school system.

The fact that interests and capacities change with age is undeniable; that the boy and girl of sixteen differ markedly from those of twelve, and those of the latter age from those of eight and the latter, in turn, from those of five and six is too evident to escape notice. But the underlying problem is whether the changes occur gradually and almost insensibly or by sharply marked off leaps which correspond to the conventional institutional school divisions. This is a question which must be investigated and the answer found by independent study of the facts of development in individuals. The need of this independent inquiry as a check and test is the more acute because the divisions that exist among school units react upon personal development. It is in consequence easy to assume that changes in personal growth are inherent, when in fact they may be the relatively artificial products of the existing school divisions and in so far abnormal and undesirable.

For this reason the study of the best methods of articulation should be checked by a comparative study of those schools in which division into units is minimized; that is, "unified schools" in which children of different ages, from primary to high school, are found together and wherein there is no administrative break between junior and senior years in the high schools. Only by such a comparative study can the elements, if any, that are artificial and conventional in the schools where units are emphasized be detected. This statement does not contradict what was said earlier about the problems of area of distribution and the need of increased variety of courses and equipment in higher grades. For, in the first place, cities vary greatly in population and there may be median range of size to which the unified school is well adapted. In the second place, the results of comparative inquiry would throw light upon the methods of organization to be adopted in the schools of towns of such a large size that the unified system can not be literally adopted. For there is a question of limits, and educators can work in either of two directions, toward opposite poles—either to that of independent units, or to the maximum possible of relative unification of the assembling of pupils—without carrying either principle to its logical extreme. This consideration seems to me to be fundamental in the whole problem of articulation. Mere convenience of administration should not be permitted to override it.

It is recognized that adequate treatment of the fundamental problem here— the mutually complementary character of the administrative and the moral psychological development of individuals—must wait upon command of greater knowledge of the actual process of normal growth than anybody now possesses. Nevertheless, reference to the latter is important, for it indicates, in the first place, the necessity of continued study of personal growth as an inherent factor in the problem of articulation from the administrative side. And in the second place, it serves a warning. It cautions us against a too ready assumption that the present institutional division into separate units has necessary inherent value on account of corresponding "epochs" of personal development. It warns us against attaching too great value, decisive value, to matters of administrative habit and inertia.

A complete examination of the question of articulation can be attained only when the experiences of classroom teachers in immediate contact with pupils are procured and utilized, as well as the experiences of administrators. This statement does not signify that principals and superintendents in their reports do not take advantage of the experiences gained in actual classroom work. It is, however, a reminder that specialized experience always creates a one-sided emphasis, in habits of thought as well as of outward action, and always needs to be checked. There is much evidence in the various reports of the extent to which conference and exchange of reports and information already obtain as necessary methods of avoiding unduly sharp breaks in subject-matter, methods, and harmful repetitions. What I am pleading for is a more direct obtaining of data on the whole subject of continuity of personal development from classroom teachers, and a direct inclusion of such reports in the gathering and interpretation of material along with those of superintendents and supervisors and principals. The findings of experimental and progressive schools must also be included, not as models, but as providing data regarding processes of personal development under different conditions.

Conceding that we have not adequate knowledge of the course of mental development in individuals, I propose now to consider the bearing of what is available in this respect upon the general problem of articulation. I begin with a statement which is so general that it can hardly arouse dissent. The ideal is that the achievements at any one period of growth supply the tools, the agencies and instrumentalities, of further growth. The statement is not one that refers simply to the transition from one unit to another. It is of constant application. That is, whatever the pupils gain at any period, whether in skill or knowledge, should be promptly funded into something actively employed in gaining new skill and knowledge. A new level of intellectual achievement should mark off each successive month and week of school life, and not be thought of as occurring only in the transition from one unit to another. The bearing of this principle upon the specific problems of articulation which the various reports of the commission bring out may be postponed until another basic principle has been stated.

The idea of ripening, maturing, is evidently fundamental in the question of individual growth. Now what needs to be especially borne in mind with reference to maturing is that it is plural, that is, various powers and interests which coexist at the same time mature at very different rates. Maturing is a continuous process; the mature fruit may appear, as with fruits on a tree, only at some later stage, even if we assume, which it is probably wrong to do, that there is ever any such completely matured fruit in the case of a human being as in a plant. But the normal maturing as a process goes on all the time; if it does not there is something the matter with conditions. Arrest of growth, incapacity to cope with subject-matter, and inability to respond to methods employed at a later period are all signs of something wrong. They need to be studied as symptoms and diagnosed with a view to constructive remedies.

Since maturing is a continuous process and also a plural one, it is not a uniform four-abreast thing. One has only to observe a baby to note how one ability ripens before another, the ability to fixate objects with the eye, to grasp, to sit up, to creep, to walk, to talk; and how each operation as it matures is utilized as a factor in bringing about some maturing of another ability and adaptation. No parent ever makes the mistake of overlooking this plural nature of maturing. When we come to schooling, however, I wonder if there is not too much of a tendency to assume an equal, uniform, four-abreast maturing, and if that does not underlie the conception of "epochs" of growth which correspond to various units of the school system. If the assumption is not made in a positive form, it is made in a negative way, that is, by overlooking the specific needs and capacities that are ripening, or that may ripen, during each year and month of school life. It is this neglect which is responsible for the idea that each stage is merely preparation for some later stage, particularly that the aim of the early years of the elementary school is chiefly the purpose of gaining social tools to be independently employed and enjoyed later on.

I am always surprised and disturbed when I find persons who insist that the high school must not be dominated by the idea of college preparation ready to assume as a matter of course that the first two or three primary years must have as their main purpose the securing of "social tools" for later use, instead of being devoted to gaining those experiences which are appropriate to the powers that are ripening at the time. I must express my profound dissent from the position taken in the general introduction that sets up a dualism between the actual experience of children in the early years and the requirements imposed and dictated by the needs of later school years.

At this point, the two principles laid down cease to be innocuous generalities. The way to get possession and command of a tool for later use is by having the experiences proper to the immediate time—experiences which awaken new needs and opportunities and which, just because they are achievements, form the natural agencies or tools for later activities. Any theory which sets out by denying that this is possible misstates the problem of articulation, and its "solution" is bound to be defective. Unless powers as they ripen are put to immediate use in acquiring new knowledge and skill, tools are not shaped for later use. The problem, from the side of earlier years, is that of discovering those particular needs, interests and capacities which are ripening then and there, not attempting a premature introduction and forcing of others; and then of finding that use and application of them which passes insensibly into the ripening of other more complex tendencies. From the side of later years, it is the same problem, but with the added factor of adjusting subject-matter and methods so that the powers already relatively ripened shall be used in developing the new powers that are showing themselves. Only in this way can the maximum of continuous growth be secured and an internal rather than mechanical articulation be secured. The point and force of the two principles laid down is found in their concrete application. I propose, accordingly, to consider some phases of isolation and waste, of non-articulation, in their light.

In the first place, they suggest that reasonable integration within the school can not be secured by limiting the problem to what goes on in the school. The fundamental problem of articulation takes us outside the school to articulation of its activities with the out-of-school experience of the pupils. It is for this reason, of course, that the curriculum is so fundamental; to articulate successive phases of subject-matter with one another there must be an articulation of the curriculum with the broadening range of experiences had at home, in the neighborhood and community. This principle applies at the beginning and all the way through. I remember hearing an intelligent parent complain that kindergarten teachers seemed to assume that children came to them blanks, and treated them as if everything had to begin afresh, thereby boring children with things they could already do and were familiar with, and failing to utilize the capital they had already acquired.

This complaint was made over thirty years ago; doubtless cause for it no longer exists. But it is typical of what is meant by the present point. Except for highly specialized matters, the ripening of powers does not go on exclusively nor mainly in school. This fact gives great significance to matters contained in the various reports which at first sight are remote from the question of school articulation; matters of health, nutrition, regularity of attendance, home life, reading and occupations out of school, economic status of parents and children, as well as the general changing demands of a rapidly changing civilization. But it extends to the whole matter of utilizing in school the experiences gained out of school.

More specific points are involved in the application of the two principles. One of these is the principle of alternate concentration and remission of work in special lines. While great improvements have taken place, there is still an undue tendency to a uniform four-abreast treatment of the subjects that make up the school program. Certain studies tend to appear in every month and in every year of a school program. There is need for flexible experimentation in periods of intensive concentration upon such things as reading and number work in the elementary grades, followed by periods of relaxation in which achievements gained are capitalized in concentration upon other studies. The same principle applies to history, geography, nature study and science. Each might be made for a time the relative centre with subordination of other factors. The effect would be to disclose better than does the uniform method special aptitudes and weaknesses, and would, I think, greatly minimize the breaks that now come with change of pupils to a new year and new unit.

Other difficulties in the present situation arise, I believe, from the isolation that comes from the confining of teachers to single years. The pupils are the only ones who come into direct contact with the whole process. Artificial breaks, sudden introduction of new demands and new methods of discipline, teaching of new kinds of subjects, duplications and need of review of subjects already supposedly mastered are the result. They are in large measure due, I think, to the isolation of the teacher resulting from too exclusive confinement to a single year. Articulation is secured only as at each stage of the school system, pupils' activities are directed in reference to a continuing wholeness of growth. One year is too short a span in which to survey the process of growth. Much has been done, as appears from the reports in exchange of records and data, and in joint committee to form the curriculums. Unified supervision helps. But these things do not cover the whole situation. There are administrative difficulties attending transfers of teachers from one grade to another, or in having a teacher give instruction during the same year in more than one grade. But I do not believe that, without a greater use of these methods, teachers can get that real appreciation of continuity of school movement which will enable them to secure articulation from within.

One aspect of this matter involves the question of having younger children in contact with more than one teacher. I recognize the objections that are so clearly pointed out in the section of chapter II of the report dealing with departmentalization in the elementary grades. But these objections have to be offset not only against the point already made regarding the need of intimate acquaintance on the part of the teacher with children at different stages of development, but against the evils of the conditioning of a child to the habits and methods of a single person, and against the fact, frequently noted, of the friction that arises when the pupils enter a unit in which departmental teaching does exist. It does not follow, because departmental teaching can easily be overdone in the early grades, that children may not profitably get used to more than one teacher even in the first grade. It is a concrete question of proportioning. We need also to bear in mind that the one-room, one-teacher plan tends to perpetuate the régimes of either formalism or undirected spontaneity in the early years. No one teacher can know enough to answer all the questions children ask that need to be followed up if that growth is to be secured which gives a firm basis for future work—although one teacher is enough to allow children to do what they please or to teach the traditional formal subjects. Nor does it follow that in high schools teaching should be rigidly departmentalized. We need a little more "give" at both ends. Still less does it follow that departmentalized teaching in high schools should be confined to a teacher having many sections of algebra or geometry or physiography in only one year of the school. Genuine correlation or integration and genuine continuity of articulation may depend upon a teacher having more than one topic and in teaching a subject through more than one year. As Ella Flagg Young used to remind teachers many years ago, what often passes for departmentalization is in reality only a subdivision of labor such as obtains in a factory where each worker is confined to making a part of a shoe, which part is then passed on to the next worker.

A point frequently mentioned in the reports is connected with the last two. Attention is called to the difficulties arising from the fact that teachers in training often specialize on some one phase or unit, to the neglect of knowledge of the system as a whole. It would seem to follow that all teachers in training should have at least one thorough course to familiarize them with the system in its entirety, with special reference to the place, in the whole, of that part of the system for which they are specially preparing. If this were a regular procedure, it is possible that the reluctance of teachers to change from one grade or one unit to another might give way to desire for a broader experience. In connection with the training of teachers there are so many problems relevant to the issue of articulation that it is possible to select only one.

Graduate schools of universities are in a large measure training schools for teachers in colleges and in an increasing degree in high schools. Through instruction given to those in colleges who go out to teach in high schools there is, in any case, a reaction into high-school teaching. These conditions account in large measure for the gaps and maladjustments frequently referred to in articulation of senior high schools with the junior, and in general of high schools with upper elementary grades. I allude to the distinction often drawn between greater attention to development of pupils on one side and to subject-matter as such on the other. No survey of the causes of bad articulation is complete that does not take into account the influence, direct and indirect, of the training of future teachers in graduate schools of universities. It is a phase of the old question of the isolation of normal schools from colleges with the greater emphasis of one upon method and of the other upon subject-matter. Although the problem is not as acute as it used to be, since there has been rapprochement from both sides, it is still an important factor.

Time permits only of these few selected illustrations. I conclude by recurring to the original statement of the problem: that of coordinating the administrative approach with the psychological-moral approach through personal development. It makes a great difference how we take up the problem of articulation. If we accept too readily any existing distribution of units as even relatively fixed, I am skeptical of any solutions being found which do more than eliminate some of the more striking cases of external friction. It is a natural trait of the human mind to "rationalize" what exists—that is, to find adventitious reasons that justify what is found. We should, it seems to me, view the problem of articulation as one of differentiation.

The metaphor of organic growth is helpful if not pressed too literally. The problem of coordinated physiological growth is not one of coordinating bones, muscles, lungs, and stomach together; not until mal-coordinations have been established does the latter problem arise. There is a gradual differentiation of different organs and functions, each cooperating with the others. The problem of educational guidance may be conceived as that of bringing about differentiation in a consecutive way. The meaning of this general statement may be briefly illustrated. For this purpose I select once more a portion of the introduction of the commission which in its implications appears to diverge from the principle. I refer to the contrast which is set forth between the earlier and later years in reference to docility of a passive type in the former and personal independence and individualistic initiation in the latter, and the conclusions about legitimate separation of units drawn from the alleged contrast. The statement seems to overlook several facts, such as that well known to parents, the fact called "contrary suggestion" in very early years: the fact that development in the school years comes through activities, and also the adoption of the method of socialized activities in the kindergarten.

Receptivity and assertive activity are *constant* functions. What differs with different stages of growth is *range* of exercise and *field* of exercise. Because a child of six or seven can not assume the same active responsibilities that he can when he is eight or nine does not mean that some field for its exercise is not available at the earlier age nor that it is not an indispensable factor in normal development. To generalize wholesale from the regions in which the capacity does not exist, and infer from them that the willingness of children to accept what is put over on them "dictates" certain subject-matters at that period is to fail to prepare pupils for greater independence in other fields later, and thus puts a premium upon excessive "individualism" later. The problem is one of constant differentiation of powers of independent action through prior utilization of those which already exist. A normal differentiation will create in pupils a willingness to recognize later their need of guidance and receptivity in respect to that in which they are not developed to the point of independence, and thus reduce an abrupt and undesirable "individualism."

The example is taken from a limited field, but it applies throughout. At each stage the pupil, whether in elementary grades, junior high school or college, has a certain region of experience in which he is relatively at home and has certain tendencies which are relatively mature. Attention to these things as the agencies to be connected with in securing new powers of independent and responsible action in wider fields of experience gives the key to a continuous process of differentiation which will place the problem of articulation in its proper light.

I can not conclude this exposition, at once too fragmentary and too general, without acknowledging my great indebtedness to the studies embodied in the report of the commission. More important, however, than any personal indebtedness is the evidence afforded that the educators of the country are alive to their responsibility. In our American system of diffused control, in the absence of any central directive body, our sole guarantee of constant improvement is the method of cooperative voluntary inquiry and mutual conference. The report of the commission is a notable contribution to the accomplishment of this task in a problem of fundamental importance in the advancement of education. We all owe them thanks for the alertness and thoroughness with which the task has been performed.

Democracy in Education (1903)

MODERN LIFE MEANS DEMOCRACY, DEMOCRACY means freeing intelligence for independent effectiveness—the emancipation of mind as an individual organ to do its own work. We naturally associate democracy, to be sure, with freedom of action, but freedom of action without freed capacity of thought behind it is only chaos. If external authority in action is given up, it must be because internal authority of truth, discovered and known to reason, is substituted.

How does the school stand with reference to this matter? Does the school as an accredited representative exhibit this trait of democracy as a spiritual force? Does it lead and direct the movement? Does it lag behind and work at cross-purpose? I find the fundamental need of the school today dependent upon its limited recognition of the principle of freedom of intelligence. This limitation appears to me to affect both of the elements of school life: teacher and pupil. As to both, the school has lagged behind the general contemporary social movement; and much that is unsatisfactory, much of conflict and of defect, comes from the discrepancy between the relatively undemocratic organization of the school, as it affects the mind of both teacher and pupil, and the growth and extension of the democratic principle in life beyond school doors.

The effort of the last two-thirds of a century has been successful in building up the machinery of a democracy of mind. It has provided the ways and means for housing and equipping intelligence. What remains is that the thought-activity of the individual, whether teacher or student, be permitted and encouraged to take working possession of this machinery: to substitute its rightful lordship for an inherited servility. In truth, our public-school system is but two-thirds of a century old. It dates, so far as such matters can be dated at all, from 1837, the

---

First published in *Elementary School Teacher* 4 (1903): 193–204.

year that Horace Mann became secretary of the state board of Massachusetts; and from 1843, when Henry Barnard began a similar work in Connecticut. At this time began that growing and finally successful warfare against all the influences, social and sectarian, which would prevent or mitigate the sway of public influence over private ecclesiastical and class interests. Between 1837 and 1850 grew up all the most characteristic features of the American public-school system: from this time date state normal schools, city training schools, county and state institutes, teachers' associations, teachers' journals, the institution of city superintendencies, supervisory officers, and the development of state universities as the crown of the public-school system of the commonwealth. From this time date the striving for better schoolhouses and grounds, improved text-books, adequate material equipment in maps, globes, scientific apparatus, etc. As an outcome of the forces thus set in motion, democracy has in principle, subject to relative local restrictions, developed an organized machinery of public education. But when we turn to the aim and method which this magnificent institution serves, we find that our democracy is not yet conscious of the ethical principle upon which it rests—the responsibility and freedom of mind in discovery and proof—and consequently we find confusion where there should be order, darkness where there should be light. The teacher has not the power of initiation and constructive endeavor which is necessary to the fulfilment of the function of teaching. The learner finds conditions antagonistic (or at least lacking) to the development of individual mental power and to adequate responsibility for its use.

1. *As to the teacher.*—If there is a single public-school system in the United States where there is official and constitutional provision made for submitting questions of methods of discipline and teaching, and the questions of the curriculum, text-books, etc., to the discussion and decision of those actually engaged in the work of teaching, that fact has escaped my notice. Indeed, the opposite situation is so common that it seems, as a rule, to be absolutely taken for granted as the normal and final condition of affairs. The number of persons to whom any other course has occurred as desirable, or even possible—to say nothing of necessary—is apparently very limited. But until the public-school system is organized in such a way that every teacher has some regular and representative way in which he or she can register judgment upon matters of educational importance, with the assurance that this judgment will somehow affect the school system, the assertion that the present system is not, from the internal standpoint, democratic seems to be justified. Either we come here upon some fixed and inherent limitation of the democratic principle, or else we find in this fact an obvious discrepancy between the conduct of the school and the conduct of social life—a discrepancy so great as to demand immediate and persistent effort at reform.

The more enlightened portions of the public have, indeed, become aware of one aspect of this discrepancy. Many reformers are contending against the conditions which place the direction of school affairs, including the selection of text-books, etc., in the hands of a body of men who are outside the school system itself, who have not necessarily any expert knowledge of education and who are moved by non-educational motives. Unfortunately, those who have noted this undemocratic condition of affairs, and who have striven to change it, have, as a rule, conceived of but one remedy, namely, the transfer of authority to the school superintendent. In their zeal to place the centre of gravity inside the school system, in their zeal to decrease the prerogatives of a non-expert school board, and to lessen the opportunities for corruption and private pull which go with that, they have tried to remedy one of the evils of democracy by adopting the principle of autocracy. For no matter how wise, expert, or benevolent the head of the school system, the one-man principle is autocracy.

The logic of the argument goes farther, very much farther, than the reformer of this type sees. The logic which commits him to the idea that the management of the school system must be in the hands of an expert commits him also to the idea that every member of the school system, from the first-grade teacher to the principal of the high school, must have some share in the exercise of educational power. The remedy is not to have one expert dictating educational methods and subject-matter to a body of passive, recipient teachers, but the adoption of intellectual initiative, discussion, and decision throughout the entire school corps. The remedy of the partial evils of democracy, the implication of the school system in municipal politics, is in appeal to a more thoroughgoing democracy.

The dictation, in theory at least, of the subject-matter to be taught, to the teacher who is to engage in the actual work of instruction, and frequently, under the name of close supervision, the attempt to determine the methods which are to be used in teaching, mean nothing more or less than the deliberate restriction of intelligence, the imprisoning of the spirit. Every well-graded system of schools in this country rejoices in a course of study. It is no uncommon thing to find methods of teaching such subjects as reading, writing, spelling, and arithmetic officially laid down; outline topics in history and geography are provided ready-made for the teacher; gems of literature are fitted to the successive ages of boys and girls. Even the domain of art, songs and methods of singing, subject-matter and technique of drawing and painting, come within the region on which an outside authority lays its sacrilegious hands.

I have stated the theory, which is also true of the practice to a certain extent and in certain places. We may thank our heavens, however, that the practice is rarely as bad as the theory would require. Superintendents and principals often encourage individuality and thoughtfulness in the invention and adoption of methods of teaching; and they wink at departures from the printed manual of study. It remains true, however, that this great advance is personal and informal. It depends upon the wisdom and tact of the individual supervisory official; he may withdraw his concession at any moment; or it may be ruthlessly thrown aside by his successor who has formed a high ideal of "system."

I know it will be said that this state of things, while an evil, is a necessary one; that without it confusion and chaos would reign; that such regulations are the inevitable accompaniments of any graded system. It is said that the average teacher is incompetent to take any part in laying out the course of study or in initiating methods of instruction or discipline. Is not this the type of argument which has been used from time immemorial, and in every department of life, against the advance of democracy? What does democracy mean save that the individual is to have a share in determining the conditions and the aims of his own work; and that, upon the whole, through the free and mutual harmonizing of different individuals, the work of the world is better done than when planned, arranged, and directed by a few, no matter how wise or of how good intent that few? How can we justify our belief in the democratic principle elsewhere, and then go back entirely upon it when we come to education?

Moreover, the argument proves too much. The more it is asserted that the existing corps of teachers is unfit to have voice in the settlement of important educational matters, and their unfitness to exercise intellectual initiative and to assume the responsibility for constructive work is emphasized, the more their unfitness to attempt the much more difficult and delicate task of guiding souls appears. If this body is so unfit, how can it be trusted to carry out the recommendations or the dictations of the wisest body of experts? If teachers are incapable of the intellectual responsibility which goes with the determination of the methods they are to use in teaching, how can they employ methods when dictated by others, in other than a mechanical, capricious, and clumsy manner? The argument, I say, proves too much.

Moreover, if the teaching force is as inept and unintelligent and irresponsible as the argument assumes, surely the primary problem is that of their improvement. Only by sharing in some responsible task does there come a fitness to share in it. The argument that we must wait until men and women are fully ready to assume intellectual and social responsibilities would have defeated every step in the democratic direction that has ever been taken. The prevalence of methods of authority and of external dictation and direction tends automatically to perpetuate the very conditions of inefficiency, lack of interest, inability to assume positions of self-determination, which constitute the reasons that are depended upon to justify the régime of authority.

The system which makes no great demands upon originality, upon invention, upon the continuous expression of individuality, works automatically to put and to keep the more incompetent teachers in the school. It puts them there because, by a natural law of spiritual gravitation, the best minds are drawn to the places where they can work most effectively. The best minds are not especially likely to be drawn where there is danger that they may have to submit to conditions which no self-respecting intelligence likes to put up with; and where their time and energy are likely to be so occupied with details of external conformity that they have no opportunity for free and full play of their own vigor.

I have dwelt at length upon the problem of the recognition of the intellectual and spiritual individuality of the teacher. I have but one excuse. All other reforms are conditioned upon reform in the quality and character of those who engage in the teaching profession. The doctrine of the man behind the gun has become familiar enough, in recent discussion, in every sphere of life. Just because education is the most personal, the most intimate, of all human affairs, there, more than anywhere else, the sole ultimate reliance and final source of power are in the training, character, and intelligence of the individual. If any scheme could be devised which would draw to the calling of teaching persons of force of character, of sympathy with children, and consequent interest in the problems of teaching and of scholarship, no one need be troubled for a moment about other educational reforms, or the solution of other educational problems. But as long as a school organization which is undemocratic in principle tends to repel from all but the higher portions of the school system those of independent force, of intellectual initiative, and of inventive ability, or tends to hamper them in their work after they find their way into the schoolroom, so long all other reforms are compromised at their source and postponed indefinitely for fruition.

2. *As to the learner.*—The undemocratic suppression of the individuality of the teacher goes naturally with the improper restriction of the intelligence of the mind of the child. The mind, to be sure, is that of a child, and yet, after all, it is mind. To subject mind to an outside and ready-made material is a denial of the ideal of democracy, which roots itself ultimately in the principle of moral, self-directing individuality. Misunderstanding regarding the nature of the freedom that is demanded for the child is so common that it may be necessary to emphasize the fact that it is primarily intellectual freedom, free play of mental attitude, and operation which are sought. If individuality were simply a matter of feelings, impulses, and outward acts independent of intelligence, it would be more than a dubious matter to urge a greater degree of freedom for the child in the school. In that case much, and almost exclusive, force would attach to the objections that the principle of individuality is realized in the more exaggerated parts of Rousseau's doctrines: sentimental idealization of the child's immaturity, irrational denial of superior worth in the knowledge and mature experience of the adult, deliberate denial of the worth of the ends and instruments embodied in social organization. Deification of childish whim, unripened fancy, and arbitrary emotion is certainly a piece of pure romanticism. The would-be

reformers who emphasize out of due proportion and perspective these aspects of the principle of individualism betray their own cause. But the heart of the matter lies not there. Reform of education in the direction of greater play for the individuality of the child means the securing of conditions which will give outlet, and hence direction, to a growing intelligence. It is true that this freed power of mind with reference to its own further growth cannot be obtained without a certain leeway, a certain flexibility, in the expression of even immature feelings and fancies. But it is equally true that it is not a riotous loosening of these traits which is needed, but just that kind and degree of freedom from repression which are found to be necessary to secure the full operation of intelligence.

Now, no one need doubt as to what mental activity or the freed expression of intelligence means. No one need doubt as to the conditions which are conducive to it. We do not have to fall back upon what some regard as the uncertain, distracting, and even distressing voice of psychology. Scientific methods, the methods pursued by the scientific inquirer, give us an exact and concrete exhibition of the path which intelligence takes when working most efficiently, under most favorable conditions.

What is primarily required for that direct inquiry which constitutes the essence of science is first-hand experience; an active and vital participation through the medium of all the bodily organs with the means and materials of building up first-hand experience. Contrast this first and most fundamental of all the demands for an effective use of mind with what we find in so many of our elementary and high schools. There first-hand experience is at a discount; in its stead are summaries and formulas of the results of other people. Only very recently has any positive provision been made within the schoolroom for any of the modes of activity and for any of the equipment and arrangement which permit and require the extension of original experiences on the part of the child. The school has literally been dressed out with hand-me-down garments—with intellectual suits which other people have worn.

Secondly, in that freed activity of mind which we term "science" there is always a certain problem which focuses effort, which controls the collecting of facts that bear upon the question, the use of observation to get further data, the employing of memory to supply relevant facts, the calling into play of imagination, to yield fertile suggestion and construct possible solutions of the difficulty.

Turning to the school, we find too largely no counterpart to this mental activity. Just because a second-handed material has been supplied wholesale and retail, but anyway ready-made, the tendency is to reduce the activity of mind to a docile or passive taking in of the material presented—in short, to memorizing, with simply incidental use of judgment and of active research. As is frequently stated, acquiring takes the place of inquiring. It is hardly an exaggeration to say that the sort of mind-activity which is encouraged in the school is a survival from the days in which science had not made much headway; when education was mainly concerned with learning, that is to say, the preservation and handing down of the acquisitions of the past. It is true that more and more appeal is made every day in schools to judgment, reasoning, personal efficiency, and the calling up of personal, as distinct from merely book, experiences. But we have not yet got to the point of reversing the total method. The burden and the stress still fall upon learning in the sense of becoming possessed of the second-hand and ready-made material referred to. As Mrs. Young has recently said, the prevailing ideal is a perfect recitation, an exhibition without mistake, of a lesson learned. Until the emphasis changes to the conditions which make it necessary for the child to take an active share in the personal building up of his own problems and to participate in methods of solving them (even at the expense of experimentation and error), mind is not really freed.

In our schools we have freed individuality in many modes of outer expression without freeing intelligence, which is the vital spring and guarantee of all of these expressions. Consequently we give opportunity to the unconverted to point the finger of scorn, and to clamor for a return to the good old days when the teacher, the representative of social and moral authority, was securely seated in the high places of the school. But the remedy here, as in other phases of our social democracy, is not to turn back, but to go farther—to carry the evolution of the school to a point where it becomes a place for getting and testing experience, as real and adequate to the child upon his existing level as all the resources of laboratory and library afford to the scientific man upon his level. What is needed is not any radical revolution, but rather an organization of agencies already found in the schools. It is hardly too much to say that not a single subject or instrumentality is required which is not already found in many schools of the country. All that is required is to gather these materials and forces together and unify their operation. Too often they are used for a multitude of diverse and often conflicting aims. If a single purpose is provided, that of freeing the processes of mental growth, these agencies will at once fall into their proper classes and reinforce each other.

A catalogue of the agencies already available would include at least all of the following: Taking the child out of doors, widening and organizing his experience with reference to the world in which he lives; nature study when pursued as a vital observation of forces working under their natural conditions, plants and animals growing in their own homes, instead of mere discussion of dead specimens. We have also school gardens, the introduction of elementary agriculture, and more especially of horticulture—a movement that is already making great headway in many of the western states. We have also means for the sake of studying physiographic conditions, such as may be found by rivers, ponds or lakes, beaches, quarries, gulleys, hills, etc.

As similar agencies within the school walls, we find a very great variety of instruments for constructive work, or, as it is frequently, but somewhat unfortunately termed, "manual training." Under this head come cooking, which can be begun in its simpler form in the kindergarten; sewing, and what is of even greater educational value, weaving, including designing and the construction of simple apparatus for carrying on various processes of spinning, etc. Then there are also the various forms of tool-work directed upon cardboard, wood, and iron; in addition there are clay-modeling and a variety of ways of manipulating plastic material to gain power and larger experience.

Such matters pass readily over into the simpler forms of scientific experimentation. Every schoolroom from the lowest primary grade up should be supplied with gas, water, certain chemical substances and reagents. To experiment in the sense of trying things or to see what will happen is the most natural business of the child; it is, indeed, his chief concern. It is one which the school has largely either ignored or actually suppressed, so that it has been forced to find outlet in mischief or even in actually destructive ways. This tendency could find outlet in the construction of simple apparatus and the making of simple tests, leading constantly into more and more controlled experimentation, with greater insistence upon definiteness of intellectual result and control of logical process.

Add to these three typical modes of active experimenting, various forms of art expression, beginning with music, clay-modeling, and story-telling as foundation elements, and passing on to drawing, painting, designing in various mediums, we have a range of forces and materials which connect at every point with the child's natural needs and powers, and which supply the requisites for building up his experience upon all sides. As fast as these various agencies find their way into the schools, the centre of gravity shifts, the régime changes from one of subjection of mind to an external and ready-made material, into the activity of mind directed upon the control of the subject-matter and thereby its own upbuilding.

Politically we have found that this country could not endure half free and half slave. We shall find equally great difficulty in encouraging freedom, independence, and initiative in every sphere of social life, while perpetuating in the school dependence upon external authority. The forces of social life are already encroaching upon the school institutions which we have inherited from the past, so that many of its main stays are crumbling. Unless the outcome is to be chaotic, we must take hold of the organic, positive principle involved in democracy, and put that in entire possession of the spirit and work of the school.

In education meet the three most powerful motives of human activity. Here are found sympathy and affection, the going out of the emotions to the most appealing and the most rewarding object of love—a little child. Here is found also the flowering of the social and institutional motive, interest in the welfare of society and in its progress and reform by the surest and shortest means. Here, too, is found the intellectual and scientific motive, the interest in knowledge, in scholarship, in truth for its own sake, unhampered and unmixed with any alien ideal. Copartnership of these three motives—of affection, of social growth, and of scientific inquiry—must prove as nearly irresistible as anything human when they are once united. And, above all else, recognition of the spiritual basis of democracy, the efficacy and responsibility of freed intelligence, is necessary to secure this union.

The Classroom Teacher (1924)

WHAT I HAVE TO SAY this afternoon is more in continuation of the talk of this morning than might seem from the title. I hope the reasons for making this connection between the two subjects will become apparent as I go on. As I suggested this morning, it is not so much in theory or philosophy of education that we need to provide greater recognition of individuality in the schools, but rather in certain practical considerations. It is easier, more convenient, and cheaper to handle persons in masses and classes than it is to deal with them individually. A very large number of people can learn to run a machine; a comparatively small number of people can be artists of a creative sort. The tendency toward treating students in masses and classes rather than individually results in the comparative ease and comfort there is in working with a smoothly-running machine. In learning the behavior of a machine, how to adjust it, much more is required.

When we come to dealing with living things, especially living characters that vary as human individuals do, and attempt to modify their individual dispositions, develop their individual powers, counteract their individual interests, we have to deal with them in an artistic way, a way which requires sympathy and interest to make all of the needed adjustments to the particular emergencies of the act. The more mechanical a thing is, the more we can manage it; the more vital it is, the more we have to use our observation and interest in order to adjust ourselves properly to it. It is not easy, in other words, to maintain a truly artistic standard, which is, of course, the real business of the teacher; hence the emphasis upon quantity rather than quality.

Our whole system of education, with the graded, classified system of inspection and examination, necessitates the handling of large numbers of students at a time, and moving them on according to some time schedule in large

First published in *General Science Quarterly* 7 (1924): 463–72, from an address given at the State Conference of Normal School Instructors, Bridgewater, Mass., 5 September 1922.

groups. These things, rather than philosophy or theory, are the great forces working against a more general recognition of the principle of individuality in education. The whole effect of organized administration sometimes seems to force a kind of standardization which is unfavorable to the development of the teacher's individuality and to the teacher's cooperating in the development of the pupil's individuality.

Wherever there is a mechanical element, wherever we are dealing with physical conditions—space, time, money conditions—there is room, and a necessity, for standardization or uniformity. The danger is, however, that those who become interested in this work of standardizing conditions—the external side of the school work—will forget the limits of standardized uniformity, and attempt to carry it over into the strictly human, spiritual element that cannot be standardized. At bottom, this is very largely a matter of money, like so many other things. But if we ask why it is that the best known and best tested educational ideas are not more widely practised than they actually are, we are quite apt to come up against the fact of professed inability of the community to supply the material means to do the best thing that is possible. I repeat this! Our whole system of examination, inspection, grading, classification, tends almost automatically to introduce a factitious factor that gets between the educator and the human individual that is being developed.

There was an English novel published a few years ago, wherein a young girl, whose parents having died, was brought up in an institution, an orphan asylum. Later on, when someone inquired about her education, she replied, "We never had any education; we were just brought up in batches." That tendency to treat children in batches instead of individually is enforced as a measure of economy.

I was very much interested in what Professor Kirkpatrick said this morning about the subject of intelligence tests. He put the emphasis in the right place, I think. There is some danger in putting the emphasis in the wrong place. I do not think the leaders in the movement put the emphasis on the wrong place, but I do think there is considerable danger in the mind of the public who have not had a share in the scientific use of the test. There is some danger that the impression should get abroad that when you have a student's intelligence quotient—his I.Q.—you have a certain insight and measurement of him as an individual. If you stop to think what these tests are and what they propose to do, you will see that an intelligence quotient is something quite different from an insight into the make-up of the individual as an individual. It is a method, as the word "quotient" shows, of getting a certain average, in order to show what class of person he belongs in, a wholly relative matter.

If you take the children of the country at large, you will find a certain number of an average of such and such ability. This particular class belongs in that group having this average intellectual ability. One might say you do not know any more about the individual than you did before. Suppose he has the mental age of 13½, while his physiological age is so and so. He is above or below the average of his age. He is one of certain hundreds of thousands of children in the country who have been tested. We would know so many hundreds of thousands of children attain a mental age of so and so, and that this child belongs in that group. This finding is valuable for purposes of classification, which places the individual where he will work most effectively with others, and prevents useless retardation, of which Dr. Kirkpatrick spoke. It guards against the mistake of trying to make an individual go at a faster pace than he is capable of moving. However, when the teacher has determined this mental level, her work is really just beginning, so far as the psychological interest is concerned.

To turn now to the announced subject for the afternoon. It is the classroom teacher who is in contact with the individuals who are being educated. We might well say that all the rest of the system, organization and administration, is really so much superstructure for enabling the classroom teacher to do his or her work more effectively. It is true that actual education, whatever there is in the way of actual teaching and learning, is done in the classroom, through vital contact, intellectual and moral, between teacher and student. Like many other things self-evident, we give this basic fact a glance of passing recognition and then do not take it further into account. We emphasize the machinery of administration, the formation and laying out of the course of study, the functions of the school board, functions of the superintendent, principals and supervisors. All these stand in the public eye, at least very often, as the most important elements in the school system. To a certain extent, all these exist for the sake of the ultimate consumers, the teacher and the pupil as they come into direct personal relationship with each other in the school. If these factors of organization, administration and supervision of instruction do not stimulate, assist and reinforce the worker in the classroom, then they are useless, or even worse, since they become encumbrances in the way of the teacher. After all, the truest thing said in education is, "As is the teacher, so is the school." We all know that. The difference between one school and another, between one class in school and another, goes back to the personality of the principal or teacher. The problem is then: How are we going to concentrate all of these more external elements so that they really will emancipate, assist and safeguard the individual teacher in the classroom? Have we not, to some extent, been looking through the wrong end of the telescope? Do we not need to look more frequently through the end that magnifies the work of the classroom teacher and places that work in a better position?

Referring briefly to the course of study. I would have the best experts in the country studying the proper course of study. I would have experts in history, geography, arithmetic, and other subjects in the curriculum. Let them meet together and discuss what is the best subject matter out of the vast range of subject matter to be had. That may be, and should be, of great assistance to the classroom teacher, but it does not wholly determine what the actual subject matter is that comes home to the pupil. The course of study should be a course; it ought to be a flowing, moving thing, for its subject matter comes into continuous contact with the minds of the pupils.

There is no way by which subject matter, as laid out by experts, can get over to the pupils, except through the medium of the teacher. We can have a text-book written in accordance with the recommendation of experts. But after all, will not the last thing that counts be how the teacher uses that text-book; how it is handled; the questions that are asked? You can have very rich, full subject matter laid down on paper, and yet the personality and intelligence of the teacher may be such that the subject matter will shrink, dry up, and become a mere trickle of dull fact when it gets to the pupil. You can have an outline of a course of study, in the form of a bare skeleton on paper, and yet that course of study, as it gets over to the pupils in the classroom, may be very full, rich and alive, because of the spirit that the teacher puts into it; the methods the teacher uses; the assignment of outside study that the teacher gives, and new points of view in the student mind. What is true here of the course of study, as it comes to the pupils through the teacher's mind and personality, is true, in my judgment, of many other things in the educational system. It is the failure to concentrate all of the various school resources upon the power of the teacher that is a fundamental cause of some stereotyped mechanizing of our educational system. I repeat. Because the classroom teacher stands for this element of personal individual contact, while administration and organization are influences which are modified as they reach the pupil through the teacher, the central problem is how to use all of our existing resources in developing the classroom teacher.

We all know that there is a very great gap between our theories and our practices. Many of the wisest and truest things about education have been said for many hundreds of years—some of them by Plato, over 2,000 years ago; others, in the educational reforms of the last three or four hundred years. Many have come through discoveries in recent years and in our own day. But we all know that, even if these discoveries had not been made, there was enough known before as true and wise by educational experts immensely to improve our schools, indeed to have revolutionized them. I remember a few years ago a young woman who, for some reason, had escaped a secondary school education, for better or worse, and decided she wished to be a teacher. She went to Teachers College to study all of the improved theories of teaching. She later took a place in a school, and she had a surprise, not to say shock, which most of us who have come through an educational system would not have. Here were those things taught by the authorities, agreed to by the authorities as true, as well as modern and up-to-date, and she assumed she was going to find schools run on the basis of these advanced theories of which she had learned. It was the discrepancy between the teaching she had and the actual practice and teaching in the schools that gave her this shock. It brought home to me how wide this gap is, after all, and how the crucial problem of the improvement of education is to make those advances that we have in theory and administration, effective upon the work of the teacher, so that they will seriously affect the life of the pupil.

A teacher, a short time ago, at the suggestion of another teacher, made a study over a number of years of the volumes of reports of the N.E.A., with a view to seeing who was making the vital contributions to educational thought; contributions that were supposed to influence practice. As perhaps you will guess, a very small percentage of the papers read at the N.E.A., the addresses made, came from classroom teachers. If we eliminate the number coming from high school classroom teachers, the number coming from elementary classroom teachers was negligible. I doubt if it was one per cent, going over a series of years. That seems to me to be a deplorable fact. It indicates that, for some reason, classroom teachers are not being the active force in the improvement of educational practice that they should be. The people who are doing the actual work of instruction, that are in personal contact, are personal influences on the character and minds of the students, are not the ones who are actively carrying forward the theory. I realize how many explanations can be given for this condition,—such as lack of time, teachers overburdened with work, etc. The university or normal school teacher or principal may have more leisure to study these things, but, after all, since it is the teachers who make the final application, ought they not to play a large part in developing and making concrete and real the ideas which they are engaged in executing?

In industry and factory life we have a sharp separation between those who plan and those who execute. I wonder, however, from the standpoint of the welfare of the country, whether, even in a factory, it is advisable to have so sharp a line of division between those who plan and those who execute. But certainly, when we come to such a vital thing as education, it is still more dangerous to have this sharp distinction between those who plan and those who do the work of execution. The result is that the teacher, who does not have part in developing ideas, cannot have that sympathetic understanding of them that one has who has taken part in working them out. The principle of learning by experience, if it is a good principle for pupils, is a good principle for teachers. If our ideas and theories ought to be arrived at inductively, if they ought to grow up out of actual experience, why should not the concrete experience of the classroom teacher develop more in the way of educational ideas and principles than it does at present? I think one reason for the gap between our modern theories and what is known and accepted in school practice, is largely due to the fact that the intellectual responsibility of the classroom teacher has not been sufficiently recognized or magnified. You know, if you are engaged in carrying out plans and ideas of one person, you do not, and cannot, throw yourself into it with the same enthusiasm and wholeheartedness, or same desire to learn and improve, that you do when you are carrying out plans and ideas which you yourself have had some share in developing.

The function of the supervisor is important and valuable. Obviously, it should be one of inspiration and of education, rather than that of simply writing prescriptions such as those the doctor writes, and which are then handed to a drug-store clerk to fill out. Teachers should not be clerks filling out recipes that are prescribed by others. They should not be like cooks in the kitchen, who take a cook-book and mix ingredients in the proportion called for by the recipe in the book, not knowing why they do this or that, or with any expectation that they are going to make any discoveries or improvement. The real cook is the one who originates all the improved dishes that we like to eat. And the permanent improvements in the course of study must be those which are either contributed to, tested by, worked out, experimented upon intelligently by the teacher in the classroom.

A good deal of supervision, so-called, especially when class supervision is the watchword of the day, seems to have a great deal of "super" in it and not much of "vision." It is the business of the supervisor to look over the field, to get a larger, wider, more thorough view of it than the conditions of the classroom teacher can permit. It is the privilege of the supervisor and directing officer to give the classroom teacher the benefit of this larger, more comprehensive vision of the field.

There are, of course, some valuable short cuts and mechanical devices. It is difficult always to be a creative artist. I think, however, that we should get on more rapidly if we realized that, if education is going to live up to its profession, it must be seen as a work of art which requires the same qualities of personal enthusiasm and imagination as are required by the musician, painter or artist. Each one of these artists needs a technique which is more or less mechanical, but in the degree to which he loses his personal vision to become subordinate to the more formal rules of the technique he falls below the level and grade of the artist. He becomes reduced again to the level of the artisan who follows the blue prints, drawings, and plans that are made by other people.

I think what first interested me in this problem of the greater freedom on the part of the teacher, was carried or transferred from an interest in more varied and creative, independent and original work on the part of the pupil. Finally, I saw how inconsistent it was to expect this greater amount of creative, independent work from the student when the teachers were still unemancipated;

when the teachers were still shackled by too many rules and prescriptions and too much of a desire for uniformity of method and subject matter.

As Mr. Baldwin said this morning, every course of study put in print is more or less out of date by the time it is in print. It can serve only as a suggestion for the teacher, and every classroom teacher ought to be regarded by others, and regard himself or herself, as responsible not only for the teaching of recognized subject matter, but for the making of new contributions to subject matter. Think of the variety of the universe we live in, the history of society and human life! There is no end to the riches of the material that it is possible to draw upon. We can only begin to attack the reservoir of subject matter in education. There is not a teacher fit for the work, who is really stimulated to do her best, who will not find in her own locality, suggested by the needs of the locality, or stimulated or aroused by the questions that pupils ask, some new field of subject matter which will satisfy the mental hunger of the pupils at the present time. We shall not make our theoretical improvements in education practically effective, we shall not realize upon them and get them over into concrete cash values, until we expect, as well as give, opportunity where every individual pupil can exercise freedom and discuss certain lines of subject matter in the school in contact with the teacher, quite irrespective of any formula or prescribed course of study.

The imagination of everybody today, their unconscious way of seeing things, is more influenced by industrial considerations than we realize. The way business is done influences unconsciously all our ideas. So we have from business practices carried over into education too much standardization, too much concentration of responsibility. There should be concentration of responsibility, but if, in a school system, you concentrate responsibility in a small number of people, what does that mean for the rest of the people? Is it not a division of irresponsibility, when you have concentrated your responsibility in a few? Responsibility needs to be concentrated, but in everybody. Every part of the school system needs to have responsibility for improvements in subject matter, in methods of instruction, in methods of discipline. When we try to place all responsibility on a few administrative officers, we are practically depriving the greater number of teachers of responsibility. That is why I say that concentration of responsibility is a division of irresponsibility. Too often the relation between pupils and teachers is reduplicated in the relation between teachers and supervisory officers. Pupils, many of them, strive to come up to the external standards that are set by the teacher, and the main question with them is whether they can get by; whether they can do enough at the proper time to satisfy the demands and expectation of the teacher. This situation is often reduplicated in the relation between teacher and the supervisory officer. The teacher is simply concerned with the things that will meet external standards that are set for her.

My attention was first called to this by one of the finest women I ever knew, Mrs. Ella Flagg Young of Chicago. Mrs. Young began as a classroom teacher, and became a supervisor, an associate superintendent, and finally, superintendent. From forty years' experience she knew from every angle the public schools of a large city. She saw the schools from the standpoint of the teacher and supervisory officer, and was acutely aware of the situation that could exist in a highly organized school system between two parts of the system.

The classroom teacher has this advantage. She is on the job all the time. There are not enough supervisory officers to go around and be on the job all the time. They can only visit now and then. But under a regime of class supervision, the teachers often develop a very great skill in doing what they like to do, and at the same time appearing to be carrying out the directions of supervisors. The advantage is on the side of the classroom teacher, because she is there all the time.

Let me repeat a story told by a teacher: "As a high school teacher in algebra I had what I thought was an unusually successful recitation, because the pupils were doing all the work. I was acting as umpire. The principal came in and did not see me doing anything. He reproved me afterwards, and said that I was lazy. I remedied that immediately. Every time he came into the room after that, I began to lecture to the pupils, and he thought I was a good teacher. Personally I do not think I was teaching so successfully."

I sometimes think the greatest human loss there is at the present time is in the loss of experience as to our human contacts with each other. Parents too often start out having to take and train their own children as if nobody had ever done it before. There is some improvement now, but, after all, how much experience goes unrecorded and unutilized that might be rendered available for others. And so in the school, because the teacher is not given a responsible position, how much in the way of experience there is that goes unused, that does not become food for their further teaching, and, because of that, other people, perhaps professors like myself in universities, who are more or less at arm's length from the situation, have to provide ideas and theories that are more or less abstract. These ideas and theories do not get translated over into vital results because the teacher has not had share enough in building them up and contributing to them.

PART FOUR. THE IDEAL SCHOOL

Introduction: The Ideal School

YOU MAY RIGHTLY WONDER IF any school can be called *ideal*. Certainly, if we did call a school ideal we would want to be clear about what we mean by using the term. For Dewey, the ideal school should indirectly guide students' growth and development of particular skills, attitudes, habits, and dispositions that shape their thinking, feeling, and acting. In order to do this most effectively and ethically, the school must see itself and be seen by others as an intimate part of the community in which it is embedded and as a dynamic, microcosmic community in its own right. Further, the school—as an organic whole—needs to be understood as a creative construction of even smaller communities or social groups (MW9.367–70; MW15.171–79). For Dewey, furthermore, the school embodies the life of the community by linking subject matter to the experiences of students. From one perspective, then, an ideal school—although there is no such entity in an unqualified or absolute sense—is an experimental one where children and educators learn to inquire, share, question, and reflect, not merely talk or listen or share information. In fostering worthwhile, holistic experiences, including aesthetic ones, an ideal school interacts with the life of the community and assists in developing habits of creative and critical inquiry wherever its influence reaches.

From another perspective, an ideal school is a place that understands its cultural context, tests teaching and learning practices, and pays attention to student interaction and growth. However, in view of different contexts, diverse students, and personalized curricula, ideal, or more nearly ideal, schools vary tremendously. They also vary because of differences in the developmental stages of students and staff. Even so, through students' interacting and working together with educators and volunteers, the school community learns the importance of democratic values, including respecting others, tolerating and testing differences of opinion, appreciating cultural diversity, and working toward solutions that make a difference in real-life situations. Dewey has even more to say about dynamic, growing, and educative schools in the following essays, which present a more complex and nuanced view of so-called ideal schools.

In "Monastery, Bargain Counter, or Laboratory in Education" (LW6.99–111), Dewey discusses a few of the historical changes that have occurred since the founding of the American public school system. By *monastery*, he means a system of classical education that catered to the elite few who were presumed to be the leaders of the future, and not the masses. The *bargain counter* metaphor alludes to a broad-based education that has been marketed to the general public, offering whatever they desire. For Dewey, the bargain counter system—despite the legitimate complaints about how it sells its cultural and vocational goods— has meant a democratization of education. And by dissolving the distinction between theory and practice, knowledge and action, it has opened the way for a third alternative. Dewey offers the example of the laboratory to suggest some features of what an ideal school might look like. Unlike the "pipeline education" of the monastery type, where the fossilized lessons to be learned are simply passed down to students, the laboratory school offers the possibility of experimentation, discovery of new knowledge, and invention of new ways of doing things.

In a speech to the Progressive Education Association, "Progressive Education and the Science of Education" (LW3.257–68), Dewey poses a paragraph-long series of questions to his audience about the nature and purpose of progressive education. He mentions among the characteristics of a progressive school respect for freedom and individuality, less formality, building on experience, activity over passivity, communicating openly, and engendering a public or common spirit whereby the student learns personal and social responsibility. In describing the progressive school as experimental, he poses a three-part question: What should a progressive or experimental school do for other schools, for a science of education, and for students? He concludes that there is room for multiple *sciences* of education and that a closed-minded, fundamentalist approach to educational theory must be avoided.

In an unusual essay, "Dewey Outlines Utopian Schools" (LW9.136–40), Dewey takes us beyond laboratory, experimental, and progressive schools to a speculative picture of a utopian school, a type of school that did not yet exist. Apparently, he was interested in seeing education transcend the traditional monastery, bargain-counter, and perhaps even laboratory-experimental-progressive types of schools to become "utopian assembly places." Knowing that his audience might find it difficult to imagine a world without schools, he argues that a society that is truly utopian would have little if any need for formal education to take place, because every aspect of life and every societal entity would have a positive educational influence. Education would take place throughout everyday life in homes, neighborhoods, museums, offices, and wherever social and intellectual interactions occur. In this utopian vision, educative life experiences themselves would be the primary teachers.

In "What Is Learning?" (LW11.238–42), Dewey is concerned that educators understand "the natural processes of learning" as they relate to human development and learning theories. First, he emphasizes the necessity of identifying and constructing conditions that are most beneficial to learning. Second, he notes that educators must understand students' psychosocial development, particularly their evolving impulses, needs, and urges. Third, contrary to the behaviorism of his time, he asserts that students actively seek out, not simply respond to stimuli that reinforce their behavior. Fourth, Dewey claims that learning is best motivated and accomplished by students' internal senses of satisfaction, accomplishment, and excitement, not by external rewards. Fifth, he emphasizes that student development is a mixture of direct and indirect guidance and reflective inquiry. Finally, he offers his synoptic definition of what a true—a genuine ideal?—school would be like when it is guided by a natural theory of learning.

In "Education, Direct and Indirect" (MW3.240–48), Dewey deals with present or desired educational realities rather than any utopian visions, but he always looks for learning situations in their ideal forms. He critiques an overly directive educational system that places too much emphasis on teachers, textbooks, grades, or tasks to be completed rather than on helping students find ways to navigate their way in the world. He objects to grades as a motivation tool and calls for alternative forms of assessment. And he favors what he terms *indirect education* that engages students in the learning process. Or, to restate the idea, he encourages a type of education that provides stimulating conditions in an environment that guides students to make discoveries about their world rather than focus on external expectations of teachers and school administrators, such as tests and grades. Tying together Dewey's closing thoughts, he seems to be saying that schools can be communities where students are indirectly educated to be their reflective best, or they can be funeral parlors where students go through the direct process of being embalmed, laid out for viewing, and eventually interred with other unreflective corpses. Undoubtedly, Dewey would have us ask, Can teachers, if they are led by informed and courageous leaders, successfully pursue the first option?

The answer to that question—and more—is partially found in "The Need for Orientation" (LW11.162–70). Writing during a time of economic collapse, political uncertainty, and educational chaos, Dewey declared that there were no genuine educational systems, and the so-called ones merely mirrored society, which was a social spasm of disparate activities. He discusses four things, in particular, that support his conclusion: a piecemeal curriculum, a mechanical pedagogy, a class-based system of oversight, and a compromised administration. Students were too often treated as "intellectual robots," were not provided with their "intellectual legs," and were lost ethically and occupationally when they left school. Those who are interested in better, even ideal, schools cannot afford to wait for society to recover, he concludes. Among Dewey's suggestions for creating high-quality schools are several that merit attention: a district or school needs a clear philosophical orientation, which involves having lucid and focused aims; educators need to understand the world in which they live and work; a curriculum needs objectives that cohere with a district's or school's orientation; oversight of schools needs to be distributed among the diverse peoples of an area; and social intelligence should characterize all endeavors of schools, districts, and boards. In a word, an ideal school is a *community* school. In this essay, then, Dewey adds to the criteria by which we should evaluate a school, including but not limited to the following: the school needs a living philosophical orientation, an indirect approach to guiding students, a natural learning theory, an experimental outlook, and a progressive view of students.

The ideal school, of course, is more than these and previous essays suggest. The school also has a view of society, including itself, that provides at once its means, curriculum, and ends: a democratic society in the process of reflective growth. Perhaps the following questions will serve as stimuli for your own questions.

REFLECTION AND DISCUSSION QUESTIONS

1. Dewey was immensely interested in the psychology of learning and the best approaches to nurture learning. How does Dewey define learning? What might learning look like in the ideal school? How would learning be substantiated?

2. Dewey stressed that a good education was more than a diploma or some sort of certification. What characteristics or dispositions does Dewey feel students should gain through their education?

3. What strengths do you see in the schools that Dewey recommended we replace? What weaknesses do you note in his preferred schools? Is a society without schools possible? How would your vision of a utopian educational setting differ from Dewey's?

4. Dewey characterized traditional education as boring, a burden, much like a corpse, grounded in fear, constraint, and embarrassment. How does your own formal education compare with Dewey's description?

5. What might the contemporary school look like if it embodied Dewey's theory of education?

6. Beyond clarifying his theory of an ideal school, what other theories do these essays help clarify? Why do you think Dewey discussed these theoretical dimensions in the context of his discussing his theory of schools?

Monastery, Bargain Counter, or
Laboratory in Education? (1932)

SOME YEARS AGO WHEN I was in the Adirondacks, I climbed Mt. Marcy, the highest peak of those mountains. There, near the top, is a marshy space with a little brook trickling down, apparently insignificant. A few rods away, after a slight rise of land, there is a second little brook, likewise apparently insignificant. I was told that the first one I speak of is the headwaters of the Hudson River; that the waters a short way off, separated by a watershed only a few feet higher than this swampy land, finally empty into the St. Lawrence. These little streams, that are hardly to be called streams but rather rivulets, at their source are only a few yards apart, but traversing very different lands and seeing very different scenes they finally reach the Atlantic Ocean hundreds of miles away from each other. This metaphor for purposes of comparison is trite, yet it seems to me that in its way it is representative of what happens historically. Great movements are not often great in their beginnings. Taken in themselves their inception is as seemingly insignificant and trivial as the little trickles of water near the top of that mountain. It is only when after long periods of time we look back to see what has come out of these little beginnings, that they appear important; just as it is when we see the Hudson River after it has become a majestic stream that the small rivulet at the top of Mt. Marcy gains importance.

You remember Emerson spoke about men who build better than they know. It seems to me that all great historic movements may be said to build either much better or much worse than those who started them knew or intended. This is true in the history of the founding of our own country. You will recall that most of the leaders in the Revolution, George Washington himself included, hoped

First published in *Barnwell Bulletin* 9 (February 1932): 51–62, from the Barnwell Address delivered at Central High School, Philadelphia, on 4 February 1932.

that there would not be a complete break with Great Britain. They had certain objects which they wanted to gain, but they did not contemplate a really new political world. They felt rather that they were protesting against abuses of the liberties which belonged to British subjects, and just as their English forefathers had protested against the tyranny of the Stuarts, so they, in protesting against the despotism of the Georges in their own day, were walking in the footsteps of their ancestors.

Certainly those who started the educational system in America had no idea and no intention of founding a new educational system. Indeed, they looked backward rather than forward. Some of them looked back to Holland, others to England; and their highest ambition was to imitate or, if possible, to reproduce those schools in which they themselves had been trained. They were in a new country, the greater part still a wilderness, and naturally their highest ambition was to come as near as possible to recreating on American soil the kind of school which they themselves had known when they were children. This attempt to continue the educational system of the Old World persisted for a long time. Upon the whole it continued in this country until—we can only speak roughly—until, say, some time after the Civil War. Up to that time our education in the main was still a perpetuator; an effort to maintain the higher culture of our European source.

That type of education had certain quite definite features. In the earlier period of the elementary school the instruction was essentially an education in the three R's, reading, 'riting and 'rithmetic, with a little history of our own country and geography of the world, but more especially the geography of our country, superadded. There was a tendency to divide the subjects and methods of instruction. The mass of pupils who had received a training in the rudiments of learning did not go on with their education in higher schools. When they left the elementary school, their education was continued mainly through serving apprenticeships in trades and callings of various kinds, entered into either by formal indenture or in an informal way. In the service of a master and from the contact arising from this relation, the apprentice acquired skill in a trade. A small number of pupils, however, continued with higher education. For them the backbone of advanced education was the ancient languages, Greek and Latin, for those going into the learned professions of law and medicine, with the addition of Hebrew for those entering the ministry. Some history was also added, but classic history, the history of Greece and Rome with the literatures of those ancient countries. In those days there was no English literature in the higher courses, and there were no modern languages. The education, as you see, for the most part was in the symbols of knowledge and in the written and printed expression, especially in the languages and literatures of antiquity. It almost seems as if it was supposed that the material was better and more precious, the further away from the present it was both in space and in time.

This type of education I have taken the liberty of calling that of the monastery. This is a metaphor which is not to be taken too literally. But it was an education intended for the few rather than for the mass of the people. It was derived from the European tradition in which it was expected that only a few would continue beyond the mere rudiments of learning into what would be really an education. And the material of it, as I have just said, was largely the symbol of learning. Mathematics was the symbol of numbers, and the written and printed word that of grammar and literature, and so on. There was an aloofness from ordinary every-day living, which perhaps does not make the term "monastery education" entirely inappropriate.

Now this type of education, derived essentially from European sources though modified in some details (since after all there was the ocean between it and its source), persisted longer than we might have expected. There were probably two main causes for the long persistence of this older education on the new soil, which in the meantime had developed a new political and to a considerable extent a new social system. One cause was that in the first decades of our Republic the practical education of the great majority of people was still obtained out of school. In the main we were still a rural and agrarian people. We were still in an age in which industry was chiefly carried on in the home and in the neighborhood by means of handicraft. If there was machinery, it was comparatively simple. There were local shops in the villages, country communities and towns to which everyone had comparatively easy access. I remember the village in which stood my grandfather's house, where in my childhood I went to spend the summer vacation. There in the village was the old-fashioned sawmill, the old-fashioned gristmill, the old-fashioned tannery; and in my grandfather's house there were still the candles and the soap which had been made in the home itself. At certain times the cobbler would come around to spend a few days in the neighborhood, making and repairing the shoes of the people. Through the very conditions of living, everybody had a pretty direct contact with nature and with the simpler forms of industry. As there were no great accumulations of wealth, the great majority of young people got a very genuine education through a kind of informal apprenticeship. They took part in the home-made duties of the household and farm and activities of the neighborhood. They saw with their eyes, and followed with their imaginations, the very real activities about them. The amount of genuine education, and of training in good habits that were obtained in this way under our earlier pioneer conditions, is not easy to overestimate. There was a real education through real contact with actual materials and important social occupations.

On the other hand, knowledge in the form of the written and printed word then had what economists call a "scarcity value." Books, newspapers, periodicals, in a word reading matter of all kinds, were much rarer and more expensive than they are today. Libraries were comparatively few. Learning, or rather the mastery of the tools of learning, the ability to read and to write and to figure, had a high value, because the school was the one place where these tools of learning could be mastered. We all have heard the story of Abraham Lincoln and other backwoodsmen and of their devotion to learning, of the great difficulties they had to contend with, of their going barefooted for miles to school, of their sitting up at night to master by candle light the rudiments of learning. For in those days, the monastery education was the only avenue to the larger world of the culture of the past. And that is why, I think, this older type of education, that seems to us today rather barren and meagre, persisted so long and relatively was so effective in achieving important results.

Gradually, with the change of those social conditions, there was brought about a very great change, a change so great as to be called a revolution in our whole educational system. I think of the old gristmill of my boyhood days in contrast with the great flour manufactories of today as symbolical. Then we could go into the mill, we could see the grain, we could watch it being ground in those great stone hoppers; we could see it passing through the pipes, and we could follow it with our eyes until it was turned into bran, flour and the rest of it. Today if we go into one of these big flour mills, we would not even see the grain going into the hopper! We may follow the whole process and see practically nothing, not even the finished flour as it is automatically put into barrels. The youth of today have no access to the basic realities of living, social, material, economic, at all to the extent to which the youth of a few generations ago had. This is what I mean by the illustration of the mills, if we take it symbolically. That fact has made it necessary for the schools to branch out in their instruction and to take up many things which used to be taken care of in the life of the boys and girls, of the young men and young women, out of school. In addition the situation is reversed in reference to language and books. Printed matter is almost a drug; it is cheap, accessible, voluminous. It would require considerable ingenuity for one growing up in the city to escape it. Machines take over the work of calculation and penmanship. On the other hand, however, opportunities have vanished for the learning and for the practical discipline which used to be had in open fields under the skies, and in shops where a few persons worked in close contact with one another, using their own judgment and receiving recognition for their personal achievements. They are now fenced-in roads where there used to be open fields inviting the inventive to take short cuts to their goals. The roads, moreover, are crowded and there is much standing in line; individual pace is regulated by the movement of the mass. There are two outstanding facts which have changed the course of our inherited education in schools. To maintain the idea of democratic equality, schooling was made universal and compulsory. In the last thirty years we have done something to make this ideal a fact. The number of boys and girls who go to high school and college is five or six times greater, in proportion to the population, than it was even thirty or forty years ago. And then the change in the character of life, the change from the agrarian to the industrial, compelled a shift of emphasis in the material of instruction. At first there was merely the attempt to give to the many the education which had in the old country been intended for the few. But as time went on, the very fact that it was the many who were to be schooled compelled a vast change; a change, which has been called a revolution, in things taught, in the ends for which they were taught, and in the methods by which they were taught.

The nature of this revolutionary change was determined largely by the economic factor of life. The great change which goes by the name of the industrial revolution, that is to say, the substitution of mechanical power for the muscular power of animals and man, began, of course, in England, not in the United States. But the relatively sparse population in our country together with the abundance of natural resources, including unused and unappropriated land, the great distances which had to be knit together in transportation and communication, stimulated and almost compelled in this country the rapid and unhindered growth of the new methods of production and distribution. Moreover there was another factor of great importance. In England and in Europe generally, the new industry not only developed more slowly, but also in and against a background of traditions and institutions which were long centuries old. The latter did more than check its rapid growth; they formed the banks within which the economic and industrial movement was confined. In the United States there were no such counterbalancing forces. The industrial conquest of a continent became almost by sheer force of circumstances the dominant occupation of the American people. Physical mastery tended to absorb, almost to monopolize, the energies which in Europe were expended in a variety of channels. It was impossible, humanly speaking, that this engrossing interest should not leave its deep impress upon education in the schools and in the interplay of forces outside of the school which shape disposition and form habits.

Moreover, the development of the arts and industries was more and more dependent upon techniques which ultimately rest upon scientific knowledge; chemistry and physics were making discoveries which displaced the routine, rule of thumb methods which earlier generations had acquired through imitation and apprenticeship. Many lines of activity which were not themselves of a high order from the intellectual point of view felt the infection. They had to seem to adopt a scientific technique whether they actually rose above the level of empirical routines or not. Science obtained such a high prestige value that every conceivable human activity now has its corresponding "science"—writing advertisements, doing laundry work, keeping accounts, cooking meals, stenography and type-writing, and so on through the whole inventory.

While many, perhaps most people, regard the broadening of education to meet the needs of the greater number, and especially the inclusion of a larger amount of the vocational element, as an enrichment of education, there are others who hold a contrary view. And this brings me to the second catchword in the caption of my remarks. The persons in the hostile group say that our education has deteriorated through catering to the needs of larger numbers; that what we now have is a bargain counter education; that the older kind of education relied upon the wisdom and the culture of the past to determine what was good for young people, inexperienced and unwise, to study; that the present theory and practice of education is rather to spread everything out on the educational counter, to provide some study and some course for every taste, so that the buyer, not the person who provides the education but the immature person who is to get the education, determines what kind it will be. Hence they say that the school is now a store where the storekeeper spreads out all kinds of goods in the hope that, by so doing, some one thing which catches the eye will appeal to the taste of one person, while some other thing will gratify the wants of another. And so they say that our education has become a scattered education; that it has been diluted and attenuated; that the elements of the earlier education, which made for discipline and culture, have been more and more eliminated; that the principle on which the schools are now conducted is simply that of giving young people what they want or what they think they want. They claim that education in meeting these demands has become utilitarian, "practical" rather than cultural; that its aim is simply to help an individual make his way industrially, so that he can earn money more easily, or get a better job than he could if he did not have this training. Accordingly, our universities and colleges, and also our high schools, and to some extent even our elementary schools, have been under attack on the grounds that this broadening out instead of being an enrichment is a thinning, while dilution and attenuation have made a course of study congested. The training which the youth now gets lacks depth—it is something merely on the surface.

While I do not wholly agree with these criticisms, I have nevertheless ventured to take the title "bargain counter education," as a characterization of certain phases of the present education. It is hardly possible to discuss how far these criticisms are really justified. The reason is that different people have such very different standards. If one person thinks that closer connection with life is an advance in education, and another thinks that it is a term of condemnation since the essence of culture is that it shall not be too closely related to the practical needs of everyday life, there is clearly no point of contact between them. They will judge what is going on very differently because they have different standards. Thus if Mr. and Mrs. Smith think it is a fine thing for education to become more vocational, since it then takes into account the fact that the majority of people have got to make their living; while on the other hand their neighbors, Mr. and Mrs. Jones, believe that this kind of education is a step backward, obviously they will appraise the present system quite differently. But this is too large a question to go into here. Some of these criticisms, I may say, seem to be justified. In several respects our present education is spread out too thin, is too scattered; it lacks definiteness of aim. Very often the courses which are called practical are not really practical except in their label. Some of these courses try to teach things which can only be learned in the actual business or calling itself, while they do not take sufficient account of the rapid changes that are going on, since the teachers are out of contact with industry and teach the way things were done five or ten years ago rather than the way they are done now in the actual callings of life. And they are still less in contact with the way things are going to be done five years from now. In consequence, even the so-called practical courses in the long run are often not very practical.

We may make all these admissions about certain tendencies in our present system of education, and may yet say that we have accomplished one very important thing; we have at least broken down the obstacles and barriers which in the traditional education, the so-called cultural education, stood between the mass of the people and the possibility of their receiving anything worthy of the name of education. We have at least taken the first step in making education universally accessible, so that there is more reality than there used to be in the ideal of equality of opportunity for all. We have also at least broken down the wall that used to exist between what was called culture and vocation; for in fact the older type, that which I have called the "education of the monastery," (or which I might have called that of the pulpit, if I had another social class as a type), assumed that the people who were to acquire culture were people of leisure. Only those who had a substantial economic background which rendered it unnecessary for them to engage in any calling or business received education. On the other hand it was assumed that people who went into the active callings of life, especially those which in any way involved the use of the body and the hands, were people who were, of necessity, shut out from any high culture, being condemned to a life of contact with physical, material things, so that in their callings there was no avenue to things of value intellectually and artistically. This bargain counter education, therefore, even taking it at its lowest level, has got rid of this dividing line, this complete separation between vocation and culture; or, in other terms, between theoretical things and practical things; between action and doing on the one hand, and knowledge and understanding on the other.

The bargain counter education has then at least prepared the way for another type of education, to which, also somewhat metaphorically, I have given the name of the "laboratory." For as the very word laboratory suggests, there is action, there is work, there is labor involved in it. The term is of course usually confined to the scientific laboratory, that of physics, chemistry or biology. But the idea inherent in the word extends further than this restriction. The first great characteristic of a laboratory is that in it there is carried on an activity, an activity which involves contact with technical equipment, as tools, instruments and other apparatus, and machinery which require the use of the hands and the body. There is dealing with real materials and not merely, as in the old, traditional education, with the symbols of learning.

There is no reason why the idea of the laboratory should not be extended to include also the workshop. There is no reason why the kitchens, if you please, where the girls learn cooking, or the rooms where they have contact with textiles, and the manual training shops where boys learn something of the arts while using their hands, eyes and bodies, should not embody the principle of learning through action by dealing with realities. There is no reason why there should not be extended to them the kind of learning which goes on in the physics laboratory or in the chemical laboratory. There is no reason why the workshop, whether in the upper grammar school or in the high school or in the college, should be confined merely to imparting manual skill and to giving an external ability to carry on a particular trade or calling. Through active contact with a wide range of materials, an opportunity is offered for an introduction into all the resources of science. Indeed, I often think that probably for the majority of young people the shops would make a better avenue of initiation into the elements of scientific knowledge than do our laboratories. For the concepts of physics and chemistry when approached directly, as in the study of the molecule, the atom or the electron, are technical, difficult and abstract, often quite as abstract and certainly as far removed from sense-perception as anything found in the older type of education. Through the medium of such things as the automobile, the airplane and the radio, there is a direct avenue to the principles of physics, chemistry, the structure of materials, which is on the line of least resistance, and yet which is capable of giving young people a personal and intelligent grasp of scientific principles. Such knowledge then comes to them in terms and through means which are associated with their daily experience; it means something to them in terms of their life instead of in abstruse and remote technical symbols.

Through the workshop when conducted as a laboratory, that is, as a means of learning and discovery, there is also the opportunity of arousing the curiosity of pupils and of equipping them with the methods for finding out things. The laboratory education also offers a means of access to an understanding of society.

For after all, our society is largely what it is today because of the scientifically controlled occupations which are carried on in it. It may not be advisable to subordinate or limit our education to the making of farmers, engineers and merchants, but since the very large majority of the young people who come to our schools go into these various callings, it does seem desirable that they who are to be farmers shall be intelligent farmers, capable of intellectual invention, having initiative and mental control of their materials; and similarly, that the persons who are to enter the other callings shall have an education which will equip them to be flexible and independent in their judgments and original in their outlook. This is the education I would call the laboratory type. Beginning with activity, it would through that activity bring the student into actual contact with real things, and would then use this contact with objects for intellectual training and for arousing a thirst to understand, and not merely to fit pupils into some narrow groove of later trade and business life.

There is one other characteristic of what I call the laboratory education. The older traditional education was based on the thought that the teacher or the textbook knew in advance what the young ought to learn. The teacher or the textbook told the student what was so. The student's effort was largely confined to passive absorption and reproduction—a process which we might call a pipeline education; the teacher and the textbook, pouring the information into the student, who was supposed to be a reservoir which received the knowledge and which on suitable occasions (chiefly those of the examination period), gave out what it had received. This method of education might also be called a phonographic education. For the mind of the student was regarded as a phonographic disc upon which certain impressions were made by the teacher, so that when the disc was put on the machine and the movement started (which, again, would be during the examination period), it might reveal what had been inscribed upon it. The laboratory education, however, to which the bargain counter type is at least a transitional stage, puts much more responsibility upon students themselves. The method of the laboratory is an experimental one. It is a method of discovery through search, through inquiry, through testing, through observation and reflection—all processes requiring activity of mind rather than merely powers of absorption and reproduction.

To go back now to my original metaphor. At first at the original water shed were the elementary district schools, started by parents in localities who wanted their children to have some of the opportunities which the Old World afforded, but which could not be had in the New World unless the parents themselves started the school. Then there were the universities, intended very largely as you will remember to train the clergy. Our ancestors were for the most part a pious folk who wanted pastors, and educated pastors to conduct the services in the churches. Within the past one hundred and fifty years, but more especially and with increasing acceleration during the last thirty or forty years, the streams originating in the traditions and conditions of past times, have been growing into a broad current. This current is often meandering, dividing up, getting thin and superficial. But still it has potentially the energy to create a new and significant kind of education; an education which will be universal not merely in the fact that everybody will have the chance of going to school, but universal in the sense that it will be adapted to all varieties of individual needs and abilities. Society, instead of having simply the benefit of the training of a limited class, then will be able, through the development of every individual composing it, to get the benefit of the vast resources of all its members, resources which in the past have been latent because so few people have had the opportunity of realizing their full capacities. Public education will then also be public not merely in the sense that it is conducted by the State at public expense through taxation, but in the sense that it really trains all individuals for some kind of social service. After all, it is through vocations of one sort or another that society is ultimately served, and not by those individuals who, however cultivated they may be, regard their culture as so personal and private a matter that it is not put into vital and organic connection with the work of the world. When these capacities and potentialities are fully brought out by our education, we shall have in this country a genuinely new type of education. This new education will also give the promise and potentiality of a new type of culture, one in which old barriers will be broken down, and in which learning and the pursuit of knowledge will be regarded as public trusts exercised for the benefit of society.

But as yet our education has not found itself; the stream has not reached port and the ocean. It has left behind traditional education; it can never return to its source. It has to meet the problems of today, and of the future, not of the past. The stream just now has gathered up a good deal of debris from the shores which it has flooded; it tends to divide and lose itself in a number of streams. It is still dammed at spots by barriers erected in past generations. But it has within itself the power of creating a free experimental intelligence that will do the necessary work of this complex and distracted world in which we and every other modern people have to live.

Progressive Education and the Science of Education (1928)

WHAT IS PROGRESSIVE EDUCATION? What is the meaning of experiment in education, of an experimental school? What can such schools as are represented here do for other schools, in which the great, indefinitely the greater, number of children receive their instruction and discipline? What can be rightfully expected from the work of these progressive schools in the way of a contribution to intelligent and stable educational practice; especially what can be expected in the way of a contribution to educational theory? Are there common elements, intellectual and moral, in the various undertakings here represented? Or is each school going its own way, having for its foundation the desires and preferences of the particular person who happens to be in charge? Is experimentation a process of trying anything at least once, of putting into immediate effect any "happy thought" that comes to mind, or does it rest upon principles which are adopted at least as a working hypothesis? Are actual results consistently observed and used to check an underlying hypothesis so that the latter develops intellectually? Can we be content if from the various progressive schools there emanate suggestions which radiate to other schools to enliven and vitalize their work; or should we demand that out of the cooperative undertakings of the various schools a coherent body of educational principles shall gradually emerge as a distinctive contribution to the theory of education?

Such questions as these come to mind on the occasion of such a gathering as this. The interrogations expressed are far from all inclusive. They are one-sided, and intentionally so. They glide over the important questions that may be asked about what these schools are actually doing for the children who attend them; how they are meeting their primary responsibility—that to the children

First published in pamphlet form by the Progressive Education Association from an address given to the Association at its Eighth Annual Conference, New York, 8 March 1928.

themselves and their families and friends. The one-sided emphasis is, as was said, intentional. The questions are shaped to take another slant; to direct attention to the intellectual contribution to be expected of progressive schools. The reasons for this one-sidedness are close at hand. It is natural that in your own exchange of experiences and ideas the question slurred over should be prominent. And that pupils in progressive schools are themselves progressing, and that the movement to establish more progressive schools is progressing, I have no doubt. Nor do I think that the old question, once a bugaboo, as to what will happen when the pupils go to college or out into life, is any longer an open one. Experience has proved that they give a good account of themselves; so it has seemed to me that the present is a fitting time to raise the intellectual, the theoretical problem of the relation of the progressive movement to the art and philosophy of education.

The query as to common elements in the various schools receives an easy answer up to a certain point. All of the schools, I take it for granted, exhibit as compared with traditional schools, a common emphasis upon respect for individuality and for increased freedom; a common disposition to build upon the nature and experience of the boys and girls that come to them, instead of imposing from without external subject-matter and standards. They all display a certain atmosphere of informality, because experience has proved that formalization is hostile to genuine mental activity and to sincere emotional expression and growth. Emphasis upon activity as distinct from passivity is one of the common factors. And again I assume that there is in all of these schools a common unusual attention to the human factors, to normal social relations, to communication and intercourse which is like in kind to that which is found in the great world beyond the school doors; that all alike believe that these normal human contacts of child with child and of child with teacher are of supreme educational importance, and that all alike disbelieve in those artificial personal relations which have been the chief factor in isolation of schools from life. So much at least of common spirit and purpose we may assume to exist. And in so far we already have the elements of a distinctive contribution to the body of educational theory: respect for individual capacities, interests and experience; enough external freedom and informality at least to enable teachers to become acquainted with children as they really are; respect for self-initiated and self-conducted learning; respect for activity as the stimulus and centre of learning; and perhaps above all belief in social contact, communication, and cooperation upon a normal human plane as all-enveloping medium.

These ideas constitute no mean contribution: It is a contribution to educational theory as well as to the happiness and integrity of those who come under the influence of progressive schools. But the elements of the contribution are general, and like all generalities subject to varied and ambiguous interpretations.

They indicate the starting point of the contribution that progressive schools may make to the theory or science of education, but only the starting point. Let us then reduce our questions to a single one and ask, What is the distinctive relation of progressive education to the science of education, understanding by science a body of verified facts and tested principles which may give intellectual guidance to the practical operating of schools?

Unless we beg the question at the outset assuming that it is already known just what education is, just what are its aims and what are its methods, there is nothing false nor extravagant in declaring that at the present time different sciences of education are not only possible but also much needed. Of course such a statement goes contrary to the idea that science by its very nature is a single and universal system of truths. But this idea need not frighten us. Even in the advanced sciences, like those of mathematics and physics, advance is made by entertaining different points of view and hypotheses, and working upon different theories. The sciences present no fixed and closed orthodoxy.

And certainly in such an undertaking as education, we must employ the word "science" modestly and humbly; there is no subject in which the claim to be strictly scientific is more likely to suffer from pretence, and none in which it is more dangerous to set up a rigid orthodoxy, a standardized set of beliefs to be accepted by all. Since there is no one thing which is, beyond question, education, and since there is no likelihood that there will be until society and hence schools have reached a dead monotonous uniformity of practice and aim, there cannot be one single science. As the working operations of schools differ, so must the intellectual theories devised from those operations. Since the practice of progressive education differs from that of the traditional schools, it would be absurd to suppose that the intellectual formulation and organization which fits one type will hold for the other. To be genuine, the science which springs from schools of the older and traditional type, must work upon that foundation, and endeavor to reduce its subject-matter and methods to principles such that their adoption will eliminate waste, conserve resources, and render the existing type of practice more effective. In the degree in which progressive schools mark a departure in their emphasis from old standards, as they do in freedom, individuality, activity, and a cooperative social medium the intellectual organization, the body of facts and principles which they may contribute must of necessity be different. At most they can only occasionally borrow from the "science" that is evolved on the basis of a different type of practice, and they can even then borrow only what is appropriate to their own special aims and processes. To discover how much is relevant is of course a real problem. But this is a very different thing from assuming that the methods and results obtained under traditional scholastic conditions form the standard of science to which progressive schools must conform.

For example it is natural and proper that the theory of the practises found in traditional schools should set great store by tests and measurements. This theory reflects modes of school administration in which marks, grading, classes, and promotions are important. Measurement of IQs and achievements are ways of making these operations more efficient. It would not be hard to show that need for classification underlies the importance of testing for IQs. The aim is to establish a norm. The norm, omitting statistical refinements, is essentially an average found by taking a sufficiently large number of persons. When this average is found, any given child can be rated. He comes up to it, falls below it, or exceeds it, by an assignable quantity. Thus the application of the results make possible a more precise classification than did older methods which were by comparison hit and miss. But what has all this to do with schools where individuality is a primary object of consideration, and wherein the so-called "class" becomes a grouping for social purposes and wherein diversity of ability and experience rather than uniformity is prized?

In the averaging and classificatory scheme some special capacity, say in music, dramatics, drawing, mechanical skill or any other art, appears only one along with a large number of other factors, or perhaps does not appear at all in the list of things tested. In any case, it figures in the final result only as smoothed down, ironed out, against a large number of other factors. In the progressive school, such an ability is a distinctive resource to be utilized in the cooperative experience of a group; to level it down by averaging it with other qualities until it simply counts in assigning to the individual child a determinate point on a curve is simply hostile to the aim and spirit of progressive schools.

Nor need the progressive educator be unduly scared by the idea that science is constituted by quantitative results, and, as it is often said, that whatever exists can be measured, for all subjects pass through a qualitative stage before they arrive at a quantitative one; and if this were the place it could be shown that even in the mathematical sciences quantity occupies a secondary place as compared with ideas of order which verge on the qualitative. At all events, quality of activity and of consequence is more important for the teacher than any quantitative element. If this fact prevents the development of a certain kind of science, it may be unfortunate. But the educator cannot sit down and wait till there are methods by which quality may be reduced to quantity; he must operate here and now. If he can organize his qualitative processes and results into some connected intellectual form, he is really advancing scientific method much more than if, ignoring what is actually most important, he devotes his energies to such unimportant by-products as may now be measured.

Moreover, even if it be true that everything which exists could be measured—if only we knew how—that which does not exist cannot be measured. And it is no paradox to say that the teacher is deeply concerned with what does not exist.

For a progressive school is primarily concerned with growth, with a moving and changing process, with transforming existing capacities and experiences; what already exists by way of native endowment and past achievement is subordinate to what it may become. Possibilities are more important than what already exists, and knowledge of the latter counts only in its bearing upon possibilities. The place of measurement of achievements as a theory of education is very different in a static educational system from what it is in one which is dynamic, or in which the ongoing process of growing is the important thing.

The same principle applies to the attempt to determine objectives and select subject-matter of studies by wide collection and accurate measurement of data. If we are satisfied upon the whole with the aims and processes of existing society, this method is appropriate. If you want schools to perpetuate the present order, with at most an elimination of waste and with such additions as enable it to do better what it is already doing, then one type of intellectual method or "science" is indicated. But if one conceives that a social order different in quality and direction from the present is desirable and that schools should strive to educate with social change in view by producing individuals not complacent about what already exists, and equipped with desires and abilities to assist in transforming it, quite a different method and content is indicated for educational science.

While what has been said may have a tendency to relieve educators in progressive schools from undue anxiety about the criticism that they are unscientific—a criticism levelled from the point of view of theory appropriate to schools of quite a different purpose and procedure—it is not intended to exempt them from responsibility for contributions of an organized, systematic, intellectual quality. The contrary is the case. All new and reforming movements pass through a stage in which what is most evident is a negative phase, one of protest, of deviation, and innovation. It would be surprising indeed if this were not true of the progressive educational movement. For instance, the formality and fixity of traditional schools seemed oppressive, restrictive. Hence in a school which departs from these ideals and methods, freedom is at first most naturally conceived as removal of artificial and benumbing restrictions. Removal, abolition are, however, negative things, so in time it comes to be seen that such freedom is no end in itself, nothing to be satisfied with and to stay by, but marks at most an opportunity to do something of a positive and constructive sort.

Now I wonder whether this earlier and more negative phase of progressive education has not upon the whole run its course, and whether the time has not arrived in which these schools are undertaking a more constructively organized function. One thing is sure: in the degree in which they enter upon organized constructive work, they are bound to make definite contributions to building up the theoretical or intellectual side of education. Whether this be called science or philosophy of education, I for one, care little; but if they do not intellectually organize their own work, while they may do much in making the lives of the children committed to them more joyous and more vital, they contribute only incidental scraps to the science of education.

The word organization has been freely used. This word suggests the nature of the problem. Organization and administration are words associated together in the traditional scheme, hence organization conveys the idea of something external and set. But reaction from this sort of organization only creates a demand for another sort. Any genuine intellectual organization is flexible and moving, but it does not lack its own internal principles of order and continuity. An experimental school is under the temptation to improvise its subject-matter. It must take advantage of unexpected events and turn to account unexpected questions and interests. Yet if it permits improvisation to dictate its course, the result is a jerky, discontinuous movement which works against the possibility of making any important contribution to educational subject-matter. Incidents are momentary, but the use made of them should not be momentary or short-lived. They are to be brought within the scope of a developing whole of content and purpose, which is a whole because it has continuity and consecutiveness in its parts. There is no single subject-matter which all schools must adopt, but in every school there should be some significant subject-matters undergoing growth and formulation.

An illustration may help make clearer what is meant. Progressive schools set store by individuality, and sometimes it seems to be thought that orderly orga-nization of subject-matter is hostile to the needs of students in their individual character. But individuality is something developing and to be continuously attained, not something given all at once and ready-made. It is found only in life-history, in its continuing growth; it is, so to say, a career and not just a fact discoverable at a particular cross section of life. It is quite possible for teachers to make such a fuss over individual children, worrying about their peculiari-ties, their likes and dislikes, their weaknesses and failures, so that they miss perception of real individuality, and indeed tend to adopt methods which show no faith in the power of individuality. A child's individuality cannot be found in what he does or in what he consciously likes at a given moment; it can be found only in the connected course of his actions. Consciousness of desire and purpose can be genuinely attained only toward the close of some fairly prolonged sequence of activities. Consequently some organization of subject-matter reached through a serial or consecutive course of doings, held together within the unity of progressively growing occupation or project, is the only means which corresponds to real individuality. So far is organization from being hostile to the principle of individuality.

Thus much of the energy that sometimes goes to thinking about individual children might better be devoted to discovering some worthwhile activity and to arranging the conditions under which it can be carried forward. As a child engages in this consecutive and cumulative occupation, then in the degree in which it contains valuable subject-matter, the realization or building up of his individuality comes about as a consequence, one might truly say, as a natural by-product. He finds and develops himself in what he does, not in isolation but by interaction with the conditions which contain and carry subject-matter. Moreover a teacher can find out immensely more about the real needs, desires, interests, capacities, and weaknesses of a pupil by observing him throughout the course of such consecutive activity than by any amount of direct prodding or of merely cross-sectional observation. And all observations are of necessity cross-sectional when made of a child engaged in a succession of disconnected activities.

Such a succession of unrelated activities does not provide, of course, the opportunity or content of building up an organized subject-matter. But neither do they provide for the development of a coherent and integrated self. Bare doing, no matter how active, is not enough. An activity or project must, of course, be within the range of the experience of pupils and connected with their needs—which is very far from being identical with any likes or desires which they can consciously express. This negative condition having been met, the test of a good project is whether it is sufficiently full and complex to demand a variety of responses from different children and permit each to go at it and make his contribution in a way which is characteristic of himself. The further test or mark of a good activity, educationally speaking, is that it have a sufficiently long time-span so that a series of endeavors and explorations are involved in it, and included in such a way that each step opens up a new field, raises new questions, arouses a demand for further knowledge, and suggests what to do next on the basis of what has been accomplished and the knowledge thereby gained. Occupational activities which meet these two conditions will of necessity result in not only amassing known subject-matter but in its organization. They simply cannot be carried on without resulting in some orderly collection and systematization of related facts and principles. So far is the principle of working toward organization of knowledge not hostile to the principles of progressive education that the latter cannot perform its functions without reaching out into such organization.

An exaggerated illustration, amounting to a caricature, may perhaps make the point clearer. Suppose there is a school in which pupils are surrounded with a wealth of material objects, apparatus, and tools of all sorts. Suppose they are simply asked what they would like to do and then told in effect to "go to it," the teacher keeping hands—and mind, too—off. What are they going to do? What assurance is there that what they do is anything more than the expression, and exhaustion, of a momentary impulse and interest? The supposition does not, you may say, correspond to any fact. But what are the implications of the opposite principle? Where can we stop as we get away from the principle contained in the illustration? Of necessity—and this is as true of the traditional school as of a progressive—the start, the first move, the initial impulse in action, must proceed from the pupil. You can lead a horse to water but you can't make him drink. But whence comes his idea of what to do? That must come from what he has already heard or seen; or from what he sees some other child doing. It comes as a suggestion from beyond himself, from the environment, he being not an originator of the idea and purpose but a vehicle through which his surroundings past and present suggest something to him. That such suggestions are likely to be chance ideas, soon exhausted, is highly probable. I think observation will show that when a child enters upon a really fruitful and consecutively developing activity, it is because, and in as far as, he has previously engaged in some complex and gradually unfolding activity which has left him with a question he wishes to prove further or with the idea of some piece of work still to be accomplished to bring his occupation to completion. Otherwise he is at the mercy of chance suggestion, and chance suggestions are not likely to lead to anything significant or fruitful.

While in outward form, these remarks are given to show that the teacher, as the member of the group having the riper and fuller experience and the greater insight into the possibilities of continuous development found in any suggested project, has not only the right but the duty to suggest lines of activity, and to show that there need not be any fear of adult imposition provided the teacher knows children as well as subjects, their import is not exhausted in bringing out this fact. Their basic purport is to show that progressive schools by virtue of being progressive, and not in spite of that fact, are under the necessity of finding projects which involve an orderly development and inter-connection of subject-matter, since otherwise there can be no sufficiently complex and long-span undertaking. The opportunity and the need impose a responsibility. Progressive teachers may and can work out and present to other teachers for trial and criticism definite and organized bodies of knowledge, together with a listing of sources from which additional information of the same sort can be secured. If it is asked how the presentation of such bodies of knowledge would differ from the standardized texts of traditional schools, the answer is easy. In the first place, the material would be associated with and derived from occupational activities or prolonged courses of action undertaken by the pupils themselves. In the second place, the material presented would not be something to be literally followed by other teachers and students, but would be indications of the intellectual possibilities of this and that course of activity—statements on the basis of carefully directed and observed experience of the questions that have arisen in connection with them and of the kind of information found useful in answering them, and of where that knowledge can be had. No second experience would exactly duplicate the course of the first; but the presentation of material of this kind would liberate and direct the activities of any teacher in dealing with the distinctive emergencies and needs that would arise in re-undertaking the same general type of project. Further material thus developed would be added, and a large and yet free body of related subject-matter would gradually be built up.

As I have touched in a cursory manner upon the surface of a number of topics, it may be well in closing to summarize. In substance, the previous discussion has tried to elicit at least two contributions which progressive schools may make to that type of a science of education which corresponds to their own type of procedure. One is the development of organized subject-matter just spoken of. The other is a study of the conditions favorable to learning. As I have already said there are certain traits characteristic of progressive schools which are not ends in themselves but which are opportunities to be used. These reduce themselves to opportunities for learning, for gaining knowledge, mastering definite modes of skill or techniques, and acquiring socially desirable attitudes and habits—the three chief aspects of learning, I should suppose. Now of necessity the contribution from the side of traditional schools to this general topic is concerned chiefly with methods of teaching, or, if it passes beyond that point, to the methods of study adopted by students. But from the standpoint of progressive education, the question of method takes on a new and still largely untouched form. It is no longer a question of how the teacher is to instruct or how the pupil is to study. The problem is to find what conditions must be fulfilled in order that study and learning will naturally and necessarily take place, what conditions must be present so that pupils will make the responses which cannot help having learning as their consequence. The pupil's mind is no longer to be on study or learning. It is given to doing the things that the situation calls for, while learning is the result. The method of the teacher, on the other hand, becomes a matter of finding the conditions which call out self-educative activity, or learning, and of cooperating with the activities of the pupils so that they have learning as their consequence.

A series of constantly multiplying careful reports on conditions which experience has shown in actual cases to be favorable and unfavorable to learning would revolutionize the whole subject of method. The problem is complex and difficult. Learning involves, as just said, at least three factors: knowledge, skill, and character. Each of these must be studied. It requires judgment and art to select from the total circumstances of a case just what elements are the causal conditions of learning, which are influential, and which secondary or irrelevant. It requires candor and sincerity to keep track of failures as well as successes and to estimate the relative degree of success obtained. It requires trained and acute observation to note the indications of progress in learning, and even more to detect their causes—a much more highly skilled kind of observation than is needed to note the results of mechanically applied tests. Yet the progress of a science of education depends upon the systematic accumulation of just this sort of material. Solution of the problem of discovering the causes of learning is an endless process. But no advance will be made in the solution till a start is made, and the freer and more experimental character of progressive schools places the responsibility for making the start squarely upon them.

I hardly need remind you that I have definitely limited the field of discussion to one point: the relation of progressive education to the development of a science of education. As I began with questions, I end with one: Is not the time here when the progressive movement is sufficiently established so that it may now consider the intellectual contribution which it may make to the art of education, to the art which is the most difficult and the most important of all human arts?

Dewey Outlines Utopian Schools (1933)

THE MOST UTOPIAN THING IN Utopia is that there are no schools at all. Education is carried on without anything of the nature of schools, or, if this idea is so extreme that we cannot conceive of it as educational at all, then we may say nothing of the sort at present we know as schools. Children, however, are gathered together in association with older and more mature people who direct their activity.

The assembly places all have large grounds, gardens, orchards, greenhouses, and none of the buildings in which children and older people gather will hold much more than 200 people, this having been found to be about the limits of close, intimate personal acquaintance on the part of people who associate together.

And inside these buildings, which are all of them of the nature of our present open-air schools in their physical structure, there are none of the things we usually associate with our present schools. Of course, there are no mechanical rows of screwed-down desks. There is rather something like a well-furnished home of today, only with a much greater variety of equipment and no messy accumulations of all sorts of miscellaneous furniture; more open spaces than our homes have today.

Then there are the workshops, with their apparatus for carrying on activities with all kinds of material—wood, iron, textiles. There are historic museums and scientific laboratories, and books everywhere as well as a central library.

The adults who are most actively concerned with the young have, of course, to meet a certain requirement, and the first thing that struck me as a visitor to Utopia was that they must all be married persons and, except in exceptional cases, must have had children of their own. Unmarried, younger persons occupy

First published in *New York Times*, 23 April 1933, Education section, p. 7, from an address on 21 April 1933 to the Conference on the Educational Status of the Four- and Five-Year-Old Child at Teachers College, Columbia University.

places of assistance and serve a kind of initiatory apprenticeship. Moreover, older children, since there are no arbitrary divisions into classes, take part in directing the activities of those still younger.

The activity of these older children may be used to illustrate the method by which those whom we would call teachers are selected. It is almost a method of self-selection. For instance, the children aged say from about 13 to 18 who are especially fond of younger children are given the opportunity to consort with them. They work with the younger children under observation, and then it soon becomes evident who among them have the taste, interest and the kind of skill which is needed for effective dealing with the young.

As their interest in the young develops, their own further education centres more and more about the study of processes of growth and development, and so there is a very similar process of natural selection by which parents are taken out of the narrower contact with their own children in the homes and are brought forward in the educational nurture of larger numbers of children.

The work of these educational groups is carried on much as painters were trained in, say, Italy, when painting was at its height. The adult leaders, through their previous experience and by the manner of their selection, combine special knowledge of children with special gifts in certain directions.

They associate themselves with the young in carrying on some line of action. Just as in these older studios younger people were apprentices who observed the elders and took part along with them in doing at first some of the simpler things and then, as they got more experience, engaged directly in the more complex forms of activity, so in these directed activities in these centres the older people are first engaged in carrying on some work in which they themselves are competent, whether painting or music or scientific inquiry, observation of nature or industrial cooperation in some line. Then the younger children, watching them, listening to them, begin taking part in the simpler forms of the action—a minor part, until as they develop they accept more and more responsibility for cooperating.

Naturally I inquired what were the purposes, or, as we say now, the objectives, of the activities carried on in these centres. At first nothing puzzled me more than the fact that my inquiry after objectives was not at all understood, for the whole concept of the school, of teachers and pupils and lessons, had so completely disappeared that when I asked after the special objectives of the activity of these centres, my Utopian friends thought I was asking why children should live at all, and therefore they did not take my questions seriously.

After I made them understand what I meant, my question was dismissed with the remark that since children were alive and growing, "of course, we, as the Utopians, try to make their lives worth while to them; of course, we try to see that they really do grow, that they really develop." But as for having any objective beyond the process of a developing life, the idea still seemed to them quite silly. The notion that there was some special end which the young should try to attain was completely foreign to their thoughts.

By observation, however, I was led to the conclusion that what we would regard as the fundamental purposes were thoroughly ingrained in the working of the activities themselves. In our language it might be said to be the discovery of the aptitudes, the tastes, the abilities and the weaknesses of each boy and girl, and then to develop their positive capacities into attitudes and to arrange and reinforce the positive powers so as not to cover up the weak points but to offset them.

I inquired, having a background of our own schools in mind, how with their methods they ever made sure that the children and youth really learned anything, how they mastered the subject matter, geography and arithmetic and history, and how they ever were sure that they really learned to read and write and figure. Here, too, at first I came upon a blank wall. For they asked, in return to my question, whether in the period from which I came for a visit to Utopia it was possible for a boy or girl who was normal physiologically to grow up without learning the things which he or she needed to learn—because it was evident to them that it was not possible for any one except a congenital idiot to be born and to grow up without learning.

When they discovered, however, that I was serious, they asked whether it was true that in our day we had to have schools and teachers and examinations to make sure that babies learned to walk and to talk.

It was during these conversations that I learned to appreciate how completely the whole concept of acquiring and storing away things had been displaced by the concept of creating attitudes by shaping desires and developing the needs that are significant in the process of living.

The Utopians believed that the pattern which exists in economic society in our time affected the general habits of thought; that because personal acquisition and private possession were such dominant ideals in all fields, even if unconsciously so, they had taken possession of the minds of educators to the extent that the idea of personal acquisition and possession controlled the whole educational system.

They pointed not merely to the use in our schools of the competitive methods of appeal to rivalry and the use of rewards and punishments, of set examinations and the system of promotion, but they also said that all these things were merely incidental expressions of the acquisitive system of society and the kind of measure and test of achievement and success which had to prevail in an acquisitive type of society.

So it was that we had come to regard all study as simply a method of acquiring something, even if only useless or remote facts, and thought of learning and scholarship as the private possession of the resulting acquisition. And the social change which had taken place with the abolition of an acquisitive economic society had, in their judgment, made possible the transformation of the centre of emphasis from learning (in our sense) to the creation of attitudes.

They said that the great educational liberation came about when the concept of external attainments was thrown away and when they started to find out what each individual person had in him from the very beginning, and then devoted themselves to finding out the conditions of the environment and the kinds of activity in which the positive capacities of each young person could operate most effectually.

In setting creation, productivity, over against acquiring, they said that there was no genuine production without enjoyment. They imagined that the ethics of education in the older period had been that enjoyment in education always had to be something deferred; that the motto of the schools, at least, was that man never is, but always is to be, blest; while the only education that really could discover and elicit power was one which brought these powers for immediate use and enjoyment.

Naturally, I inquired what attitudes they regarded as most important to create, since the formation of attitudes had taken the place with the young of the acquisition of information. They had some difficulty in ranking attitudes in any order of importance, because they were so occupied with an all-around development of the capacities of the young. But, through observation, I should say that they ranked the attitude which would give a sense of positive power as at least as basic and primary as the others, if not more so.

This attitude which resulted in a sense of positive power involved, of course, elimination of fear, of embarrassment, of constraint, of self-consciousness; eliminated the conditions which created the feeling of failure and incapacity. Possibly it included the development of a confidence, of readiness to tackle difficulties, of actual eagerness to seek problems instead of dreading them and running away from them. It included a rather ardent faith in human capacity. It included a faith in the capacity of the environment to support worthwhile activities, provided the environment was approached and dealt with in the right way.

What Is Learning? (1937)

TO DISCOVER THE REALITY BEHIND such educational terms as study, teaching, learning, reference to their meaning in outside life will be helpful. How then does the professional or business man or other adult learn and, as judged by these, what conditions are most favorable to learning?

Occupation implies consecutive activity bringing man into contact with materials, instrumentalities, and persons. For success there must be constant observation, reflection, and search for new information. Learning is the product of the exercise of powers needed to meet the demands of the activity in operation. Consideration of the qualifications necessary in the physician and of his actual activities shows that he is not merely externally busy but that his faculties are always on the alert, sharpened by constant use, and that he is constantly enlarging his information. His primary aim is to do his work better, but learning is a necessary accompaniment, the more so as being largely the unconscious effect of other acts and experiences. To the pupil in school the knowledge that he is, or should be, studying actually distracts his attention from his work.

It may be urged that the child has no parallel occupation, but he has various urgent lines of activity corresponding in function if not in contents. They are less unified and organized though, in fact, most adults have more than one axis of activity. The young, however, have to find their way about and become at home in a complex world, and to do so must learn by experiments their own powers and the uses of these. Nor are their activities sporadic and dispersed; their separate acts are linked along a number of axes. An infant is urged to do a number of things involving ordered procession in time. No one operation is a single disconnected act. All are accomplishments demanding a continuous knitting together of individual doings in a sequence moving steadily forward in

First published as part of chapter 4, "Curriculum Problems," in *Educational Adaptations in a Changing Society*, ed. E. G. Malherbe (Capetown and Johannesburg: Juta and Co., 1937), 91–93.

a given direction. The impetus that threads the impulses together until definite abilities or habits emerge comes from an inner, though unconscious, purpose as truly as do the actions of the adult.

In no three later years of life does any human being learn as much as in the first three years of infancy. If we realize the complexity of the task, its obstacles, and its seemingly slight equipment, the achievements of standing, walking, talking, are by comparison with those of the adult marvelous.

Analysis of this spontaneous learning in the young shows the presence of "active needs," which are not conscious purposes but none the less dynamic moving forces. Needs are not merely negative—lacks awaiting external satisfaction, but positive—actually searching for the materials which will bring satisfaction. Hunger is not merely emptiness but also active uneasiness, seeing implies hunger for light or color, hearing implies hunger for sound, reaching implies hunger for contact. A need is thus a demand working unceasingly for its own satisfaction, which can only be met by external objects and forces. External stimulus does not come first; outgoing activity seeks for this and decides whether this or that will stimulate further activity. An adult ignores events around him, if they do not bear upon his immediate activity, and the difficulty of distracting an infant from some object which it has at heart brings the lesson home still more clearly.

In learning then first, in time and importance, is an inner pressure in some direction which constitutes the reality of need. The infant learns so rapidly because his needs are so intense and of such a nature that surrounding things naturally and almost inevitably provide means of satisfaction and hence of that continual forward movement or growth which is learning. An adult may wonder at the fascination to a child of the repetition of some process of noise-making, which is really only the way in which, in response to his inner urge and demand, he learns the properties of things and the nature and meaning of his own powers and acts.

A second need in learning, then, is the existence of materials and objects, or means of realizing impulses. Environment takes us to a certain point, possibly a minimum if we observed carefully dawning activities and gave conscious thought to provision of conditions which would evoke a graded series of new stages of behavior to be mastered. Growth, however, comes as infant activities prompted by inward pressure make contact with external conditions which make possible their successful exercise.

In the third place, in the infant the criterion of success is internal rather than external. Satisfaction is personal; an unaided success in an attempt to stand or walk gives the sense of elation in accomplishment and victory, and this same sense of progressive achievement is the motive power which, joined to need, will carry the child on to greater external perfection of execution.

In school education on the other hand there is comparative neglect of the element of inner need, as is shown in the external imposition and authority exercised without reference to such need. The parent, however, does not leave the hungry infant to forage for himself, and it is for the teacher to cooperate with the child's needs to enable him to achieve execution and satisfaction to the maximum of fulfilment possible.

A more common error is the assumption that there is one set body of subject matter and of skills to be presented to the young, only requiring to be presented to and "learned" by the child, whose failure to meet the material supplied is attributed to his own incapacity or wilfulness, not to failure of the educator to understand what needs are stirring him.

A comparison between the natural processes of learning to speak and to understand the speech of others and the old methods of teaching reading and writing is instructive. In the better modern schools great progress has been achieved by wise and ingenious teachers in assimilating the process of learning to read to that of acquiring ability to talk by finding the occasions and creating the situations in which the pupil finds a need and a satisfaction in meeting this.

Even in the home the negative aspects of behavior and failure are apt to be stressed with the result that fear to try new modes of action is induced, while, if failures are passed over lightly and a line of action, involving some measure of difficulty, is provided in which the child can make progress and have the glow of positive achievement, he will be better enabled to develop his own intimate standards of achievement. Standards of external accomplishment tend to the laying of stress on failure which breeds lack of confidence, while stress on external good achievement fosters conceit and pride, which also arrest development.

The presence of objects which respond naturally to activities leads to intelligence and purpose. The formalities of the old class-room are artificial and develop the truant disposition which also operates through exercise with an adequate variety of materials. At the same time, while the materials must be of the right kind, they must not be so numerous as to lead to distraction or confusion nor shut out opportunity for seeing the needs for further instruments to carry an activity further and the demand for constructive imagination and manual skill in supplying what is needed.

This implies that there must be selection and organization, not haphazard provision, of material for the young. There must be variety to meet different capacities, and plans of work must be sufficiently worked out to prevent casual flitting from one thing to another. The child is not consciously aware of what he wants, and the educator by careful study must judge the dominant and enduring needs as distinct from passing whims which the child might, in response to direct enquiry, state as his wants.

Learning under these conditions is an inevitable result. In the learner it is a product rather than a conscious aim, to the teacher it is an aim but to be realized on defined principles. In teaching effects follow causes, and the attempt to get the effect without first setting up the conditions may at best meet with accidental success but at the worst leads to loss of time, dissipation of energy, dulling of curiosity, and establishment of corrupting and weakening habits.

The character of activity changes as development matures. In early years it is mainly direct and, as viewed from without, is largely physical. Gradually it becomes more indirect as imagination, stimulated by intercourse with others and informed by communications of ideas and facts, plays a greater part. In later years reflective thought operating by artificial symbols plays the larger part, but all three elements, though the proportion varies, are involved in all stages of development. The ratio varies in different individuals and the teacher must realize this fact and be guided accordingly, whereas in the past the schools have provided mainly for those to whom activity along the road of symbols is congenial more adequately than for imaginative expression or concrete instruction, the individual thus suffering through thwarting of natural tendencies and the community losing through failure to turn to account distinctive talents. Too often only in later life does the individual find the conditions which make whole-hearted learning possible, conditions which all too many never find at all.

A well-balanced curriculum means, then, one in which there is adequate provision for all the elements of personality, for the manual and overtly constructive powers, for the imaginative and emotional tendencies that later take form in artistic expression, and for the factors that respond to symbolic statement and that prepare the way for distinctively abstract intellectual pursuits. A genuine school of learning is a community in which special aptitudes are gradually disclosed and the transition is made to later careers, in which individuals find happiness and society is richly and nobly served because individuals have learned to know and use their own powers.

Education, Direct and Indirect (1904)

THE OTHER DAY A PARENT of a little boy who recently entered our elementary school, after having been in a public school, told me that her son came to her and said, "I think we learn almost as much at that school as we did at the John Smith school—I believe, maybe, we learn more, only we have such a good time that we do not stop to think that we are learning anything." This story I tell to help illustrate the meaning of the term "indirect education." We have our choice between two methods. We may shape the conditions and direct the influences of school work so that pupils are forever reminded that they are pupils—that they are there to study lessons and do tasks. We may make the child conscious at every point that he is going to school, and that he goes to school to do something quite different from what he does anywhere else—namely, to learn. This is "direct education." Put in this bald way, however, the idea may well arouse some mental searchings of heart. Are we really willing to admit that the child does not learn anything outside of school—that he is not getting his education all the time by what he is thinking and feeling and doing, and in spite of the fact that his consciousness is not upon the fact that he is learning? This, then, is the other alternative—the child may be given something fixed up for purposes of learning it, and we may trust to the learning, instruction and training which results out of and along with this doing and inquiring for its own sake. This is "indirect education."

Having got thus far, we are ready to ask the question as to whether and how this indirect education has a place inside the school walls. Shall we show the door of the school as that kind of development which comes with doing things that are worth doing for their own sake, the growth that comes with contact with the realities of the physical and social world, which is had for the sake of

First published in *Progressive Journal of Education* 2 (1909): 31–38, from an address at the Francis W. Parker School, Chicago, January 1904.

the fullness and reality of the contact? Shall we frame our school in such a way that the child is perpetually and insistently reminded that here is the place where he comes to learn things, to study, to get and recite lessons?

Before trying to answer this question, let us ask some of the ways in which we succeed in making so prominent, so overpowering in the consciousness of the child, the fact that in school he is undergoing education. I begin with one of the most obvious aspects of the matter, not because it is so very important in itself, but because it is such an admirable symbol and index of what lies back. I refer to all of the school machinery that hinges around the giving of marks—the eternal presence of the record book, the never-absent consciousness on the part of the child that he is to be marked for the poorness or goodness of his lesson, the sending home of graded reports upon purely conventional, mathematical or alphabetical schemes, the comparing by the children of their respective grades and all the scheming (sometimes cheating) thereby called forth.

That acute humorist who wrote under the name of John Phoenix tells a story of how he became disgusted with the inaccuracy of our descriptive language, having in mind such terms as little, remarkably, exceedingly, etc., etc., and evolved a scheme, which he thought would meet the whole difficulty, of substituting a decimal system of notation. The idea was that instead of saying that it was a moderately fine day, one would say that the weather was about 53 per cent good, while a particularly fine sunset might be described as a 95 per cent sunset. He goes on to say that, much elated with his project, he submitted it to his wife, who replied that she thought it was a fine scheme, and that she would put it in operation by telling him that he was a 99 per cent idiot.

I do not know whether this was intended as a caricature of the methods of our schools or not, but it may stand as a parody. Suppose we were to watch the child at his sports and games, and not having any confidence in an inherent development of power and knowledge through the very experience, thought it necessary to accentuate in his mind the fact that he had something to learn by giving him a mark of 60 per cent upon his game of marbles, and marking him "A" for his excellence in baseball. Suppose we tried to apply the same scheme to what the child gets from his daily conversation with older people; to the results accruing from the necessity he is under of adapting his modes of behavior to the demands of the social circle in which he lives and moves and has his being; suppose when our boy comes home fresh and elated from what he has seen in the park, or from a trip to the country, that after seeing his interest expressed by his telling, in his animated way, of his experiences, we were under obligation to decide that he was entitled to 82 per cent upon his accuracy of observation, while we should be compelled to give him not above 60 per cent upon his grammatical accuracy—all this so that he might be tested upon his growth or stimulated to further learning!

This is so clearly ridiculous that it may seem extremely unfair to the marking system in the schools. But what I want to point out is that the marking system implies as a fundamental and unquestionable axiom that the actual subject-matter with which the child is engaged, and the responsive play of his own emotional and mental activities upon it, do not suffice to supply educative motive and material—that over and above them some further stimulus in the way of an externally imposed conventional scheme of rating is required to keep attention fixed upon the importance of learning.

Now this assumption that education is not natural and attractive—inherently so—reacts most disastrously upon the responsibility of both the teacher and the child. Human nature being what it is, any teacher who works under the conditions imposed by considering the school just as a place to learn lessons, comes to feel that he has done his whole duty by the individual (so far as judging and estimating the work and worth of that individual is concerned) when he has, after full and impartial investigation as possible, given that student his mark—i.e., determined his success in learning lessons. If some scheme had been intentionally devised in order to prevent the teacher from assuming the full responsibility he ought to feel for keeping constant watch and ward over the life of the child, for relating the child's work to his temperament, capacities, and to totality of influences operating him—if the scheme, I say, had been intentionally devised for relieving the teacher of the necessity of the most intimate and unremitting acquaintance with the child, nothing better could have been found.

I should not have the slightest hesitation in making the statement that, given two schools of otherwise equal conditions, in one of which the marking system prevailed, and in the other did not, the latter would in time possess the teachers who had the most thorough and sympathetic knowledge of all the children, both as to their weak points and their strong points. All the influences at work, unconscious as well as conscious, compel the teachers to know the individuals with whom they are dealing, and to judge not merely their external work, to consider fairly how it should rank between the letters A and E, or zero and 100, but to judge the individual himself as a living, struggling, failing and succeeding individual. In one case, the individual has to be known and judged in terms of his own unique self, unrepeatable in any other self; and in the last analysis, incomparable with any other self just because he is his own self. The other scheme permits and encourages the teacher to escape with the feeling that he has done his whole duty when he has impartially graded the external and dead product of such a personality.

The same tendency to lack of full responsibility imposes itself upon the children and spreads among them. I have seen a powerful indictment against the marking and examination system, as ordinarily conducted, to the effect that it sets up a false and demoralizing standard by which the students come to judge their own work. Instead of each one considering himself responsible for the highest excellency to which he can possibly attain, the tendency is to suppose that one is doing well enough if he comes up to the average expectation; and that, indeed, everything above the required pass mark is so much to the student's credit—representing a sort of accumulation of merit, which in case of an emergency justifies a falling off. The point here is a far-reaching one. I have sometimes heard arguments which imply that there is something particularly strenuous in the disciplinary ideals of rigid tests and marks, and that their surrender means the substitution of a less severe and exacting standard—that it is a part of what is sometimes called "soft pedagogy." As I see it, the exact contrary holds. Where there is a system which fastens upon learning set lessons, the student cannot be reasonably held up to the best of which he himself is capable. All but the obvious failures can point in justification of themselves to the fact that they have come up to the standard which the school itself has officially set. If the student has done what the school proclaims it exacts of him, what further right to blame him? The "average" is a false and demoralizing standard.

Please do not think I am over-concerned about marks. They are indeed an evil, yet not in themselves of supreme importance. But they externally symbolize what I have said about the situation in the schools where the learning of lessons is made the measure of education. Any standard which can be stated, which can be put in external form, is by the necessity of the case a mechanical and quantitative thing. It points out to students certain particular things which are to be done and certain particular things which are to be avoided. And it not only permits but encourages them to believe that the whole duty of man is done when just these special things have been performed, and just these special things avoided. Neither the intellectual nor moral standard of life is capable of any such restriction. What the laws of life demand of everyone is that he always do absolutely the best that he can under all circumstances. The only reasonable, and, in the long run, the only effective standard by which students should learn to judge their own work is whether they have developed the subject that is given them to the utmost; whether they have seen all in the subject of study that it is possible for them to see; and whether by engaging it with their full attention may have got out of it all gain or power which is possible. To let the student substitute the standard of "passing," of coming up to a certain external limit, is to let him off altogether too easily; and the worst of it is that this easy-going standard tends to become habitual—it radiates to other spheres of life and makes itself at home in them.

The marking system in itself is a minor matter. It is an effect rather than a cause; a symptom rather than an underlying disease. The root of the evil lies much deeper. The artificial division of subject-matter, and the assignment of particular chopped-off sections of it as tasks to be accomplished in the form of lessons, lies much nearer the centre of the evils of this "direct education." Subjects are first rigidly marked off from each other, and then this arbitrarily selected subject-matter is arranged so as to provide the material which will make the student most conscious that he has before him just and only something which is to be learned by him. The reality of experience, the substance of truth or beauty that may be involved, becomes a wholly secondary matter. The main thing is that so many lines or pages have been assigned for the next lesson, and that the educational work is judged not by the refinement and growth of the organ of vision which it brings, not by the strengthening of the hunger and thirst after what is fine and true, but by exhibition of the mastery of specific tasks assigned.

It ought not to be necessary to point to the crippling and paralysis that result. There is, after all, a presumption that there are certain great currents of truth and rightness flowing through all subject-matter which has any right to occupy a place in the school curriculum. It is true, is it not, that the universe is really a wonderful place, and that history is a record of all the absorbing struggles, failures and successes of human aspiration and endeavor? If this be true, are we doing quite the fair thing by either the world of nature or of history, or the child, the newcomer into this wonderful world, when we manage to present all this to him as if it constituted just so many lessons which for no very obvious and vital reason have to be learned? If it were not pathetic, it would make one smile to hear the argument used sometimes against having eager and alert interest play a part in the school room. The argument rests on supposing that interest is something which simply attaches to the child's side of the educational problem—as if the things in themselves, the realities of nature and human life and art through which the child receives his education, were themselves quite uninteresting or even repulsive! The purpose of the newer movement in education is not to make things interesting to the child by environing him with a sort of vaudeville divertisement, with all sorts of spectacular accompaniments. The aim is to permit the intrinsic wonder and value which attach to all the realities which lie behind the school curriculum to come home to the child, and to take him up and carry him on in their own onward sweep. It is true that we adults get too easily blasé, overcome by the mere routine of living, and somehow constitutionally distrustful of the surprising values that reside in the bare facts of living. But it requires, I think, an unusually hardened pessimism to assume that the universe of nature and society, which, after all, is the only thing which can form the material of studies and lessons, is without inherent inspiration and appeal to the child, or that the child, of all beings, is so made as to be dull and slow in responding to this appeal. Yet this is the assumption which underlies the treatment of the material of education as if it were something only fit to be given out in lessons and tasks—the assumption which underlies the notion that education is a purely and direct conscious process—conscious to him who receives as well as to him who gives. The simile of a friend who was herself a teacher always occurs to my mind. Education, she said, reminded her of nothing so much as a corpse. It was all so silent, composed and laid out, and so dead.

Here also I should resent the interpretation that that idea of education which believes in educating by bringing boy and girl into proper relations of contact and responsiveness to the things in experience which are best worth seeing and doing, represents a lowering of standards, a decrease of severity intellectually or morally. It is the converse which is true. The standard which the truth and order of the universe set up when they are given a fair chance, an open and free field, when they secure adequate access to the individual, is infinitely more exacting than the conventions which text-book and school teacher can manage to agree upon and to set up. The responsibility of responding to what is right and worthy is a much more significant thing than the responsibility for reciting a given lesson. And the influence of the teacher becomes much more real and lively when it takes the form of cooperating with the influences that proceed from occupations and subject-matter than when it is felt purely as an independent and direct source.

More particularly, "direct education" involves a low standard because it fixes the attention of pupils upon the demands which teacher and text-book make, instead of the demands of the subject-matter, moving in the medium of individual thought and endeavor. It substitutes the standard, "Have I got this well enough to recite today? What are the chances of my being called upon to recite today, anyway, since I recited yesterday?" for the standard of "What is there in this that is so real as to make it imperative that I rise to it and move along with it?" There is one inevitable tendency of treating subject-matter simply as lessons or tasks: the desires, wishes or real expectations of the teacher, the teacher's own peculiar interests, tastes and standards become the controlling element. For moral purposes it makes comparatively little difference whether the pupils look at these expectations and demands from the standpoint of seeing in how many cases and by what ingenious methods they may evade them and still go through the show of conformity, or whether (because of greater skill of the teacher, or what is called tact) the children devote themselves to measuring up in the most amiable way possible—and children rightly approached are amiable to the level of the teacher's methods and ideals. In either case, the children are getting set in external habits of morality, and are learning to find their centre of intellectual gravity outside their own selves.

I know by experience that even after we come to believe in certain modes of educational practice, because we find that in spite of our theories they actually work well with our own children, we are yet somewhat "hard of heart and slow to believe" in their underlying theory and ideals. I am reminded of a gentleman who used periodically to insist that his children be taken out of the school where the method that I have called indirect education was in vogue, and be sent to a school where they would really have to learn lessons (to work, as he called it), but who, after he had won his wife's assent, always ended by stating that although the theory of the thing was absurd and demoralizing, at just that time it seemed to be working so well that he thought they had better leave the children where they were a little longer. Indeed, the point of view is so relatively recent in educational practice that I think that even the most ardent believers in it need to at times remind themselves of its fundamental reasonableness, and of the basic realities upon which it rests. We need to remind ourselves that the newer types of study, the various forms of social occupations, the cooking, the shop work, weaving, music, painting and clay modeling, are not merely devices for making old studies more pleasing, nor for disguising the inherent disagreeableness they have for boys and girls, that they are not simply effective methods for getting children to study more and learn their lessons easier and better than they used to, but that they stand for something which is fundamentally moral. They stand for the belief that the only final educative force in the world is participation in the realities of life, and that these realities are inherently moral in effect. It is because the various studies and occupations, which play so prominent a part in what is called the new education, are just modes of participating in the moving forces of truth and rightness that they insist upon being made central in everything that has a right to be termed a school. When this centre is the heart of school life, I have no fears as to the quality of education that is the outcome.

The Need for Orientation (1935)

FOR ONE WHOSE LIFE HAS been given in one form or another to education, it is no gratification to say things that may be construed as an attack on our educational system. But we are living in a time when discriminating criticism is a necessary condition both for progress and for cashing in on the many good things that are already in the schools. And it is not teachers that are primarily criticized but the system under which they work. I am glad to believe there were never so many teachers in this country as there are now who are trained for their work and who are eager to improve themselves professionally. But the setup of the system distracts and confuses their minds as well as their work. It is to these things I shall refer.

The system is a system only by courtesy. In fact, it is more like a patchwork, and a patchwork whose pieces do not form a pattern. It is a patchwork of the old and the new; of unreconstructed survivals from the past and of things introduced because of new conditions. This statement applies equally to the things taught, the ways they are taught, the social control of the educational system, and its administration. In consequence, the new studies that have been introduced have split up the curriculum into unrelated parts and created congestion. There are too many studies and too many courses of study, and the result is confusion.

Return to the strict and narrow curriculum of the past is urged by some as a remedy. But there is no use in discussing its desirability, because it is impracticable. The forces of the modern world are here, and they are going to continue to act upon the schools. The demands of an industrialized and technological society cannot be ignored. The old education, even in this country, was a con-

First published in *Forum* 93 (June 1935): 333–35, as part 1 of a debate with Tyler Dennett entitled "Education and Our Society: A Debate."

tinuation or an imitation of an education designed for a small and select class. The number in high schools and colleges has increased sixfold and more in about a generation. This irruption is something unprecedented in the history of any nation. Its members proceed from those who do not have the background, traditions, or needs of the class to which the old system catered. New studies and courses are brought in as a response to their needs. But they are brought in piecemeal, without a unified aim. And the old studies persist, with little modification, side by side with the new ones. Only those pupils who have a strong natural bent come out with any clear idea either of their own capacities or of the world in which they are to live. The schools are a drift rather than a system.

The methods of discipline and instruction in such schools as are adequately supported have been revolutionized in a generation or so, and mostly for the better—though the rural schools in a large part of the country are still in a condition that should be a public scandal. There is much more recognition of the make-up of individuals and much more adaptation to individual needs than there used to be. But in our large cities, with their inhuman aggregations of students and their overstuffed classes, the change has affected the general spirit of the teaching much more than its actual impact upon students. Methods are still largely mechanical—even more so oftentimes than in many of the old, small rural schools. The worst thing is that, even in the schools where pupils are not treated as intellectual robots, their individual traits are stimulated more or less at haphazard, rather than directed.

It is certainly not the fault of teachers that so many of the recent graduates of the schools now find themselves at a tragic standstill, without an occupation and without prospect of one. It is not the fault of teachers that so many young men and women still in high schools and colleges find themselves in a state of painful and bewildering insecurity about the future. But it is the fault of the system that so many of these young persons have no intellectual legs of their own to stand upon, no sense of perspective by which to take their bearings, no insight into the causes of the economic and social breakdown, and no way of orienting themselves. It is bad enough to be without a job. The evil is increased when these young people find themselves with no clue to the situation in which they are to live and are at a loss intellectually and morally, as well as vocationally and industrially.

I do not mean that the schools should have prepared the young to understand the problems that baffle mature and experienced persons. But I do mean that education, if it is really education, should send them forth with some unified sense of the kind of world in which they live, the directions in which it is moving, and the part they have to play in it. The schools should have given them some sort of intellectual and moral key to their contemporary world. But the hodge-podge of studies pursued for so-called cultural, vocational, and disciplinary aims (that conflict moreover with one another) and by methods that in part appeal to individual powers and that in part mechanize their minds and activities are poor preparations for facing the scene that now confronts the young. In other countries, the combination of economic insecurity with lack of insight into the forces and movements of society have made the young the readiest and most enthusiastic adherents of Fascism. We shall be fortunate if the same sort of thing does not take place here.

What I have said is general in character. But anyone who knows much about our schools can make it concrete, considering how much of the time and energy of pupils is still spent in mere accumulation of information and the acquisition of mechanical forms of skill. Moreover the information that is first memorized and then poorly remembered is selected upon no particular principle; much of it simply on the ground that it was taught in the past. There is little attempt to overhaul the whole structure with a view to selection and organization that would send out students with a sense of the bearing of what they learn upon the present world.

As for methods, the prime need of every person at present is capacity to think; the power to see problems, to relate facts to them, to use and enjoy ideas. If a young man or woman comes from school with this power, all other things may be in time added to him. He will find himself intellectually and morally. But, in the mass of things that have to be "learned," the ability of individuals to think is submerged. In consequence, too large a part of our citizens has left our schools without power of critical discrimination, at the mercy of special propaganda, and drifting from one plan and scheme to another according to the loudest clamor of the moment. Many who have escaped this tendency have found that they had to start their own education afresh. In this connection, I may say that our present system is highly defective in opportunities for directed continuation of education. It is no disparagement of present efforts in "adult education" to say that the continued education of those who have left school should long ago have been made a paramount interest of public education.

There is little genuine relation between the existing social control of the school system and its educative work. In fact, the connection that exists is detrimental to the truly educative work of the schools. School boards at present, taking the country as a whole, are representative of a special class or group in the community, not of community interests. They regard themselves after the analogy of private employers of labor and the teaching staff as their hired men and women.

This situation is reflected in the administrative organization of the schools. On the one hand, there is little real cooperation between administrative officers and classroom teachers. The former make out courses of study, prepare syllabuses for instruction, and lay down methods of instruction. The latter take orders, and, in the degree in which they do so, their professional initiative is blunted, and their own work rendered routine and mechanical. On the other hand, the administrators are dependent for their jobs upon undue conformity to the desires of the economic class that is dominant in school boards as the agents of social control.

It should now be clear why I am not engaged in wholesale indictment of teachers. The defects of the school are reflections within the school of the disorder and confusion of our society. It mirrors social planlessness and drift. But the mirror is not passive. It serves to perpetuate the social and economic conditions out of which it arises. I do not mean that teachers and administrators are impotent in this situation. There is no present event more significant than the assertion on the part of courageous and intelligent educators of the responsibility of the schools for a definite share in the evolution of a reconstructed social order. This assertion is as necessary for society as for educational advance. But it is met by a campaign of newspaper vilification, notably on the part of the Hearst press. It is met also by repressive legislation. The responsibility of those engaged in these movements for production of still-greater social chaos is enormous. At the time when intelligence in social matters, in their widest meaning, political and economic, is imperative, there are persons striving to reduce even the amount of social intelligence that now exists. "After me, the deluge," as long as my immediate power remains, is as truly their principle of action as it was that of any Bourbon king.

PART FIVE. THE DEMOCRATIC SOCIETY

Introduction: The Democratic Society

WHAT DO WE MEAN BY democracy and what are its implications for teachers, leaders, students, and society in general? The word *democracy* derives from the Greek *demos*, meaning "people," and *kratos,* or "strength, power," so literally it means "the power of the people to rule themselves," or "government by the people." Dewey understood that government by the people was not a given, a simple matter, or a purely governmental question. It was more than a political process or one form among the many possible forms of government. It is a form of ethical association, an ideal that challenges people to interact, communicate, develop community, respect diversity, nurture commonalties, and create culture. Dewey saw it as an active endeavor, a process of engagement and inquiry, never the mere acceptance of beliefs, values, or structures, certainly not without questioning them. An admirer of Thomas Jefferson, Dewey reveals in *The Public and Its Problems* (LW2.365) and other works his faith in the ability of the general population to learn to judge events and to make intelligent decisions, and he argues that leaders create most of the societal problems through their misuse of power and disregard for democratic values (LW2.365).

Dewey believed that education plays a crucial role in providing the kinds of conditions to cultivate a climate of experimental inquiry. Education in a democratic society, he insisted, also needed to be democratic to prepare the student for deliberative participation in school and societal concerns. This type of education pays attention to the world of students, their communities, and their cultures. Moreover, it is rooted in a respect for all students, their ability to become reflective thinkers, and their capacity of playing an active role in community and societal development. And this kind of education ties together students' out-of-school and in-school experiences with the selection, teaching, and learning of subject matter.

Accordingly, Dewey's emphasis on democracy has political, social, and individual dimensions. Political democracy includes the political process and the structure of government and underscores such values as respect, equality, justice, tolerance, and freedom. Social democracy implies an enactment of the values of political democracy throughout a society at the level of common interests, interaction, compassion, and communication. The personal dimension of democracy refers to individuals' personal attitudes, dispositions, habits, and behaviors that make social and political democracy possible. Without the personal dimension of democracy, the social dimension is superficial and the political is hollow. When all three dimensions of democracy are strong and vibrant, the educative forces of society are coherent, active, and complementary. But this has seldom been the case and certainly an ideal democracy has yet to materialize in human history. Nevertheless, this is not grounds for pessimism. Instead, it is an opportunity for intentional, intelligent development, both individually and socially.

Democracy, in its several dimensions and manifold complexities, is vitally related to education and the growth of desirable dispositions and habits of thinking and acting. Dewey believed the democratic community called *school* should guide the development of open communication, common interests, mutual respect, and shared goals. Within this environment, administrators, students, teachers, and other stakeholders would learn to live, think, and act democratically by experiencing democratic processes on a regular basis. Inquiry into fields of understanding would be similarly democraticized in that claims, information, data, and arguments would be considered and evaluated on the basis of relevant public criteria, not irrelevant matters, such as a person's social class, religion, economic status, age, race, sexual orientation, or gender.

A genuinely democratic educator integrates the political, social, and personal aspects of democracy into daily activities whether in the classroom, the principal's office, or the superintendent's suite. The three dimensions are woven together to form an intricate and developing culture of democracy. In this way, freedom of inquiry, mutual respect, and friendly communication form a nexus of experience. For these reasons, Dewey believed that freedom of intelligence (freedom of inquiry) and freedom of speech were cornerstones of the democratic way of life and education. But these freedoms need to be buttressed by the value of respect for the rights of others to their opinions, including the right to disagree. Hence, students as inquirers and young citizens should learn to listen to others, consider others' interests, discuss issues, and, frequently, dispute so-called facts, findings, and interpretations. Whether in familial surroundings, school classrooms, neighborhood gatherings, corporate boardrooms, civic engagements, or government chambers, the values of democracy—guided by a free social intelligence—should be manifested habitually in order to ensure that government by the people is a reality.

Dewey's democratic ethic, therefore, is an encompassing approach to governing, living, and growing both in schools and the rest of society. In all of its ramifications, democracy is grounded in a reflective faith rather than a pessimistic cynicism. It is a faith that believes that listening to the voices of others will lead to a better understanding of all community members and the needs of everyone. In the interlacing of personal and community concerns, the individual realizes that even within free societies, choices and actions have consequences on groups as well as individuals. Personal and social democracy are intimately joined with political democracy, the form of government that should protect the values of freedom, justice, opportunity, equality, tolerance, openness, and participation. Each of these values needs to be protected from those who have the power—political, economic, religious, social, and so on—to undermine, weaken, truncate, or destroy them. One of the functions of citizens and schools is to question and critique governmental, social, and educational structures that undercut democratic processes, structures, policies, and values.

In the light of Dewey's philosophy of democracy, government, business, and school activities should never be haphazard or the result of an unthinking process. Instead every entity should see itself as an educational body that plays a vital role in teaching democratic lessons. Educational and democratic agencies should be in constant renewal or rebirth. If not, they weaken and wither away even in societies that claim that they prize both education and democracy. As a consequence, Dewey urged educators, politicians, business leaders, parents, students, and other stakeholders to be part of the formal or informal educative process. Fostering freedom, equality, justice, community, and communication, however, should be based on a clear understanding of these ideas. Anyone can claim to support and practice democratic values and processes. But claims and concepts must be questioned and clarified. The school, therefore, should be at least a key formal educational agency for the clarification and demonstration of democratic ideas, values, and processes. The essays that follow highlight a threefold obligation of education: clarifying, demonstrating, and fostering democratic ideas, ideals, and processes.

The first two essays introduce some of Dewey's basic ideas about democracy. In "What *Is* Democracy?" (LW17.471–74), written shortly after World War II, he avers that there are two cardinal concerns of a democracy. The first concern is that a nation respect freedom of intelligence, which is inseparable from and underwritten by freedom of thought, speech, publication, assembly, and inquiry. The second indispensable concern of democracy is that government be for and by the people as a whole, not for and by powerful cliques, corporations, cultural elites, financial demagogues, and so forth. Dewey's point is that freedom of intelligence—or what we might today call *inquiry* and *reflection*—is used for the betterment of society.

In the second article, "Democracy Is Radical" (LW11.296–99), Dewey asserts that true democracy should be distinguished both from state control over the means of production and from a bourgeois or purely capitalistic democracy that privileges the economic freedom of individuals above the interests of the society as a whole. Indeed, he might well have asked how any nation that is largely controlled by financial capitalists looking out solely for their own interests or by those who employ distortion, oppression, brutality, inequity, and war to manage society could be deemed a democracy. Although he recognizes that even those who are not wealthy sometimes profit from unbridled capitalism, he insists that democracy must remain radical: it must insist that both the means and the ends of democracy be respected. That is to say, it must be achieved by means that show respect for all people, honor freedom of speech, demonstrate open consultation, and prize individuality. For educators, one of the issues becomes: Will I use my professional power to indoctrinate my students into my ideology, or will I employ it to introduce diverse ideas to my students? Will I impose my important values and ideas on students to counteract the socially engrained beliefs they already hold?

Another idea that is intrinsic, although frequently misunderstood, to the concept of democracy is freedom. The essay "Freedom" (LW11.247–55) is Dewey's attempt to clarify his understanding of that notion. As is evident in humanity's many struggles for independence and political freedom, freedom in democracy involves a personal and social association, one with great responsibility. He was concerned that our earlier pioneer spirit of freedom and exploration had led in the modern era to rampant individualism, consumerism, and laissez-faire capitalism that fears government and threatens democracy. He argues that schools can play a vital role in preparing students to understand and respect freedom, including intellectual freedom. But many schools act as if they fear freedom of inquiry, speech, and expression. In a time when freedom and schools were being co-opted by nationalists and socialists for purposes of propaganda, Dewey urged them to protect a democratic way of life and of education, reminding educators that negative freedom—that is, absence of constraint, or freedom from government—is secondary to positive freedom—when government contributes to the well-being of citizens because it reflects their interests and equalizes opportunities. Writing at the time of the Great Depression, he points to the bitter lesson that unconstrained individualistic enterprise can be harmful not only to the individual whose fortune is at risk, but to society in general. Thus, freedom is not solely an economic or political issue, but a moral one. And no one has more responsibility—or opportunity—to nurture democratic ideals in young people than teachers.

In "Intelligence and Power" (LW9.107–11), Dewey describes intelligence as a great potential force in social affairs. Rejecting what he considers the extreme positions, he argues that intelligence alone does not constitute power but that it may become a power when integrated into a political or social action. To bring about change, one needs to understand the different kinds and sources of power. But if intelligence is not welcomed and combined with a deliberative system of interests rooted in communication and persuasion, the remaining alternatives are reduced to antidemocratic measures: coercion, force, violence, manipulation. Then we have wars—political, social, military, and other kinds—over class, religious, economic, racial, gender, and political interests. Education, he concludes, may play a role in bringing intelligence and power together, but it offers no panacea to society's entrenched power cartels. Educated citizens in all walks of life must join in the process of protecting and extending democracy.

In "Nationalizing Education" (MW10.202–210), Dewey sidesteps the idea suggested by his title—having the central government take over the management of education—to address the underlying issue: using education to promote our national idea, "the idea of democracy." He argues that our choices come down to two: we can either engage in democratizing education to create greater and more equal opportunities for all Americans or we can refeudalize it, bolstering class divisions and becoming more isolationist. Both options are forms of *nationalism* one the negative, xenophobic sense of a nation that is self-absorbed and develops internal cohesiveness by depicting other peoples as enemies, and a positive one (a nation interested in the common needs of all of its peoples as well as those in other countries). If society selects the former, negative option, it will probably become dominated by a partisan spirit, and the wealthy who promote an education to prepare future workers for jobs will promote a new feudalism. If society selects the later, positive alternative, it will stress that its nationalism is characterized by interracial and international peoples and provide all with educational opportunity. The latter option, however, can no longer rely on a geographical accident (the size and location of the country) to promote opportunity, freedom, and democracy. Democracy must become an intentional goal of public schools where educators see themselves as civic servants who promote the development of tolerance, goodwill, respect, friendship, and courage. But is this a sufficient pedagogical agenda? Not if we listen to Dewey.

Answering a series of questions regarding workers and their importance in "The Teacher and the Public" (LW11.158–61), Dewey contends that teachers are workers who should produce social goods and that they should unite with other workers, producers of both material and social goods, to acquire the power needed to help construct a democratic social order. He condemns economic leaders who make their living off of the work of others and for their markedly limiting classroom teachers in their roles of producers of social intelligence. On the other hand, he implies that classroom teachers who want to separate themselves from those who work with their hands and who conform to the expectations of economic elites are in reality the enemies of education and democracy—and the servants of a small, select faction in society. An ideal society, then, is one that is growing toward democratic ideals and practices and has educators who are courageous and collaborative as they work with others to promote education and democracy.

In "The Duties and Responsibilities of the Teaching Profession" (LW5.326–330), Dewey raises many questions and offers few answers, but that was his purpose. He asks, Should schools in a democratic society deal with controversial issues? What constitutes freedom in our schools? What is hindering democratic cooperation? Should schools fit individuals to the existing social order or should school have a responsibility to think about planning for a different society? Does the teaching of patriotism result in antagonism to other peoples? Through these questions, Dewey opens a wider range of ideas about the duties of teachers, including some that are strenuously objected to by some educators, administrators, parents, and policymakers. He argues that teachers, their representatives, and educators as a whole should become deeply involved in *discussions*—a critical democratic concept for him—about the direction of schools themselves, the determination of educational objectives, the selection of curricula, and the inclusion of controversial studies. Moreover, he seeks to stimulate teachers to encourage critical thinking and open discussion in classrooms about racial, class, immigration, patriotic, and international issues in ways that do not distort facts in favor of a romantic picture of national identity. In essence, he pushes teachers to become advocates for teacher preparation and professionalism and the freedom and responsibility entailed in them, not to be content to perpetuate existing practices and structures that are undemocratic.

One of Dewey's most quoted essays is "Creative Democracy: The Task Before Us" (LW14.224–230), an address he wrote for his eightieth birthday celebration. He highlights the point that difficult times require a new energy and determination to *re-create* democratic values, values that had been taken for granted or believed to be self-perpetuating. War, racism, classism, and other atrocities, hatreds, and prejudices are the challenges to democracy that prove there is work to be done. Thus, simply promoting or voicing belief in democracy is inadequate. It has to be re-created by creative means, and its scope extended to every facet of life. Democracy, Dewey insists, is only operative when it becomes a way of life, a personal way of everyday life that permeates all aspects of society. In stating the idea of democracy in philosophical terms, Dewey ties it finally to the means and ends of education: "democracy is belief in the ability of human experience to generate the aims and methods by which further experience will grow in ordered richness." What better definition of education could we ask for?

REFLECTION AND DISCUSSION QUESTIONS

1. Dewey envisioned the primary purpose of the school as nurturing democracy and thought the purpose was a moral ideal. How does he make the connection between democracy and ethics?

2. Dewey showed concern that modern society had distorted the true meaning of freedom in a democratic society. What were some of these distortions and how did Dewey reconceptualize the concept of freedom?

3. Many progressive schools that practiced Dewey's ideas studied pioneer life. Dewey often referred to the need for a new pioneer spirit. What do you think he meant by a new pioneer spirit, and why would the old pioneer spirit no longer suffice?

4. Dewey believed that democracy was still "the task before us." Is that a task that is in front of us today? What role can teachers, administrators, students, and others play in what Dewey terms "freeing the human experience" through education?

5. What constitutes a democratic school in a democratic society? Should decisions be made by a majority vote? Should students be allowed to do as they please because we respect them as persons and want them to develop the ability to make intelligent choices?

6. Beyond clarifying his theory of a democratic society, what other theories do these essays help clarify? Why do you think Dewey discussed these theoretical dimensions in the context of his discussing his theory of a good society? If you were to summarize his overall educational theory on the basis of your studies, what key ideas would you mention and how would you show the relationships of these ideas?

What *Is* Democracy? (ca. 1946)

AT NO TIME IN THE past has the world faced as many and as serious problems as at the present time. For at no past time has the world in which man lives been so extended and so complicated in its interconnected parts. This statement is made, however, not for its own sake but as an introduction to the aspect of the world's problems that will be here considered. The recent historical scene would have been regarded as impossible not more than half a century ago. For at that time the progressive triumph of democracy, both as an idea of political philosophy and as a political fact, seemed fairly assured. Of late years its very existence has been so challenged that its fate seemed to hang in the balance and even now its future is far from settled. The first attack made upon it was open, unconcealed. The military assault of Japan, Italy, and Germany and their satellites was attended and supported by the ever-repeated charge that the democratic ideal had outlived its usefulness, and that new and different order was urgently required.

The nations that made the military attack suffered a crushing defeat. The present state of the world proves, without need for extended argument, that the underlying ground of social, economic, and political principles is far from being crushed. The struggle between democratic beliefs as they have been understood and put into practice in the past is more overt and acute than before or during the military conflict. The question "What is Democracy?" is not in the existing state of the world's affairs an academic question. Nor at present is it a matter of defending democratic principles and policies against attack by those who openly, avowedly, treated them with complete scorn. The conflict is now between two radically different, completely opposed, systems each of which claims to be faithful to the cause of democracy.

Typescript in the John Dewey Papers, Box 55, folder 3, Special Collections, Morris Library, Southern Illinois University Carbondale, ca. 1946.

A conflict which is of direct practical importance to hundreds of millions of people and upon which the issue of world-wide war or peace may depend is not a theoretical question to be settled by the arguments of political scientists. One of the national states which was an ally of the states that represent democracy as it has been traditionally understood and practiced now engages in an attack upon the latter which is both ideological and diplomatic and which, by common consent, might pass into strife of armed forces. For it accuses the traditionally democratic peoples of the West in Europe and America of betraying the cause of democracy and holds itself up as representing in its policies and principles the fulfillment of the democratic idea now misrepresented and betrayed by peoples who profess democracy but who fail to carry it into practice in one very important part of human relationships.

That part is, of course, that of human relations as they are affected by the economic order, by the conditions under which industry and finance are conducted. However, I do not intend to discuss the conflict as if its focus and centre is primarily located in the matter of economic policies. It is my belief, for instance, that economic policies have been in the past the weakest aspect of traditional western democracies. Nor do I propose to defend these democracies on the ground that each one of them, not excluding the United States which has perhaps been the country the most attached to an "individualistic" economic order, is actively modifying in its own behalf its traditional economic system. The fact that "capitalism" is so far from being a rigidly fixed system that in fact it is in almost a fluid state is pertinent to some of the charges brought against this and other western democracies but not to the issue I am discussing;—namely, what is the centre and the foundation of the democratic idea and policies?

This centre and base is, in my judgment, thrown into clear and impressive relief by the fact that the nation from which the assaults now proceed has taken over and improved upon the general totalitarian philosophy and practice, one species of which it was actively fighting only a few years ago—and which in fact is historically continuous with the anti-democratic history of its own political past. For this totalitarianism reveals with startling clearness that the central issue is that of respect for freedom of intelligence versus disrespect for it so great as to amount to its effective denial and suppression when it stands, even passively, in the way of political-economic totalitarian policy.

That no professedly democratic country has in the past been without flaw in its devotion to freedom of intelligence as carried out in freedom of the various ways in which it is publicly manifested is of course true. In my own country, for example, its Bill of Rights inserted there by the efforts of our first great and typical Democrat, Thomas Jefferson, is a guarantee of freedom of speech, writing, publication, and assembly for discussion, with respect to all public issues. Moreover, the Supreme Court of the Federation was charged in effect with ability to declare null and void all laws passed by the political units of the Federation which infringed upon the working effectiveness of this guaranteed freedom of intelligence in operation. As I have suggested, we have not always lived up in times of trouble and stress to this guarantee. But it is true that the idea is so embodied not just in the written legal Constitution of the country but in the hearts and minds of the people that every period of reaction has called out a successful period of protest and restoration.

This last remark is not made for the purpose of defense much less of a boast. It is made to indicate that this principle of respect for free intelligence in action goes so deep and extends so far that it has to be continually re-asserted and re-invigorated as conditions change. It is so far from being self-executing that in every period of crisis it has to be actively fought for though, happily, so far not by recourse to arms. The present assault made by a state in the interest of policies executed by totalitarian methods of violent (as well as ideological opposition) suppression of any departure in press, literature, public assembly, even private conversations, and even conduct of physical and biological inquiries, from officially established totalitarian doctrines, points to maintenance of free intelligence in public operation as the focal issue in the various problems of intelligence.

Another great American democrat, Abraham Lincoln, left as his heritage the statement that democracy is Government of, for, and *by* the people. I have italicized the preposition "by" because government cannot possibly be by the people save when and where the freedom of intelligence is publicly and actively supported. It is debatable whether it can for any long period be for the people and not for a governing clique or bureaucracy save where the rights of public discussion and criticism are held inviolate. Revolutionary periods, of which from a world-wide point of view the present is one, tend toward a concentration of power. The concentration claims for itself that it is in the best interests of the people at large. At the outset, that may be the case in fact. But nothing is more certain than unless its movement is attended by scrupulous attentive observance of the principle of freedom of intelligence in action it will rapidly degenerate into the rule of a small section, maintained by use of force, in its own special interest. It is for this reason that it is so peculiarly, almost uniquely, important at the present time not to be distracted into allowing any issue, no matter how useful in itself, to displace freedom of intelligence in public communication by means of speech, publication in daily and weekly press, in books, in public assemblies, in scientific inquiry, as the centre and burning focus of democracy. Nothing will be more fatal in the end than surrender and compromise on this point. Now, more than ever, it is urgently necessary to hold it in steady view as the heart from which flows the life-blood of democracy.

I should not close without definite recal of the fact that it was the pioneers of freedom of thought and speech in France in the eighteenth century, who in spite of every sort of interference by those professing to speak in the name of moral authority and social stability made that century the period of The Éclaircisse-ment, The Enlightenment, out of which has issued all that is best and truest in the democratic spirit first in the civilization of the West and now in promise if not yet in execution of the entire world. If the peoples who have behind them and still with them the living tradition of supreme and steady regard for free-dom of intelligence in operation in all channels of communication now live up to their heritage, they, we, shall issue from the present crisis with purification of the life-blood of democracy. In surmounting the cruel trials of the present crisis we shall have opened the way to a nobler, because freer, manifestation of the human spirit.

Democracy Is Radical (1937)

THERE IS COMPARATIVELY LITTLE DIFFERENCE among the groups at the left as to the social ends to be reached. There is a great deal of difference as to the means by which these ends should be reached and by which they can be reached. This difference as to means is the tragedy of democracy in the world today. The rulers of Soviet Russia announce that with the adoption of the new constitution they have for the first time in history created a democracy. At almost the same time, Goebbels announces that German Nazi-socialism is the only possible form of democracy for the future. Possibly there is some faint cheer for those who believe in democracy in these expressions. It is something that after a period in which democracy was scorned and laughed at, it is now acclaimed.

No one outside of Germany will take seriously the claim that Germany is a democracy, to say nothing of its being the perfected form of democracy. But there is something to be said for the assertion that the so-called democratic states of the world have achieved only "bourgeois" democracy. By "bourgeois" democracy is meant one in which power rests finally in the hands of finance capitalism, no matter what claims are made for government of, by and for all the people. In the perspective of history it is clear that the rise of democratic governments has been an accompaniment of the transfer of power from agrarian interests to industrial and commercial interests.

This transfer did not take place without a struggle. In this struggle, the representatives of the new forces of production asserted that their cause was that of liberty and of the free choice and initiative of individuals. Upon the continent and to a less degree in Great Britain, the political manifestation of free economic enterprise took the name of liberalism. So-called liberal parties were those which strove for a maximum of individualistic economic action with a minimum of

---

First published in *Common Sense* 6 (January 1937): 10–11.

social control, and did so in the interest of those engaged in manufacturing and commerce. If this manifestation expresses the full meaning of liberalism, then liberalism has served its time and it is social folly to try to resurrect it.

For the movement has definitely failed to realize the ends of liberty and individuality which were the goals it set up and in the name of which it proclaimed its rightful political supremacy. The movement for which it stood gave power to a few over the lives and thoughts of the many. Ability to command the conditions under which the mass of people have access to the means of production and to the products that result from their activity has been the fundamental feature of repression of freedom and the bar to development of individuality through all the ages. It is silly to deny that there has been gain to the masses accompanying the change of masters. But to glorify these gains and to give no attention to the brutalities and inequities, the regimentation and suppression, the war, open and covert, that attend the present system is intellectual and moral hypocrisy. Distortion and stultification of human personality by the existing pecuniary and competitive regime give the lie to the claim that the present social system is one of freedom and individualism in any sense in which liberty and individuality exist for all.

The United States is the outstanding exception to the statement that democracy arose historically in the interest of an industrial and commercial class, although it is true that in the formation of the federal constitution this class reaped much more than its fair share of the fruits of the revolution. And it is also true that as this group rose to economic power it appropriated also more and more political power. But it is simply false that this country, even politically, is merely a capitalistic democracy. The present struggle in this country is something more than a protest of a new class, whether called the proletariat or given any other name, against an established industrial autocracy. It is a manifestation of the native and enduring spirit of the nation against the destructive encroachments of forces that are alien to democracy.

This country has never had a political party of the European "liberal" type, although in recent campaigns the Republican party has taken over most of the slogans of the latter. But the attacks of leaders of the party upon liberalism as one form of the red menace show that liberalism has a different origin, setting and aim in the United States. It is fundamentally an attempt to realize democratic modes of life in their full meaning and far-reaching scope. There is no particular sense in trying to save the word "liberal." There is every reason for not permitting the methods and aims of democracy to be obscured by denunciations of liberalism. The danger of this eclipse is not a theoretical matter; it is intensely practical.

For democracy means not only the ends which even dictatorships now assert are their ends, security for individuals and opportunity for their development as personalities. It signifies also primary emphasis upon the means by which these ends are to be fulfilled. The means to which it is devoted are the voluntary activities of individuals in opposition to coercion; they are assent and consent in opposition to violence; they are the force of intelligent organization versus that of organization imposed from outside and above. The fundamental principle of democracy is that the ends of freedom and individuality for all can be attained only by means that accord with those ends. The value of upholding the banner of liberalism in this country, no matter what it has come to mean in Europe, is its insistence upon freedom of belief, of inquiry, of discussion, of assembly, of education: upon the method of public intelligence in opposition to even a coercion that claims to be exercised in behalf of the ultimate freedom of all individuals. There is intellectual hypocrisy and moral contradiction in the creed of those who uphold the need for at least a temporary dictatorship of a class as well as in the position of those who assert that the present economic system is one of freedom of initiative and of opportunity for all.

There is no opposition in standing for liberal democratic means combined with ends that are socially radical. There is not only no contradiction, but neither history nor human nature gives any reason for supposing that socially radical ends can be attained by any other than liberal democratic means. The idea that those who possess power never surrender it save when forced to do so by superior physical power, applies to dictatorships that claim to operate in behalf of the oppressed masses while actually operating to wield power against the masses. The end of democracy is a radical end. For it is an end that has not been adequately realized in any country at any time. It is radical because it requires great change in existing social institutions, economic, legal and cultural. A democratic liberalism that does not recognize these things in thought and action is not awake to its own meaning and to what that meaning demands.

There is, moreover, nothing more radical than insistence upon democratic methods as the means by which radical social changes be effected. It is not a merely verbal statement to say that reliance upon superior physical force is the reactionary position. For it is the method that the world has depended upon in the past and that the world is now arming in order to perpetuate. It is easy to understand why those who are in close contact with the inequities and tragedies of life that mark the present system, and who are aware that we now have the resources for initiating a social system of security and opportunity for all, should be impatient and long for the overthrow of the existing system by any means whatever. But democratic means and the attainment of democratic ends are one and inseparable. The revival of democratic faith as a buoyant, crusading and militant faith is a consummation to be devoutly wished for. But the crusade can win at the best but partial victory unless it springs from a living faith in our common human nature and in the power of voluntary action based upon public collective intelligence.

Freedom (1937)

THE OLD SAYING THAT "eternal vigilance is the price of liberty" has especial significance at the present time. Freedom from oppression was such a controlling purpose in the foundation of the American Republic, and the idea of freedom is so intimately connected with the very idea of democratic institutions, that it might seem as if in our own country it could be taken for granted as a social goal of education and, being taken for granted, be dismissed with a few words. But the lesson of history is that the forces which limit and restrict the life of individuals and thereby hinder freedom change with every great change in human relations. Consequently, freedom is an eternal goal and has to be forever struggled for and won anew. It does not automatically perpetuate itself and, unless it is continually rewon in new effort against new foes, it is lost.

The forces which work to undermine freedom appear in even subtler form as society grows more complex and operate more insidiously. They are more effective just because in their first appearance they do not seem to be oppressive of liberty. Indeed, in their first appearance and early stages of operation they are likely to be welcomed for some obvious advantages they bring with them—possibly even as a promise of greater freedom. The freedom for which our forefathers fought was primarily freedom from a fairly gross and obvious form of oppression, that of arbitrary political power exercised from a distant centre. In consequence, there developed among us the tradition that the chief enemy of liberty is governmental power. The maintenance of freedom came to be almost identified with jealous fear of and opposition to any and every extension of governmental action.

First published as chapter 9 in National Education Association, *Implications of Social-Economic Goals for Education: A Report of the Committee on Social-Economic Goals of America* (Washington, D.C.: National Education Association, 1937), 99–105.

It took generations to realize that a government of and by the people might be a positive and necessary organ for securing and extending the liberties of the individuals who both govern and are governed, instead of being an instrument of oppression. The lesson is still far from being completely learned.

The immediate result of the conditions under which the people of the United States won their independence was, then, to identify freedom for the most part with political freedom, and to think of even this form of freedom largely in a negative way. Its positive expression was confined pretty much to the right to vote, to choose public officials and thereby share indirectly in the formation of public policies, and perchance to be elected to office oneself. The ballot became the glorified symbol of freedom and every Fourth of July speech conjured up the spectacle of the procession of freemen wending their way to the polls to exercise the priceless gift of freedom. Meantime, the conditions under which citizens exercised the right of suffrage, conditions which in large measure so circumscribed and controlled the right as to reduce it for many, perhaps for the masses, to something like an empty formality, were neglected. Corruption became rife; bosses and factional political machines managed from behind the scenes by bosses grew and flourished. One who idealizes the early days of the Republic has but to read the writings and speeches of Horace Mann one hundred years ago to note the extent to which he made the evil political conditions which then prevailed a large part of the ground of his appeal for the foundation and extension of public common schools. Many of the evils of which he complained have been reduced although not eliminated. But the present political situation as well as the historic past should convince us that exclusive identification of freedom with political freedom means in the end the loss of even political freedom.

During the earlier history of our country the important freedom of its inhabitants was located in actuality in the non-political sphere. With free land, a sparse and scattered population, largely rural, and a continent to subdue, there was room for everyone—not merely physical room, but room for energy and personal initiative, room to carve out a career, seemingly boundless opportunity for all who had the vigor, wit, and industry to take advantage of it. The frontier constantly beckoned onwards. While the frontier was geographical and called for physical movement, it was more than that. It was economic and moral. It proclaimed in effect that America is opportunity; it held out the promise of the reward of success to all individuals who put forth the individual effort which would bring success. This freedom of opportunity more than political freedom created the real "American dream." Even after conditions changed and changed radically, it left its enduring impress in the distinctively American idea of freedom of opportunity for all alike, unhampered by differences in status, birth and family antecedents, and finally, in name at least, of race and sex.

But the situation did change and changed radically. Free land practically disappeared. The beckoning geographical frontier vanished. The habits of the people changed from those suited to agrarian conditions to those demanded by mechanized industry. The population became predominantly urbanized, not only in location but in standards and tastes. Industry for mass machine production became more and more centralized and with this centralization came more and more under the control of concentrated finance. Freedom inherent in equal opportunity is no longer something to be taken for granted as it could be when it was in large measure an expression of actual conditions. It is something to be striven for by every means at command. If it is not attained, the distinctive American dream becomes a memory and the most characteristic feature of the American democratic ideal of freedom goes down in ship-wreck. Until the battle for freedom of equal opportunity is won, freedom is indeed a social and economic goal to the attainment of which the American educational system must bend all its energies.

Even during the period in which economic and social conditions rendered freedom of opportunity a sufficiently close approximation to actual fact so that it could be complacently assumed to be inherent in the working of American institutions, these same conditions placed an inordinate emphasis upon one aspect of opportunity, namely, upon that narrow phase of economic opportunity which is material and pecuniary. Success came to be popularly measured by acquisition of property, enlargement of income, and increase of size and quantity generally. Under the influence of the conditions which created this one-sided emphasis upon material opportunity, there developed the idea that all individuals by nature already possess equal liberty as long as formal legal regulations apply equally to all and as long as government refrains from what was called interference with their natural liberties of action. This conception of liberty as the equal right of every individual to conduct business and make money free from social restraint, so long as he broke no law on the statute book, coincided with the notion that government is the chief source of oppression. The result of the union of the two beliefs was identification of liberty with laissez faire individualism. In words which Charles A. Beard quotes from John R. Commons in *The Unique Function of Education in American Democracy*, it was a philosophy in which democratic freedom was made equivalent to "mechanical principles of individualism, selfishness, division of labor, exchange of commodities, equality, fluidity, liberty, and that divine providence which led individuals to benefit each other without intending to do so." Representatives of privileged classes took these ideas to be the very essence of the philosophy of liberty. They have exercised an enormous, at times a supreme, influence upon courts of law and upon popular moral beliefs. The more influential was this conception of liberty, the more rapidly proceeded encroachments upon the actual freedom of the mass of individuals.

It is under such conditions as these (which have been barely sketched) that freedom has become a goal to be struggled for instead of being a fact to be taken for granted.

It is under such conditions that the problem of attaining freedom has become complex and intricate, touching practically every phase of life. It is beyond the scope of this article even to begin to mention the many facets the issue of attaining the goal of freedom now presents. A few are mentioned by way of illustration.

The time of the heyday of economic individualistic freedom undoubtedly promoted invention, initiative, and individual vigor, as well as hastened the industrial development of the country. But it also encouraged a spirit of reckless speculation which has placed a heavy burden upon the present and future generations. It furthered reckless and extravagant exploitation of natural resources, as if they were literally incapable of being exhausted. Conservation of not only the public domain but restoration of worn-out land to fertility, the combating of floods and erosion which have reduced vast portions of our national heritage to something like a desert, are the penalties we have to pay for past indulgence in an orgy of so-called economic liberty. Without abundant store of natural resources, equal liberty for all is out of the question. Only those already in possession will enjoy it. Not merely a modification but a reversal of our traditional policies of waste and destruction is necessary if genuine freedom of opportunity is to be achieved.

There is little genuine freedom possible without a reasonable degree of security of work and of income. The last great depression has brought this lesson home to us so that it is not necessary to dwell upon it. Millions of unemployed, with savings exhausted, who are dependent upon private charity and public relief, is a bitter commentary upon the identification of liberty with socially unconstrained individualistic enterprise. Nor does the restriction of freedom end with the immediate victims of unemployment and insecurity. The rising tide of protest on the part of business men against the burden of taxation imposed by public relief shows that they too feel that their range of productive activities is being limited.

Unfortunately, however, few of them show any disposition to go into the causes which have produced the situation. They are for the most part content to utter complaints about symptoms which they do not like.

Concentration and centralization of industry have also brought in their train perils to genuine freedom of thought and action. It is well to point out dangers from regimentation that have their source in undue political centralization. But it is not well to overlook the immense amount of regimentation that proceeds from industrial and financial centralization. One great reason why Thomas Jefferson extolled the agrarian régime and that of small independent producers and shopkeepers, and why he prophesied the evils that would come with industrialization, was the moral reason. Under the earlier régime there were opportunity and demand for making personal decisions to be personally carried out, with experience of the satisfaction that attends such conduct. Under a régime of highly centralized finance and industry, the mass of individuals, who are subordinates, tend to become cogs in a vast machine whose workings they do not understand, and in whose management they have no part or lot. If universal freedom is to become anything like a reality, methods must be found by which the mass of individuals will have a much larger share in directing industrial processes than they have at present. Merely procuring for them a greater share in the material and pecuniary products of industrial production will not of itself secure genuine freedom for them.

One further illustration of the way in which existing conditions so limit individual freedom as to constitute it a goal to be attained is found in the rapid growth of narrow nationalism. An extreme form of this limitation carried to the point of complete denial of personal freedom is found in the totalitarian countries of Europe which are governed by dictators. But it would be a great mistake to suppose that constraint of freedom is confined to these countries. Because of acute nationalism every nation at present lives under the burden imposed by past wars and under the pall of threat of future wars. There is no other single force so completely destructive of personal freedom as is modern war. Not merely the life and property of individuals are subjected by war to external control, but also their very thoughts and their power to give them expression. War is a kind of wholesale moral enslavement of entire populations. Peace is a necessary and urgent condition of attainment of the goal of freedom.

There is, however, one domain in which fear of governmental action never became dominant in American life. That is the domain of education. In this field, the founding fathers proclaimed with well-nigh unanimous voice that government, local and state if not national, should act positively and constructively. This voice has been constantly re-echoed throughout the course of our history by political and educational statesmen alike. The voice has awakened a warmer response in the hearts of the American people than any other appeal made to them. Doubtless many parents have responded to the appeal because they felt that school education opened doors to material opportunity and success that were otherwise closed to their children. But the appeal and the response have not been merely material. The American faith in education has been grounded in the belief that without education the ideal of free and equal opportunity is an idle fantasy; that of all the guarantees of free development, education is the surest and the most effective.

This fact imposes a great responsibility upon the schools and upon the educators who conduct them. What have the schools done to bring the social-economic goal of freedom nearer to realization? What have they failed to do?

What can and should they do to combat the threats which imperil freedom? The mere raising of these questions calls attention to one phase of freedom, a fundamental one which has not been touched upon in the previous discussion—Intellectual Freedom. The Bill of Rights in the federal Constitution (unfortunately not found in all state constitutions) guarantees, as far as law can guarantee anything, freedom of belief, of speech, of the press, of assembly, and of petition. These are aspects of what I have called intellectual freedom, but which perhaps would better be called moral freedom. Eternal vigilance is even more the price of liberty with respect to these liberties than in the case of liberty of external action. The enemies of liberty of thought and expression in fields where it is felt that this liberty might encroach upon privileges possessed and might disturb the existing order, are organized and determined. The ultimate stay and support of these liberties are the schools. For it is they which more than any other single agency, are concerned with development of free inquiry, discussion and expression.

Nor is it enough that the schools by example and precept should instill faith in the precious character of these forms of freedom, or even that they should themselves be living models of the practise of freedom of inquiry, experimentation, and communication. These things are indeed to be cultivated. But the schools have also the responsibility of seeing to it that those who leave its walls have ideas that are worth thinking and worth being expressed, as well as having the courage to express them against the opposition of reactionaries and standpatters. It is quite possible that in the long run the greatest friend of censorship, whether public and explicit or private and insidious, and the greatest foe to freedom of thought and expression, is not those who fear such freedom because of its possible effect upon their own standing and fortune, but is the triviality and irrelevancy of the ideas that are entertained, and the futile and perhaps corrupting way in which they are expressed.

It is indeed necessary to have freedom of thought and expression. But just because this is necessary for the health and progress of society, it is even more necessary that ideas should be genuine ideas, not sham ones, the fruit of inquiry, of observation and experimentation, the collection and weighing of evidence. The formation of the attitudes which move steadily in this direction is the work and responsibility of the school more than of any other single institution. Routine and formal instruction, undemocratic administration of schools, is perhaps the surest way of creating a human product that submits readily to external authority, whether that be imposed by force or by custom and tradition, or by the various forms of social pressure which the existing economic system produces. It is idle to expect the schools to send out young men and women who will stand actively and aggressively for the cause of free intelligence in meeting social problems and attaining the goal of freedom unless the spirit of free intelligence pervades the organization, administration, studies, and methods of the school itself.

Educators have a primary responsibility in this respect. In the words of the original brief formulation of the Social-Economic Goals of America, "more and more should teachers become community leaders of thought." But teachers cannot accomplish this task alone. In the further language of the same formulation, "In that role they will need group solidarity and the support of public opinion, aroused to appreciate the fundamental importance of this aspect of freedom." The emphasis that is placed upon a greater measure of economic freedom for the mass of the people is not final. It does not stand alone. Ultimately, the economic freedom (which is dependent upon economic security) is a means to cultural freedom, to the release of the human spirit in all its capacities for development through science, art, and unconstrained human intercourse. The school is par excellence the potential social organ for promoting this liberation.

In ultimate analysis, freedom is important because it is a condition both of realization of the potentialities of an individual and of social progress. Without light, a people perishes. Without freedom, light grows dim and darkness comes to reign. Without freedom, old truths become so stale and worn that they cease to be truths and become mere dictates of external authority. Without freedom, search for new truth and the disclosure of new paths in which humanity may walk more securely and justly come to an end. Freedom which is liberation for the individual, is the ultimate assurance of the movement of society toward more humane and noble ends. He who would put the freedom of others in bond, especially freedom of inquiry and communication, creates conditions which finally imperil his own freedom and that of his offspring. Eternal vigilance is the price of the conservation and extension of freedom, and the schools should be the ceaseless guardians and creators of this vigilance.

Intelligence and Power (1934)

THOSE WHO CONTEND THAT INTELLIGENCE is capable of exercising a significant role in social affairs and that it would be well if it had a much larger influence in directing social affairs can readily be made to appear ridiculous. From the standpoint of past human history it not only appears but is ridiculous. It takes little acquaintance with the past to realize what the forces have been that have determined social institutions, arrangements and changes. There has been oligarchical despotic power, political, ecclesiastic and economic, sometimes exercised openly, more often by all sorts of indirect and subtle means. Habit, custom and tradition have had a weight in comparison with which that of intelligence is feeble. Custom and tradition have originated in all sorts of ways, many of them accidental. But, once established, they have had weight independent of the conditions of their origin and have reinforced the power of vested interests. At critical times, widespread illusions, generated by intense emotions, have played a role in comparison with which the influence of intelligence is negligible.

What critics overlook is that there would be no point in urging the potential claims of intelligence unless the latter had been submerged in such ways as have been indicated. The net outcome of the domination of the methods of institutional force, custom and illusion does not encourage one to look with great hope upon dependence on new combinations among them for future progress. The situation is such that it is calculated to make one look around, even if from sheer desperation, for some other method, however desperate. And under such circumstances, it also seems as if the effort to stimulate resort to the method of intelligence might present itself as at least one desperate recourse, if not the only one that remains untried. In view of the influence of collective illusion in

First published in *New Republic* 78 (25 April 1934): 306–7.

the past, some case might be made out for the contention that even if it be an illusion, exaltation of intelligence and experimental method is worth a trial. Illusion for illusion, this particular one may be better than those upon which humanity has usually depended.

The success of this method in obtaining control over physical forces and conditions has been offered as evidence that the case for trying it in social matters is not altogether desperate nor yet illusory. This reference has also been misunderstood by critics. For it is not held that the particular techniques of the physical sciences are to be literally copied—though of course they are to be utilized wherever applicable—nor that experimentation in the laboratory sense can be carried out on any large scale in social affairs. It is held that the attitude of mind exemplified in the conquest of nature by the experimental sciences, and the method involved in it, may and should be carried into social affairs. And the force of the contention depends on the consideration already mentioned: What are the alternatives? Dogmatism, reinforced by the weight of unquestioned custom and tradition, the disguised or open play of class interests, dependence upon brute force and violence.

It is stated, however, that a fundamental difference in the two cases of physical and social intelligence is ignored. "The physical sciences, it is said, gained their freedom when they overcame the traditionalism based on ignorance, but the traditionalism which the social sciences face is based upon the economic interest of the dominant social classes who are trying to maintain their special privileges in society" (Niebuhr). Of course it is. But it is a naïve view of history that supposes that dominant class interests were not the chief force that maintained the tradition against which the new method and conclusions in physical science had to make their way. Nor is it supposed for a moment that the new scientific method would have won its way in a comparatively few centuries—not that it has completely conquered even yet in the physical field—unless it had found a lodgment in other social interests than the dominant ones and been backed by the constantly growing influence of other interests.

Here we come to the nub of the matter. Intelligence has no power per se. In so far as the older rationalists assumed that it had, they were wrong. Hume was nearer the truth, although guilty of exaggeration on the other side, when he said "reason is and always must be the slave of passion"—or interest. But dominant interest is never the exclusive interest that exists—not when there is a struggle taking place. The real problem is whether there are strong interests now active which can best succeed by adopting the method of experimental intelligence into their struggles, or whether they too should rely upon the use of methods that have brought the world to its present estate, only using them the other way around.

Intelligence becomes a *power* only when it is brought into the operation of other forces than itself. But power is a blanket term and covers a multitude of different things. Everything that is done is done by some form of power—that is a truism. But violence and war are powers, finance is a power, newspapers, publicity agents and propaganda are powers, churches and the beliefs they have inculcated are powers, as well as a multitude of other things. Persuasion and conference are also powers, although it is easy to overestimate the degree of their power in the existing economic and international system. In short, we have not said anything so long as we have merely said power. What first is needed is discrimination, knowledge of the distribution of power.

Intelligence becomes a power only as it is integrated into some system of wants, of effective demands. The doctrine that has prevailed in the past regarding the nature of intelligence is itself a reflex of its separation from action. It has been conceived as something complete in itself, action following after and upon it as a merely external expression of it. If I held that notion of intelligence I should more than agree with the critics who doubt that intelligence has any particular role in bringing about needed social change. For the notion is simply one aspect of the divorce of theory and practice that has obtained throughout most of the history of mankind. The peculiar significance of the method of the physical sciences is that they broke through this idea that had for so long hypnotized mankind, demonstrating that action is a necessary part of intelligence—namely, action that changes conditions that previously existed.

Hence the first effect of acceptance of the idea that the operation of control of social forces has something to learn from the experimental method of the physical sciences is a radical alteration in the prevailing conception of social knowledge. The current assumption is that knowledge comes first and then action may—or may not—proceed from it. Critics who have attacked the idea that intelligence has an important role to play have based their attack upon acceptance of this idea; they have criticized me on the basis of attributing to me the very idea that I have been concerned to overthrow. Thus on the basis of a passage in which I denied that any amount of fact-finding apart from action aiming at control of social processes—in other words, a planned economy—could ever build up social knowledge and understanding, Mr. Niebuhr imputes to me middle-class prejudices in ignoring the role of class interest and conflict in social affairs! He imputes to me a great exaggeration of the potentialities of education in spite of the fact that I have spent a good deal of energy in urging that no genuine education is possible without active participation in actual conditions, and have pointed out that economic interests are the chief cause why this change in education is retarded and deflected.

The question at issue is not a personal one, however, and it is not worth notice on personal grounds. Just because dominant economic interests are the chief cause for non-use of the method of intelligence to control social change, opponents of the method play into the hands of these interests when they discourage the potentialities of this method. In my judgment they perpetuate the present confusion, and they strengthen the forces that will introduce evil consequences into the result of any change, however revolutionary it may be, brought about by means into which the method of intelligence has not entered. "Education" even in its widest sense cannot do everything. But what is accomplished without education, again in its broadest sense, will be badly done and much of it will have to be done over. The crucial problem is how intelligence may gain increasing power through incorporation with wants and interests that are actually operating. The very fact that intelligence in the past has operated for narrow ends and in behalf of class interests is a reason for putting a high estimate upon its possible role in social control, not a reason for disparaging it.

Nationalizing Education (1916)

THE WORDS NATION AND NATIONAL have two quite different meanings. We cannot profitably discuss the nationalizing of education unless we are clear as to the difference between the two. For one meaning indicates something desirable, something to be cultivated by education, while the other stands for something to be avoided as an evil plague. The idea which has given the movement toward nationality which has been such a feature of the last century its social vitality is the consciousness of a community of history and purpose larger than that of the family, the parish, the sect and the province. The upbuilding of national states has substituted a unity of feeling and aim, a freedom of intercourse, over wide areas for earlier local isolations, suspicions, jealousies and hatreds. It has forced men out of narrow sectionalisms into membership in a larger social unit, and created loyalty to a state which subordinates petty and selfish interests.

One cannot say this, however, without being at once reminded that nationalism has had another side. With the possible exception of our own country the national states of the modern world have been built up through conflict. The development of a sense of unity within a charmed area has been accompanied by dislike, by hostility, to all without. Skilful politicians and other self-seekers have always known how to play cleverly upon patriotism, and upon ignorance of other peoples, to identify nationalism with latent hatred of other nations. Without exaggeration, the present world war may be said to be the outcome of this aspect of nationalism, and to present it in its naked unloveliness.

In the past, our geographical isolation has largely protected us from the harsh, selfish and exclusive aspect of nationalism. The absence of pressure from without, the absence of active and urgent rivalry and hostility of powerful neighbors, has perhaps played a part in the failure to develop an adequate

First published in *Journal of Education* 84 (1916): 425–28.

unity of sentiment and idea for the country as a whole. Individualism of a go-as-you-please type has had too full swing. We have an inherited jealousy of any strong national governing agencies, and we have been inclined to let things drift rather than to think out a central, controlling policy. But the effect of the war has been to make us aware that the days of geographical isolation are at an end, and also to make us conscious that we are lacking in an integrated social sense and policy for our country as a whole, irrespective of classes and sections.

We are now faced by the difficulty of developing the good aspect of nationalism without its evil side; of developing a nationalism which is the friend and not the foe of internationalism. Since this is a matter of ideas, of emotions, of intellectual and moral disposition and outlook, it depends for its accomplishment upon educational agencies, not upon outward machinery. Among these educational agencies, the public school takes first rank. When sometime in the remote future the tale is summed up and the public as distinct from the private and merely personal achievement of the common school is recorded, the question which will have to be answered is, What has the American public school done toward subordinating a local, provincial, sectarian and partisan spirit of mind to aims and interests which are common to all the men and women of the country—to what extent has it taught men to think and feel in ideas broad enough to be inclusive of the purposes and happiness of all sections and classes? For unless the agencies which form the mind and morals of the community can prevent the operation of those forces which are always making for a division of interests, class and sectional ideas and feelings will become dominant, and our democracy will fall to pieces.

Unfortunately at the present time one result of the excitement which the war has produced is that many influential and well-meaning persons attempt to foster the growth of an inclusive nationalism by appeal to our fears, our suspicions, our jealousies and our latent hatreds. They would make the measure of our national preparedness our readiness to meet other nations in destructive war rather than our fitness to cooperate with them in the constructive tasks of peace. They are so disturbed by what has been revealed of internal division, of lack of complete national integration, that they have lost faith in the slow policies of education. They would kindle a sense of our dependence upon one another by making us afraid of peoples outside of our border; they would bring about unity within by laying stress upon our separateness from others. The situation makes it all the more necessary that those concerned with education should withstand popular clamor for a nationalism based upon hysterical excitedness or mechanical drill, or a combination of the two. We must ask what a real nationalism, a real Americanism, is like. For unless we know our own character and purpose we are not likely to be intelligent in our selection of the means to further them.

I want to mention only two elements in the nationalism which our education should cultivate. The first is that the American nation is itself complex and
compound. Strictly speaking it is interracial and international in its make-up.
It is composed of a multitude of peoples speaking different tongues, inherit-
ing diverse traditions, cherishing varying ideals of life. This fact is basic to our
nationalism as distinct from that of other peoples. Our national motto, "One
from Many," cuts deep and extends far. It denotes a fact which doubtless adds
to the difficulty of getting a genuine unity. But it also immensely enriches the
possibilities of the result to be attained. No matter how loudly any one proclaims
his Americanism, if he assumes that any one racial strain, any one component
culture, no matter how early settled it was in our territory, or how effective it
has proved in its own land, is to furnish a pattern to which all other strains and
cultures are to conform, he is a traitor to an American nationalism. Our unity
cannot be a homogeneous thing like that of the separate states of Europe from
which our population is drawn; it must be a unity created by drawing out and
composing into a harmonious whole the best, the most characteristic which
each contributing race and people has to offer.

I find that many who talk the loudest about the need of a supreme and unified
Americanism of spirit really mean some special code or tradition to which they
happen to be attached. They have some pet tradition which they would impose
upon all. In thus measuring the scope of Americanism by some single element
which enters into it they are themselves false to the spirit of America. Neither
Englandism nor New-Englandism, neither Puritan nor Cavalier any more than
Teuton or Slav, can do anything but furnish one note in a vast symphony.

The way to deal with hyphenism, in other words, is to welcome it, but to
welcome it in the sense of extracting from each people its special good, so
that it shall surrender into a common fund of wisdom and experience what it
especially has to contribute. All of these surrenders and contributions taken
together create the national spirit of America. The dangerous thing is for each
factor to isolate itself, to try to live off its past, and then to attempt to impose
itself upon other elements, or, at least, to keep itself intact and thus refuse to
accept what other cultures have to offer, so as thereby to be transmuted into
authentic Americanism.

In what is rightly objected to as hyphenism the hyphen has become something which separates one people from other peoples—and thereby prevents
American nationalism. Such terms as Irish-American or Hebrew-American
or German-American are false terms because they seem to assume something
which is already in existence called America to which the other factor may be
externally hitched on. The fact is the genuine American, the typical American,
is himself a hyphenated character. This does not mean that he is part American,
and that some foreign ingredient is then added. It means that, as I have said, he

is international and interracial in his make-up. He is not American plus Pole or German. But the American is himself Pole-German-English-French-Spanish-Italian-Greek-Irish-Scandinavian-Bohemian-Jew-and so on. The point is to see to it that the hyphen connects instead of separates. And this means at least that our public schools shall teach each factor to respect every other, and shall take pains to enlighten all as to the great past contributions of every strain in our composite make-up. I wish our teaching of American history in the schools would take more account of the great waves of migration by which our land for over three centuries has been continuously built up, and made every pupil conscious of the rich breadth of our national make-up. When every pupil recognizes all the factors which have gone into our being, he will continue to prize and reverence that coming from his own past, but he will think of it as honored in being simply one factor in forming a whole, nobler and finer than itself.

In short, unless our education is nationalized in a way which recognizes that the peculiarity of our nationalism is its internationalism, we shall breed enmity and division in our frantic efforts to secure unity. The teachers of the country know this fact much better than do many of its politicians. While too often politicians have been fostering a vicious hyphenatedism and sectionalism as a bid for votes, teachers have been engaged in transmuting beliefs and feelings once divided and opposed into a new thing under the sun—a national spirit inclusive not exclusive, friendly not jealous. This they have done by the influence of personal contact, cooperative intercourse and sharing in common tasks and hopes. The teacher who has been an active agent in furthering the common struggle of native born, African, Jew, Italian and perhaps a score of other peoples to attain emancipation and enlightenment will never become a party to a conception of America as a nation which conceives of its history and its hopes as less broad than those of humanity—let politicians clamor for their own ends as they will.

The other point in the constitution of a genuine American nationalism to which I invite attention is that we have been occupied during the greater part of our history in subduing nature, not one another or other peoples. I once heard two foreign visitors coming from different countries discuss what had been impressed upon them as the chief trait of the American people. One said vigor, youthful and buoyant energy. The other said it was kindness, the disposition to live and let live, the absence of envy at the success of others. I like to think that while both of these ascribed traits have the same cause back of them, the latter statement goes deeper. Not that we have more virtue, native or acquired, than others, but that we have had more room, more opportunity. Consequently the same conditions which have put a premium upon active and hopeful energy have permitted the kindlier instincts of man to express themselves. The spaciousness of a continent not previously monopolized by man has stimulated vigor and has also diverted activity from the struggle against fellow-man into the struggle against nature. When men make their gains by fighting in common a wilderness, they have not the motive for mutual distrust which comes when they get ahead only by fighting one another. I recently heard a story which seems to me to have something typical about it. Some manufacturers were discussing the problem of labor; they were loud in their complaints. They were bitter against the exactions of unions, and full of tales of an inefficiency which seemed to them calculated. Then one of them said: "Oh, well, poor devils! They haven't much of a chance and have to do what they can to hold their own. If we were in their place, we should be just the same." And the others nodded assent and the conversation lapsed. I call this characteristic, for if there was not an ardent sympathy, there was at least a spirit of toleration and passive recognition.

But with respect to this point as well as with respect to our composite make-up, the situation is changing. We no longer have a large unoccupied continent. Pioneer days are past, and natural resources are possessed. There is danger that the same causes which have set the hand of man against his neighbor in other countries will have the same effect here. Instead of sharing in a common fight against nature, we are already starting to fight against one another, class against class, haves against have-nots. The change puts a definite responsibility upon the schools to sustain our true national spirit. The virtues of mutual esteem, of human forbearance and well-wishing which in our earlier days were the unconscious products of circumstances must now be the conscious fruit of an education which forms the deepest springs of character.

Teachers above all others have occasion to be distressed when the earlier idealism of welcome to the oppressed is treated as a weak sentimentalism, when sympathy for the unfortunate and those who have not had a fair chance is regarded as a weak indulgence fatal to efficiency. Our traditional disposition in these respects must now become a central motive in public education, not as a matter of condescension or patronizing, but as essential to the maintenance of a truly American spirit. All this puts a responsibility upon the schools which can be met only by widening the scope of educational facilities. The schools have now to make up to the disinherited masses by conscious instruction, by the development of personal power, skill, ability and initiative, for the loss of external opportunities consequent upon the passing of our pioneer days. Otherwise power is likely to pass more and more into the hands of the wealthy, and we shall end with this same alliance between intellectual and artistic culture and economic power due to riches which has been the curse of every civilization in the past, and which our fathers in their democratic idealism thought this nation was to put an end to.

Since the idea of the nation is equal opportunity for all, to nationalize education means to use the schools as a means for making this idea effective. There was a time when this could be done more or less well simply by providing schoolhouses, desks, blackboards and perhaps books. But that day has passed. Opportunities can be equalized only as the schools make it their active serious business to enable all alike to become masters of their own industrial fate. That growing movement which is called industrial or vocational education now hangs in the scales. If it is so constructed in practice as to produce merely more competent hands for subordinate clerical and shop positions, if its purpose is shaped to drill boys and girls into certain forms of automatic skill which will make them useful in carrying out the plans of others, it means that instead of nationalizing education in the spirit of our nation, we have given up the battle, and decided to refeudalize education.

I have said nothing about the point which my title most naturally suggests—changes in administrative methods which will put the resources of the whole nation at the disposition of the more backward and less fortunate portions, meaning by resources not only money but expert advice and guidance of every sort. I have no doubt that we shall move in the future away from a merely regional control of the public schools in the direction of a more central regulation. I say nothing about this phase of the matter at this time not only because it brings up technical questions, but because this side of the matter is but the body, the mechanism of a nationalized education. To nationalize American education is to use education to promote our national idea,—which is the idea of democracy. This is the soul, the spirit, of a nationalized education, and unless the administrative changes are executed so as to embody this soul, they will mean simply the development of red tape, a mechanical uniformity and a deadening supervision from above.

Just because the circumstances of the war have brought the idea of the nation and the national to the foreground of everyone's thoughts, the most important thing is to bear in mind that there are nations and nations, this kind of nationalism and that. Unless I am mistaken there are some now using the cry of an American nationalism, of an intensified national patriotism, to further ideas which characterize the European nations, especially those most active in the war, but which are treasonable to the ideal of our nation. Therefore, I have taken this part of your time to remind you of the fact that our nation and democracy are equivalent terms; that our democracy means amity and good will to all humanity (including those beyond our border) and equal opportunity for all within. Since as a nation we are composed of representatives of all nations who have come here to live in peace with one another and to escape the enmities and jealousies which characterize old-world nations, to nationalize our education means to make it an instrument in the active and constant suppression of the war spirit, and in the positive cultivation of sentiments of respect and friendship for all men and women wherever they live. Since our democracy means the substitution of equal opportunity for all for the old-world ideal of unequal opportunity for different classes and the limitation of the individual by the class to which he belongs, to nationalize our education is to make the public school an energetic and willing instrument in developing initiative, courage, power and personal ability in each individual. If we can get our education nationalized in spirit in these directions, the nationalizing of the administrative machinery will in the end take care of itself. So I appeal to teachers in the face of every hysterical wave of emotion, and of every subtle appeal of sinister class interest, to remember that they above all others are the consecrated servants of the democratic ideas in which alone this country is truly a distinctive nation—ideas of friendly and helpful intercourse between all and the equipment of every individual to serve the community by his own best powers in his own best way.

The Teacher and the Public (1935)

WHO IS A WORKER? Are teachers workers? Do workers have common ties to unite them? Should these ties be expressed in action? These are some of the questions I want to discuss with you for a few moments this evening.

Who is a worker? I answer this question by saying that all who engage in productive activity are workers. It is customary to speak of a certain class of criminals as "second-story workers." The appellation is obviously humorous, and so it is when we speak of one person "working" another to get something out of him. Not every form of activity, even if it brings in some return to the person engaged in it, is work. It is work only when it is productive of things that are of value to others, and of value not simply in a particular case but when that kind of activity, is generally of service. Those who live upon the work of others without rendering a return are parasites of one kind or another. The man who lives upon interest, dividends or rent is, so far as that includes what he does, a parasite. There is something intellectually and morally, as well as economically, topsy-turvy when honor, esteem and admiration go to a section of society because its members are relieved from the necessity of work. To believe otherwise is to believe that those who subtract from the real wealth of society instead of adding to it are the highest type. Everybody assents to this statement in theory, but in fact the attention given in this country to the rich just because they are rich, proves that we do not live up to our theoretical belief.

Are teachers workers? The basis for answering this question has been given. Are they engaged in productive activity? Are only those persons who turn out material products producers?

Physicians who maintain the health of the community are certainly producers of a fundamental social good. The business of the teacher is to produce a

First published in *Vital Speeches of the Day* 1 (28 January 1935): 278–79, from a speech broadcast 16 January 1935 over radio station WEVD, New York City, as part of the NBC University of the Air series.

higher standard of intelligence in the community, and the object of the public school system is to make as large as possible the number of those who possess this intelligence. Skill, ability to act wisely and effectively in a great variety of occupations and situations, is a sign and a criterion of the degree of civilization that a society has reached. It is the business of teachers to help in producing the many kinds of skill needed in contemporary life. If teachers are up to their work, they also aid in production of character, and I hope I do not need to say anything about the social value of character.

Are teachers producers, workers? If intelligence, skill and character are social goods, the question answers itself. What is really important is to see how the production of material things depends finally upon production of intellectual and moral goods. I do not mean that material production depends upon these things in quantity alone, though that is true. The quality of material production depends also upon moral and intellectual production. What is equally true and finally even more important is that the distribution and consumption of material goods depends also upon the intellectual and moral level that prevails. I do not need to remind you that we have in this country all the means necessary for production of material goods in sufficient quantity, and also, in spite of the low grade often produced because of desire for profit, that we have all the resources, natural and technical, for production of sufficient quantities of good quality. Nevertheless, we all know without my telling you that millions have no work, no security and no opportunity either to produce or to enjoy what is produced. Ultimately, the state of affairs goes back to lack of sufficient production of intelligence, skill and character.

Why do I say these things which are, or should be, commonplace? I say them because of their bearing on the third question I raised. Do teachers as workers, as producers of one special kind of goods, have close and necessary ties with other workers, and if they do, how shall these ties be made effective in action?

Some of the facts that indicate the answer to these questions are found in the fact that schools and teachers, education generally, have been one of the chief sufferers from that vast industrial and economic dislocation we call the depression. Salary or wage cuts are almost universal; multitudes of schools have been closed. Classes have been enlarged, reducing the capacity of teachers to do their work. Kindergartens and classes for the handicapped have been lopped off. Studies that are indispensable for the production of the skill and intelligence that society needs have been eliminated. The number of the unemployed has been increased in consequence, and the mass consuming power necessary for recovery has been contracted. But along with these consequences, there has been a greater injury. The productive work that is the special business of teachers has been greatly impaired, and impaired at just the time when its products of intelligence, skill and character are most needed.

The cause is well known. It is in part the inability of large numbers to pay taxes, combined, however, with the desire of those able to pay taxes to escape what they regard as a burden. In other words, it is due to the depression on one side and on the other side to the control exercised by the small class that represents the more parasitical section of the community and nation, those who live upon rent, interest and dividends. If something striking, striking home, was necessary to demonstrate to teachers that they are workers in the same sense in which farmers, factory employees, clerks, engineers, etc., are workers, that demonstration has been provided. The same causes that have created the troubles of one group have created those of the other group. Teachers are in the same boat with manual, white collar workers, and farmers. Whatever affects the power of the latter to produce, affects the power of teachers to do their work. By the same token whatever measures will improve the security and opportunity of one, will do the same thing for the other. In both the causes that produce the trouble and the remedies that will better and prevent the recurrence, teachers are bound by necessity to workers in all fields.

Teachers have been slow to recognize this fact. They have felt that the character of their work gave them a special position, marked off from that of the persons who work with their hands. In spite of the fact that the great mass of their pupils come from those who work with their hands on farms, in shops and factories, they have maintained an aloof attitude toward the primary economic and political interests of the latter. I do not need to go into the causes of this attitude that has been so general. One phase of it, however, is definitely related to my main topic. I have said that the business of the teachers is to produce the goods of character, intelligence and skill. I have also said that our present situation shows and is proof of lack of these goods in our present society. Is not this fact a proof, it may be asked, of a widespread failure of teachers to accomplish their task?

The frank answer to this question is, Yes. But neither the question nor the answer gives the cause of the failure. The cause goes back to the excessive control of legislation and administration exercised by the small and powerful class that is economically privileged. Position, promotion, security of the tenure of teachers has depended largely upon conformity with the desires and plans of this class. Even now teachers who show independence of thought and willingness to have fair discussion of social and economic questions in school are being dismissed, and there is a movement, sponsored by men of wealth to label (bolsheviks, reds, and subversives) all those who wish to develop a higher standard of economic intelligence in the community.

This fact brings me to the answer of the last question asked. If teachers are workers who are bound in common ties with all other workers, what action do they need to take? The answer is short and inclusive. Ally themselves with their friends against their common foe, the privileged class, and in the alliance develop the character, skill and intelligence that are necessary to make a democratic social order a fact. I might have taken for my text the preamble of the constitution of the national American Federation of Teachers. A part of it reads as follows: "We believe that the teacher is one of the most highly productive of workers, and that the best interests of the schools and of the people demand an intimate contact and an effective cooperation between the teachers and the other workers of the community—upon whom the future of democracy must depend."

In union is strength, and without the strength of union and united effort, the state of servility, of undemocratic administration, adherence to tradition, and unresponsiveness to the needs of the community, that are also pointed out in the same document, will persist. And in the degree in which they continue, teachers will of necessity fail in the special kind of productive work that is entrusted to them.

The Duties and Responsibilities of the
Teaching Profession (1930)

AMONG THOSE WHO ACCEPT THE principle of general objectives, there seems to be at the present time a general consensus as to the nature of these objectives. On the psychological or individual side, the aim is to secure a progressive development of capacities, having due regard to individual differences, and including a physical basis of vigorous health, refined esthetic taste and power to make a worthwhile use of leisure, ability to think independently and critically, together with command of the tools and processes that give access to the accumulated products of past cultures. On the social side, this personal development is to be such as will give desire and power to share in cooperative democratic living, including political citizenship, vocational efficiency and effective social goodwill. Disagreement seems to concern the relative emphasis to be given the different elements among these aims and the best means for attaining them, rather than the objectives themselves.

On the other hand, there is a marked tendency in other groups to discard all general objectives and to seek instead for specific aims. In this case, the latter are usually sought for in analysis of existing social occupations and institutions (present adult life in general). Their unstated general objective appears to be that education should prepare, by means of blue prints of society and the individual, students to fit efficiently into present life.

I. Under these circumstances, the first need is that the teaching profession as a body should consider the nature of the social function of the school. The question of general versus specific objectives goes back to the question of whether the schools should aim to fit individuals for the existing social order,

First published in *School and Society* 32 (9 August 1930): 188–91. Used as a basis for discussion at the meeting of the National Council of Education, June 28, 1930.

or whether they have a responsibility for social planning. The latter objective clearly involves preparation of students to take part in changing society, and requires consideration of the defects and evils which need to be changed.

The first thesis or proposition is, accordingly, that apart from and prior to consideration of changes in actual school programs, curricula and methods, the teaching body, as a body, should arrive through discussion within itself at conclusions concerning the direction which the work of the school should take with respect to social conditions. Does this involve responsibility for planning and leadership or only for producing conformity?

II. As far as the conclusion points in the former direction, the question arises as to the handicaps and obstacles from which the American public school suffers in performing this function. (A) It is stated that social sentiment, especially that of influential interests, will not permit the discussion of controversial questions in the schools and is even opposed to the introduction of objective and impartial subject-matter relating to them. (B) It is also stated that teachers as a class are not equipped to take part intelligently in the discussion of such questions or to lead in consideration of them. My second proposition, accordingly, is that there should be a clearer idea obtained, through discussion within the teaching body, of the existing handicaps to the realization by the school of its social function. This would include the state of the teaching body, and the question of how far it may be better prepared for social participation and leadership, including both teachers in service and the changes which would be required in training schools. The discussion should involve attention to the problems of adult education and of how far there is at present a lack of harmony between the processes of child education and those of adult education, since the ideal of continuity of education implies that there should be consonance and not conflict.

III. There is the problem of how objectives should be determined and formulated. There is the tendency, illustrated perhaps by the present paper, to begin at the top and pass the formulations arrived at down through a series of intervening ranks until they are handed over to the classroom teacher. This procedure conflicts with the principle of democratic cooperation. It suggests the proposition that there is need that classroom teachers, who have immediate contact with pupils, should share to a much greater extent than they do at present in the determination of educational objectives as well as of processes and material.

These three main propositions may be rendered more concrete and definite by raising questions which are involved in them.

1. How far should the educational process be autonomous and how can it be made such in fact? Is it the duty of the schools to give indoctrination in the economic and political, including nationalistic principles that are current in contemporary society? Should criticism of the existing social order be permit-

ted? If so, in what ways? Can pupils really be educated to take an effective part in social life if all controverted questions are excluded?

2. To what extent is it true that in spite of formulation of objectives by leaders, the educational system as a whole is goalless, so much so that there is no common and contagious enthusiasm in the teaching body, a condition due to lack of consciousness of its social possibilities? Do students go forth from the school without adequate consciousness of the problems and issues they will have to face? As far as it is true, can this state of affairs be remedied without a realization of responsibility for social planning on the part of the teaching body and administrators?

3. Can a vital professional spirit among teachers be developed unless there is (a) greater autonomy in education and (b) a greater degree of realization of the responsibility that devolves upon educators for the social knowledge and interest which will enable them to take part in social leadership?

4. It has been stated from high quarters that the individuality and freedom of the classroom teacher are lessening; that "the teacher is becoming more and more of a cog in a vast impersonal machine." How far is this statement correct? What are its causes and remedies? Is the work of administrators too far removed from that of teachers? What is the tendency of the present administration of standardized tests? Does it tend to fix the attention of classroom teachers upon uniformity of results and consequently produce mechanization of instruction? Does it foster a grading and division of pupils with respect to mastery of standardized and predetermined subject-matter at the expense of individual development? What tests and what method of their administration would tend to greater release of creative work on the part of teachers? How much of present administrative procedures is based upon distrust of the intellectual capacities of class-room teachers? Can these capacities be increased without giving these teachers a greater degree of freedom?

5. Can the power of independent and critical thinking, said to be an objective, be attained when the field of thought is restricted by exclusion of whatever relates to controverted social questions? Can "transfer" of thinking habits be expected when thinking is restricted to technical questions such as arise when this social material is excluded?

6. What are the concrete handicaps to development of desire and ability for democratic social cooperation?—for this is also stated to be a cardinal objective. Can such questions as the relation of capital and labor, the history and aims of labor organization, causes and extent of unemployment, methods of taxation, the relation of government to redistribution of national income, cooperative vs. competitive society, etc., be considered in the school room? Similar questions arise in connection with family relations, prohibition, war and peace.

7. The principle is generally accepted that learning goes on most readily and efficiently when it grows out of actual experience and is connected with it. How far does this principle imply, logically and practically, that the structure of economic and political activities, which affect out of school experience, should receive systematic attention in school?

8. How far is the working purpose of present school work to prepare the individual for personal success? How far are competitive incentives relied upon? How far are these factors compatible with the professed objective of democratic cooperation?

9. How far can and should the schools deal with such questions as arise from racial color and class contact and prejudice? Should questions relating to Negroes, North American Indians, the new immigrant population, receive definite consideration? What should be the attitude of the schools to differences of cultural tradition and outlook in the schools? Should they aim to foster or to eliminate them? What can and should the schools do to promote greater friendliness and mutual understanding among the various groups in our population?

10. The same questions come up regarding our international relations. Does the teaching of patriotism tend toward antagonism toward other peoples? How far should the teaching of American history be designed to promote "Americanism" at the expense of historical facts? Should definite questions of international relations, such as our relation to the Caribbean region, the use of force in intervention in financial and economic questions, our relation to the World Court, etc., be introduced?

These questions are suggested as means of making the three principles laid down more concrete in their meaning. They are tied together by certain convictions. First, the formulation of objectives, whether general or specific, tends to become formal, empty and even verbal, unless the latter are translated over into terms of actual school work. Secondly, the isolation of the school from life is the chief cause for both inefficiency and lack of vitality in the work of instruction and for failure to develop a more active professional spirit. Third, the closer connection of school with life can not be achieved without serious and continued attention by the teaching body to the obstacles and handicaps that lie in the way of forming such a connection. Fourth, it is necessary to enlist the entire educational corps, including the class-room teacher, in consideration of the social responsibilities of the school, especially with reference to the larger issues and problems of our time.

Underlying these convictions is a faith that the public will respond positively to the assumption by teachers of recognition of their social function; that much of the present adverse reaction of the public to free consideration of social questions is due to the failure of the teaching profession to claim actively and in an organized way its own autonomy.

Creative Democracy—The Task before Us (1939)

UNDER PRESENT CIRCUMSTANCES I CANNOT hope to conceal the fact that I have managed to exist eighty years. Mention of the fact may suggest to you a more important fact—namely, that events of the utmost significance for the destiny of this country have taken place during the past four-fifths of a century, a period that covers more than half of its national life in its present form. For obvious reasons I shall not attempt a summary of even the more important of these events. I refer here to them because of their bearing upon the issue to which this country committed itself when the nation took shape—the creation of democracy, an issue which is now as urgent as it was a hundred and fifty years ago when the most experienced and wisest men of the country gathered to take stock of conditions and to create the political structure of a self-governing society.

For the net import of the changes that have taken place in these later years is that ways of life and institutions which were once the natural, almost the inevitable, product of fortunate conditions have now to be won by conscious and resolute effort. Not all the country was in a pioneer state eighty years ago. But it was still, save perhaps in a few large cities, so close to the pioneer stage of American life that the traditions of the pioneer, indeed of the frontier, were active agencies in forming the thoughts and shaping the beliefs of those who were born into its life. In imagination at least the country was still having an open frontier, one of unused and unappropriated resources. It was a country of physical opportunity and invitation. Even so, there was more than a marvelous conjunction of physical circumstances involved in bringing to birth this new nation. There was in existence a group of men who were capable of readapting

First published in *John Dewey and the Promise of America*, Progressive Education Booklet No. 14 (Columbus, Ohio: American Education Press, 1939), 12–17, from an address read by Horace M. Kallen at a dinner in honor of Dewey, New York City, 20 October 1939.

older institutions and ideas to meet the situations provided by new physical conditions—a group of men extraordinarily gifted in political inventiveness.

At the present time, the frontier is moral, not physical. The period of free lands that seemed boundless in extent has vanished. Unused resources are now human rather than material. They are found in the waste of grown men and women who are without the chance to work, and in the young men and young women who find doors closed where there was once opportunity. The crisis that one hundred and fifty years ago called out social and political inventiveness is with us in a form which puts a heavier demand on human creativeness.

At all events this is what I mean when I say that we now have to re-create by deliberate and determined endeavor the kind of democracy which in its origin one hundred and fifty years ago was largely the product of a fortunate combination of men and circumstances. We have lived for a long time upon the heritage that came to us from the happy conjunction of men and events in an earlier day. The present state of the world is more than a reminder that we have now to put forth every energy of our own to prove worthy of our heritage. It is a challenge to do for the critical and complex conditions of today what the men of an earlier day did for simpler conditions.

If I emphasize that the task can be accomplished only by inventive effort and creative activity, it is in part because the depth of the present crisis is due in considerable part to the fact that for a long period we acted as if our democracy were something that perpetuated itself automatically; as if our ancestors had succeeded in setting up a machine that solved the problem of perpetual motion in politics. We acted as if democracy were something that took place mainly at Washington and Albany—or some other state capital—under the impetus of what happened when men and women went to the polls once a year or so—which is a somewhat extreme way of saying that we have had the habit of thinking of democracy as a kind of political mechanism that will work as long as citizens were reasonably faithful in performing political duties.

Of late years we have heard more and more frequently that this is not enough; that democracy is a way of life. This saying gets down to hard pan. But I am not sure that something of the externality of the old idea does not cling to the new and better statement. In any case we can escape from this external way of thinking only as we realize in thought and act that democracy is a personal way of individual life; that it signifies the possession and continual use of certain attitudes, forming personal character and determining desire and purpose in all the relations of life. Instead of thinking of our own dispositions and habits as accommodated to certain institutions we have to learn to think of the latter as expressions, projections and extensions of habitually dominant personal attitudes.

Democracy as a personal, an individual, way of life involves nothing fundamentally new. But when applied it puts a new practical meaning in old ideas.

Put into effect it signifies that powerful present enemies of democracy can be successfully met only by the creation of personal attitudes in individual human beings; that we must get over our tendency to think that its defense can be found in any external means whatever, whether military or civil, if they are separated from individual attitudes so deep-seated as to constitute personal character. Democracy is a way of life controlled by a working faith in the possibilities of human nature. Belief in the Common Man is a familiar article in the democratic creed. That belief is without basis and significance save as it means faith in the potentialities of human nature as that nature is exhibited in every human being irrespective of race, color, sex, birth and family, of material or cultural wealth. This faith may be enacted in statutes, but it is only on paper unless it is put in force in the attitudes which human beings display to one another in all the incidents and relations of daily life. To denounce Naziism for intolerance, cruelty and stimulation of hatred amounts to fostering insincerity if, in our personal relations to other persons, if, in our daily walk and conversation, we are moved by racial, color or other class prejudice; indeed, by anything save a generous belief in their possibilities as human beings, a belief which brings with it the need for providing conditions which will enable these capacities to reach fulfilment. The democratic faith in human equality is belief that every human being, independent of the quantity or range of his personal endowment, has the right to equal opportunity with every other person for development of whatever gifts he has. The democratic belief in the principle of leadership is a generous one. It is universal. It is belief in the capacity of every person to lead his own life free from coercion and imposition by others provided right conditions are supplied.

Democracy is a way of personal life controlled not merely by faith in human nature in general but by faith in the capacity of human beings for intelligent judgment and action if proper conditions are furnished. I have been accused more than once and from opposed quarters of an undue, a utopian, faith in the possibilities of intelligence and in education as a correlate of intelligence. At all events, I did not invent this faith. I acquired it from my surroundings as far as those surroundings were animated by the democratic spirit. For what is the faith of democracy in the role of consultation, of conference, of persuasion, of discussion, in formation of public opinion, which in the long run is self-corrective, except faith in the capacity of the intelligence of the common man to respond with commonsense to the free play of facts and ideas which are secured by effective guarantees of free inquiry, free assembly and free communication? I am willing to leave to upholders of totalitarian states of the right and the left the view that faith in the capacities of intelligence is utopian. For the faith is so deeply embedded in the methods which are intrinsic to democracy that when a professed democrat denies the faith he convicts himself of treachery to his profession.

When I think of the conditions under which men and women are living in many foreign countries today, fear of espionage, with danger hanging over the meeting of friends for friendly conversation in private gatherings, I am inclined to believe that the heart and final guarantee of democracy is in free gatherings of neighbors on the street corner to discuss back and forth what is read in uncensored news of the day, and in gatherings of friends in the living rooms of houses and apartments to converse freely with one another. Intolerance, abuse, calling of names because of differences of opinion about religion or politics or business, as well as because of differences of race, color, wealth or degree of culture are treason to the democratic way of life. For everything which bars freedom and fullness of communication sets up barriers that divide human beings into sets and cliques, into antagonistic sects and factions, and thereby undermines the democratic way of life. Merely legal guarantees of the civil liberties of free belief, free expression, free assembly are of little avail if in daily life freedom of communication, the give and take of ideas, facts, experiences, is choked by mutual suspicion, by abuse, by fear and hatred. These things destroy the essential condition of the democratic way of living even more effectually than open coercion which—as the example of totalitarian states proves—is effective only when it succeeds in breeding hate, suspicion, intolerance in the minds of individual human beings.

Finally, given the two conditions just mentioned, democracy as a way of life is controlled by personal faith in personal day-by-day working together with others. Democracy is the belief that even when needs and ends or consequences are different for each individual, the habit of amicable cooperation—which may include, as in sport, rivalry and competition—is itself a priceless addition to life. To take as far as possible every conflict which arises—and they are bound to arise—out of the atmosphere and medium of force, of violence as a means of settlement into that of discussion and of intelligence is to treat those who disagree—even profoundly—with us as those from whom we may learn, and in so far, as friends. A genuinely democratic faith in peace is faith in the possibility of conducting disputes, controversies and conflicts as cooperative undertakings in which both parties learn by giving the other a chance to express itself, instead of having one party conquer by forceful suppression of the other—a suppression which is none the less one of violence when it takes place by psychological means of ridicule, abuse, intimidation, instead of by overt imprisonment or in concentration camps. To cooperate by giving differences a chance to show themselves because of the belief that the expression of difference is not only a right of the other persons but is a means of enriching one's own life-experience, is inherent in the democratic personal way of life.

If what has been said is charged with being a set of moral commonplaces, my only reply is that that is just the point in saying them. For to get rid of the habit of thinking of democracy as something institutional and external and to acquire the habit of treating it as a way of personal life is to realize that democracy is a moral ideal and so far as it becomes a fact is a moral fact. It is to realize that democracy is a reality only as it is indeed a commonplace of living.

Since my adult years have been given to the pursuit of philosophy, I shall ask your indulgence if in concluding I state briefly the democratic faith in the formal terms of a philosophic position. So stated, democracy is belief in the ability of human experience to generate the aims and methods by which further experience will grow in ordered richness. Every other form of moral and social faith rests upon the idea that experience must be subjected at some point or other to some form of external control; to some "authority" alleged to exist outside the processes of experience. Democracy is the faith that the process of experience is more important than any special result attained, so that special results achieved are of ultimate value only as they are used to enrich and order the ongoing process. Since the process of experience is capable of being educative, faith in democracy is all one with faith in experience and education. All ends and values that are cut off from the ongoing process become arrests, fixations. They strive to fixate what has been gained instead of using it to open the road and point the way to new and better experiences.

If one asks what is meant by experience in this connection my reply is that it is that free interaction of individual human beings with surrounding conditions, especially the human surroundings, which develops and satisfies need and desire by increasing knowledge of things as they are. Knowledge of conditions as they are is the only solid ground for communication and sharing; all other communication means the subjection of some persons to the personal opinion of other persons. Need and desire—out of which grow purpose and direction of energy—go beyond what exists, and hence beyond knowledge, beyond science. They continually open the way into the unexplored and unattained future.

Democracy as compared with other ways of life is the sole way of living which believes wholeheartedly in the process of experience as end and as means; as that which is capable of generating the science which is the sole dependable authority for the direction of further experience and which releases emotions, needs and desires so as to call into being the things that have not existed in the past. For every way of life that fails in its democracy limits the contacts, the exchanges, the communications, the interactions by which experience is steadied while it is also enlarged and enriched. The task of this release and enrichment is one that has to be carried on day by day. Since it is one that can have no end till experience itself comes to an end, the task of democracy is forever that of creation of a freer and more humane experience in which all share and to which all contribute.

Index

activity approach: art studies, 97; for character development, 68, 93; in curriculum philosophy, 111–13; as education method, 30, 150–51; as fundamental, 28–29; and home life, 26–27; and individuality, 182–84; and learning processes, 191–94; as progressive school characteristic, 178, 182–84; science study, 101, 104; utopian school model, 188–89. *See also* experience concept

Addams, Jane, 4

administrative approach, education efficiencies, 134–43

aesthetic experiences. *See* art study; literature

American Federation of Teachers, 244

apprenticeships, 168, 169, 188

Archambault, Richard, 118

Aristotle, 53

Arnold, Matthew, 100

articulation efficiencies, education processes, 120, 129, 134–43

art of teaching, 21–22, 35–36, 44–45

art study, 67–69, 82–84, 95–98, 113, 151. *See also* literature

aspiring teachers, questions for, 20, 33–36

Associated Charities, 48

bargain counter approach, schools, 164, 170–74

Beard, Charles A., 225

bourgeois democracy, 220

Burlington, Vermont, 2–3

character formation, role of schools, 68, 88–94. *See also* ethics

Chipman, Alice (later Dewey), 3, 5

classification schemes: as direct education foundation, 195–201; grading systems, 165, 196–99; student, 135–38, 153–55, 180–81; teacher assignments, 139–41. *See also* curriculum subjects

classroom teachers. *See* teachers

Cold War era, 7

Columbia University, 5

Commons, John R., 225

community life and individualism, 4, 9–10, 212. *See also* democratic society; schools, ideal; social learning

conservative/progressive conflict, as philosophy development incentive, 53

Cooke County Normal School, 4–5

curriculum subjects: overview, 28–29, 65–70; art, 67–69, 82–84, 95–98, 113, 151; and character formation, 68, 88–94; ethics, 21–22, 46–51; languages, 102–3, 113, 168; mathematics, 86–87, 112–13; moral value, 81–87; and out-of-school experiences, 93–94, 139; and philosophy of education, 107–13; in progressive schools, 181, 182–85; psychological factor, 71–80, 194; teacher power, 39, 121, 145–47, 155–59, 204–5. *See also* literature; schools, ideal; science

dance, 96

demands question, aspiring teachers, 33, 34–36

democratic ideals, schools: overview, 123–26; administrative leadership, 119, 126–30, 144–47; student role, 148–50; teacher role, 19–23, 32, 37–38, 145–48

Douglas J. Simpson holds the Helen DeVitt Jones Chair in Teacher Education at Texas Tech University, where he teaches in the areas of curriculum studies and curriculum theory with emphasis on the anthropological, pedagogical, epistemological, and ecological dimensions of school and societal curricula. His previous publications include *John Dewey Primer* (2006), *John Dewey and the Art of Teaching: Toward Reflective and Imaginative Practice* (coauthored with Michael J. B. Jackson and Judy C. Aycock, 2005), and *Educational Reform: A Deweyan Perspective* (coauthored with Michael J. B. Jackson, 1997).

Sam F. Stack Jr. received his BA in sociology from Furman University and his PhD in social and cultural foundations from the University of South Carolina. He is the author of *Elsie Ripley Clapp (1879–1965): Her Life and the Community School* (2004). His recent publications include "John Dewey and the Question of Race: The Fight for Odell Waller" (*Education and Culture*, 2009) and "Implementing *Brown v. Board of Education* in West Virginia: The Southern School News Reports" (*West Virginia History*, 2008).